"David Moe's book is an important addition to the growing literature on the dialogue between Western theology and Asian theologians. It is most significant that he chooses to focus on the concept of suffering/*Dukkha*, which is central to both Christianity and Buddhism. Furthermore, Moe's special attention to Myanmar/Burma offers a rich resource to Christians engaged in dialogue with Buddhists in this country with a fast-growing Christian community."

—Peter C. Phan, Professor of Theology and Ignacio Ellacuria Chair of Catholic Social Thought, Georgetown University

"Nuanced and comprehensive, David Moe's proposal for a Christian dialectical theology of divine and human *Dukkha* (suffering) makes a seminal contribution. As a Christian from Myanmar, David Moe poignantly addresses a theme common to both Buddhists and Christians in Asia: *Dukkha* (suffering), or in Burmese, *Pyithu*. Drawing on biblical sources and Asian and European theologians of the cross, Moe makes the case for a distinctively Burmese *Pyithu-Dukkha* theology that gives witness to the compassion and passion of a crucified Messiah who both reconciles and resists evil and injustice."

—Lois E. Malcolm, Professor of Systematic Theology, Luther Seminary

The Asbury Theological Seminary Series in Christian Revitalization Studies

In this study, David Moe demonstrates the growing reality that, in the words of Walter Brueggemann, "neither Rome nor Wittenberg nor Geneva nor Canterbury is any longer the epicenter of theological work." This is because Moe, using a contextual theological methodology, has here brought into prominence the distinctives of a Southeast Asian and Buddhist interpretation of Christian faith, which had long been unknown outside its own culture, and which correspondingly has for us far-reaching and ecumenical significance. It may well become a pivotal volume in bringing Western readers face to face with the heretofore undisclosed liberationist theology which is ascending in Myanmar (Burma). In so doing, this well researched study may also offer insight for contemporary movements of revitalization and church renewal. For that reason we present *Pyithu-Dukkha Theology* as an appropriate contribution to the Intercultural Studies Subseries of this project devoted to research in movements of Christian revitalization.

    J. Steven O'Malley
    General Editor

Intercultural Studies Sub-Series

The behavioral science approach to the study of revitalization movements has a long history that has developed several models. Anthropologists, among others, observed that people responded to colonialism and the expansion of the West in various ways: armed resistance, selective acceptance and passive resistance, among others. The problems of the colonial frontier led to a memorandum on acculturation written by Robert Redfield, Ralph Linton and Melville Herskovits in 1936. Elsewhere in the world, anthropologists observed "nativistic" or "cultural renewal" movements as well: cargo cults in Melanesia, messianic movements in South Africa, and political revolutions in Latin America. Anthony F. C. Wallace brought some order to this area of study with his 1956 article where he named the stages and subsumed the movements under the name of "revitalization movements." Harold Turner contributed the notion of New Religious Movements to focus on the indigenous responses to mission work seen in every continent. This can be seen as part of a larger development, from the 1960s on, to develop Social Movement Theory where people are seen as agents intentionally acting to renew and reform society by organizing others to resist or dethrone the powers that be. Such movements develop a culture and social organization that give meaning and impetus to action on behalf of the leader and/or the program.

In this book, David Moe has brought together a concern for a colonized and suffering people who need a Christian theology that speaks to their condition. Certainly a colonizing theology from the West cannot identify with this suffering, but Jesus can. Moe adapts the concept of suffering, *Dukkha*, from Buddhist theology, then mines previous contributions to an Asian Theology, and produces a helpful and healthy message for Burmese people based on the suffering of Christ, centered in the cross of Christ.

Michael A. Rynkiewich
Editor for the sub-series on Intercultural Studies.

Pyithu-Dukkha Theology

A Paradigm for Doing Dialectical Theology of Divine Suffering and Human Suffering in The Asian-Burmese Context

David Thang Moe

*Asbury Theological Seminary Series:
The Study of World Christian Revitalization Movements in
Interculutral Studies*

EMETH PRESS
www.emethpress.com

Pyithu-Dukkha Theology: A Paradigm for Doing Dialectical Theology of Divine Suffering and Human Suffering in the Asian-Burmese Context

Copyright © 2017 David Thang Moe
Printed in the United States of America on acid-free paper

All rights reserved. No part of this book may be reproduced, or stored in a retrieval system or transmitted in any form or by any means, electronic, mechanical, photocopying, recording, scanning or otherwise, except as permitted by the 1976 United States Copyright Act, or with the prior written permission of Emeth Press. Requests for permission should be addressed to: Emeth Press, P. O. Box 23961, Lexington, KY 40523-3961. http://www.emethpress.com.

Library of Congress Cataloging-in-Publication Data

Name: Moe, David Thang, 1983- author.
Title: *Pyithu-Dukkha* theology : a paradigm for doing dialectical theology of divine suffering and human suffering in the Asian-Burmese context / David Thang Moe.
Description: Lexington, KY : Emeth Press, [2017]
Identifiers: LCCN 2017020405 | ISBN 9781609471132 (acid-free paper)
Subjects: LCSH: Suffering--Religious aspects--Christianity. | Suffering--Religious aspects--Buddhism. | Dialectical theology. | Christianity and other religions--Buddhism. | Buddhism--Relations--Christianity. | Theology, Doctrinal--Burma. | Christianity--Burma.
Classification: LCC BT732.7 .M625 2017 | DDC 231/.809591--dc23
LC record available at https://lccn.loc.gov/2017020405

Dedicated To:

The late Daw Khang Lee—
My beloved mother—
who kindled my passion for theology,
encouraged me to serve the Lord,
and taught me the ethics of life whose faith I was too small to reach!

Table Of Contents

Foreword / xi
Preface / xiii
Acknowledgment / xvii
Chapter 1 *Pyithu-Dukkha*: Theology from the Wounded Heart of Myanmar / 1
Chapter 2 A Biblical Concept of Divine and Human *Dukkha* / 21
Chapter 3 A Theological Concept of Divine-Human *Dukkha* in the Global Context: Theology between West and East / 41
Chapter 4 *Pyithu-Dukkha* Theology for New Ecumenical and Evangelical Horizons / 65
Conclusion / 111
Bibliography / 113

Foreword

A great central reality of contemporary church theology is that Western hegemony has been decentered by the growth and vitality of gospel faith elsewhere in the world. This decentering of Western theology—with its imperial assumptions and its Enlightenment epistemology (either in the affirmations of progressivism or in the resistance of evangelicals) —means that theology can and will be expressed in other terms. This in turn means that neither Rome nor Wittenberg nor Geneva nor Canterbury is any longer the epicenter of theological work.

In his wide-ranging study, David Moe brings a fresh voice to the theological conversation from his home base of Myanmar (Burma). To be sure he makes important appeal to Western theology, but seeks to recast it in terms of Asian, specifically Burmese categories. This rearticulation of faith pivots on "the suffering mission people." This core concept permits Moe to appeal to Western theologians who have focused on God's 'suffering (Moltmann, Volf), but also to consider an interface with Korean *Minjung theology* and Indian *Dalit theology* and the chorus of Asian voices that have articulated such thought. Before he finishes, Moe's discussion moves in the direction of a liberation hermeneutic with its political implications.

The accent on suffering, moreover, suggests an important interface with Buddhist categories that move in the same direction. What becomes clear in Moe's discussion is that the articulation of faith in Asian categories is not an easy translation for Western theology, because the terms of expression are not readily commensurate. The rich cultural pluralism of Asia, the absence of Enlightenment rationality, and the pervasive availability of Buddhism all function to recognize interpretive dimensions that inescapably resist Western reductionism.

In our Western reading of this suggestive discussion, two moves are necessary. The first is to recognize and allow the legitimacy of Moe's alternative articulation. The second is to consider what we might learn from Moe's version of faith that will be instructive in the context of fading Western Christendom. Because Western Christendom (unwittingly?) fostered a "theology of glory" that has served hegemonic purposes, we may relearn from this Burmese alternative a "theology of the cross" that takes cultural form and expression. Since we Western Christians are now engaged in institutional and epistemological *kenosis,* that instruction could be genuinely important for us.

Moe finishes with an important urging addressed to Burmese readers:

> I urge Christians in Myanmar to consider the components of Christ's suffering and solidarity with the sufferers in an interaction with the Buddhist view of *Dukkha* and *Karuna*.

We in the West might likewise reflect on the components of "suffering and solidarity" as a defining vocation. It is no wonder that Moe ends with a liberationist hermeneutic concerning a preferential option that frontally critiques Western habits of racism, sexism, classism, nationalism, and abuse of creation. Self-emptying is the summons. We may learn it in a Buddhist mode or alternatively we may learn it from *the Friday Messiah*. Either way Moe invites us to fresh reflection and discipline.

—Walter Brueggemann
Columbia Theological Seminary
April 10, 2017

Preface

The uniqueness of Asia lies in its two realities: *pluralistic religiosity* (in which Christianity is a minority)[1] and *suffering* (Christians and other faiths suffer together). As a nation in Asia, Myanmar experiences these two existing realities. Consequently, *Dukkha* (suffering) becomes the daily and common spoken term of all Burmese (*Pyithu*) to express their agony and suffering. The influence of language, *Dukkha* has no boundary at all and it can be heard and seen in every realm of social-political and religious-cultural milieus. Strictly speaking, *Dukkha* is very central to both Buddhism and Christianity.

Buddha said, "life is full of *Dukkha*" in the sense that *Dukkha* is an essential part of human existence" while Christians believe that *Dukkha* is an essential part of Messianic identity (Isa. 53; Lk. 24:26). Thus, *Pyithu-Dukkha* theology is formulated by Christian theology of divine *Dukkha* in dialogue with the Buddhist notion of humanistic *Dukkha* as to how we speak about the "Crucified Christ" (1Cor. 1:22) in Myanmar.

The idea that God suffers for us is unique to the Christian faith. However, this central truth is not always a part of the dominant faith of Christians today. This study meets this need through a contextual inquiry for the suffering of Christ and the suffering of people in Myanmar and provides new insight to the emphatic God in the crucified Christ, who is present in the midst of those who suffer. This study sheds new light on how *Pyithu-Dukkha* theology is connected to the history of Israel through Jesus Christ as the Messiah, which is explained theologically and contextually within the larger framework of God's ontological creation and redemption in the biblical world.

It is with great passion that I am working on this difficult project, mainly because I believe this is what, a follower of the crucified Christ ought to do, and partly, because I set out to work on this project in order to give an account to myself about how I, as one of the members who has been struggling for the justice and truth, ought to react to God's holistic salvation as the central point of Christian theology in my home country.

The two dialectical Messianic images: the *innocent Jesus* crying out to God, "my God, my God why have you forsaken me?"(Mk.15:34) and the *sacrificial Lamb* offering as the gift of reconciliation (Jn. 1:29) are evident throughout this

---

[1] According to the census in 2010, Asian Christianity is about 9%, see Scott W. Sunquist, *The Unexpected Christian Century: Reversal and Transformation of Global Christianity 1900-2010* (Grand Rapids, MI: Baker Academic, 2015), xvii.

study. The former image calls for the command to bring about justice for outcasts and the latter calls for the demand to embrace religious outsiders.[2] This study is divided into four chapters:

Chapter 1 presents the general overview of Myanmar, its main tenets and definition of *Pyithu-Dukkha,* and its challenges from social and religious-cultural perspectives. This chapter mentions the *genesis* and *telos* of Asian theology (why and when Asian theology came to be born), in dialogue with an Asian-*Minjung* theology and *Dalit* theology to prove how *Pyithu-Dukkha* theology can be part of Asian theology.

Chapter 2 examines the biblical theme of the divine and human suffering from the perspectives of the Old and New Testaments, special attention being given to the drama of God's deliverance of the Israel and God's covenant with them, the prototype of the messianic Jesus. Next, this study deals with the New Testament Messiah who starts His ministry at the *lowest* level of the life of the poor through being in solidarity with the outcast and ends with the *highest* point of sacrifice for others on the cross.

Together with the biblical themes on the God-human relationship in context of *Dukkha,* this chapter engages the two sets of images: (1) the crucified Christ and the dying Buddha; (2) the Cross in the rose and the Lotus on which the Buddha sits or stands. As the beautiful Lotus on which the Buddha sits is a primordial symbol of world genesis, so the cross of the resurrected Christ points to the beauty of God's new creation. Here I also seek some connections of basic principles of ethics and the ultimate question of *Dukkha* in response to the liberation from the philanthropic suffering.

Chapter 3 describes a theological concept of divine and human *Dukkha* in a global context, selecting influential western and Asian theologians who inspired me most in my theological journeys. They include Martin Luther, Karl Barth, Dietrich Bonhoeffer, Jürgen Moltmann and Miroslav Volf in dialogue with the Asian theologians: Kazoh Kitamori, C.S. Song, Kosuke Koyama and Aloysius Pieris and Jung Young Lee.

Chapter 4 explores the ecumenical and evangelical perspectives on the three related themes—God's mission (*Missio Dei*). God's church (*Ecclesio Dei*) and God's Kingdom (*Regnum Dei)* in combination with Jesus' threefold office: the *prophetic* office of justice, the *priestly* office of sacrifice and the *kingly* office of Lordship. Within this framework, the theological proposals are made what perspective is relevant in response to the cries of people in the wilderness. This study sums up with the sense of *Dukkha* unto *Thukkha,* proving that divine *Dukkha* does not stop at the cross, but goes beyond and opens a new world through the risen Christ in whom we find our hope. Finally, in the postscript, I explore the interrelation between the passion and compassion of God and sin of the oppressors and suffering of the oppressed in the context of the *Pyithu-Dukkha* and propose the need of a holistic and inclusive liberation theology.

---

[2]Miroslav Volf, *Exclusion and Embrace*: *A Theological Exploration of Identity, Otherness and Reconciliation* (Nashville, TN: Abingdon, 1996). 9.

To the *tveak* (sufferer) I became *weak* (suffer), so that I might tvin the *weak*. I have become all tlrings to all people *(Pyithu-Dukkha)* Ulat I might by all means *save* some. I do it all 1(,r the sake of the gospel, so that I might share in its blessings (lCor. 9:22ft}. From this, I vvill proceed to meet the needs of my people by taking *Dukkha* as a point of contact between Christians and Buddhists.

Acknowledgment

At the outset, there are many to place on record my special debts, most of them so immense that I can repay them only with a word of heartfelt thanks: beginning with my parents, from the cradle of their tender and nursing I have grown up. Coming thousands of miles away from my homeland Myanmar, the far corner of Southeast Asia, I wish to acknowledge my heartfelt thanks to all my friends and relatives, especially my small local church, Presbyterian Church in my native village of Khin Phong and Presbyterian Church in the town of Mindat, for their unceasing prayers for my studies in the States.

My interest in the topic and the theological framework of this book was born and flowered as the fruit of my engagement with Martin Luther's *theologia crucis* at Luther Seminary in 2011-2013. A Burmese version of *Pyithu-Dukkha* theology was born as the fruit of some professors and students who often asked me what a Burmese theology is. When we do contextual theology, we must use some common words and experiences as the local sources for articulating the gospel. *Dukkha* or suffering is central to both Buddhism and Christianity. The influence of language, *Dukkha* has no boundary and it can be heard in every realm of social-political and religious-cultural milieus in Myanmar. *Pyithu-Dukkha* theology is, therefore, formulated by a Christian theology of divine *Dukkha* (suffering) in critical dialogue with the Burmese Buddhist notion of human suffering for addressing the collective suffering of *Pyithu* or the masses.

I extend thanks to all the faculty members of Luther Seminary, St. Paul, Minnesota, USA for giving me the great opportunity of theological studies and of articulating *Pyithu-Dukkha* theology. In particular, my uttermost thanks goes to Professors Amy E. Marga (thesis adviser), Lois E. Malcolm and Guillermo Hansen (readers). They all have been not only sources of wisdom for my M.Th's degree but also models of oversight for my further Ph.D studies. They gave me space to find God and myself in my journeys of academics and faith. Also, Peter Susag's kind assistance in proofreading is evident throughout this project; I convey my appreciations to him.

I must also express my special indebtedness to Dick Stone and Judy Stone (the then seminary librarian), who have become my family friends. I also wish to convey my thanks to the Presbyterian Church of the Way, (PC, USA) for their hospitality and welcoming me into their open-ended community to become a church member. Their continued supports of financial and spiritual needs are the immense blessings to my journey of academics and faith. I must extend my thanks to my brother- and sister-in-law, Gerald M. Richmond, Jr (Terry) and Shu Ha Richmond (Monica) in Syracuse, New York, for their warm hospitality during my school breaks.

Thanks must necessarily be extended to the Emeth Press, Lexington, KY, USA for publishing my book. I would also like to express the deepest senses of gratitude to five distinguished scholars: Professor Peter C. Phan of Georgetown University in Washington DC, Professor Amos Yong of Fuller Theological Seminary in California, Professor Lois Malcolm of Luther Seminary in Minnesota, Professor James H. Cone of Union Theological Seminary in the City of New York for their kind endorsements and Professor Walter Brueggemann for his wonderful foreword for this book.

I am most grateful to my longsuffering wife, Prissila Moe ("the prudent wife from the Lord," Proverbs 19:14) for her constant encouragement and patience throughout my study. Since she is not interested in a theology of suffering, she challenges me why I am working on this topic. Her challenge deepens a horizon of my articulation of a theology of suffering. Last, but most importantly, the triune God has been faithful and gracious in the course of my study at Luther Seminary. Without Him, I would not have been able to complete my study, and apart from Him, I would have nothing to say here!

May this humble work be blessed to the glory of the triune God!

Chapter 1

Pyithu-Dukkha: Theology from the Wounded Heart of Myanmar

Introduction

Myanmar is a country in S.E. Asia. Being sandwiched between the world's two great nations, China and India, Myanmar is a nebulous territory for many in the world. Many outsiders know almost nothing about what the Burmese Christians are doing and thinking. The obscurity increased when the name Burma was changed to Myanmar on June 19, 1989.[1] I am torn between using Burma or Myanmar. However, "Myanmar" will be used for the name of the country while "Burmese" will be used to indicate the people and language. Some proposed to use *Myanmese* as the people and language. Interestingly, Kosuke Koyama is right when he has said, "Myanmar is an isolated country."[2]

Due to social political oppression, Myanmar has not had the privilege of expressing her living theology to the world, especially over the past three decades. Instead, she has done theology by the witness of individual believers in the lives of the churches. Christians in Myanmar have done theology by way of what Walter Hollenweger has called "oral theology."[3] Yet, isolation does not necessarily mean there is no theology in Myanmar; it simply means the quiet testimony within the given matrix of the churches. During those turbulent periods, the churches seemed to be declining both quantitatively and qualitatively and became an arena for both Evangelical and Ecumenical theologies, wrestling with theologies imported from the west.

---

[1] The military government changed the name Burma to Myanmar on June 19, 1989, arguing that Burma is an Anglicized term.

[2] Kosuke Koyama, *Water Buffalo Theology*, 25th anniversary edition, revised and expanded (Maryknoll, NY: Orbis Books, 1999), 9-10.

[3] Walter J. Hollenweger, "Ecumenical Significance of Oral Christianity, *"Ecumenical Review* 41, no. 2 (1989): 261. Walter refers to *Oral theology* as *pulpit theology* without public engagement.

Now is high time for churches in Myanmar to search for doing a contextual theology that is concerned with the needs of all churches and societies and to project the local churches as one to the global churches in the world. I will therefore employ *Dukkha* (suffering) as a paradigm for doing a Burmese theology of suffering. Taking *Dukkha* as a paradigm for doing a dialectical theology of divine and human suffering in Myanmar, I will review the collective suffering of Israel in the OT as a prototype of Jesus in the NT who is in solidarity with the oppressed and ultimately becomes a crucified Christ.

Survey of Racial-Religious and Social-Political Existences

Racial-Religious Existence

In order to be familiar with the context of Myanmar and the content of *Pyithu-Dukkha*, it would be appropriate to begin by presenting a survey of religious-social political settings. Interestingly, Myanmar has a union of 7 native *Barma* divisions and 7 ethnic states consisting of 135 racial groups. The native "Barmas" or "Burmans" are used to refer to the Buddhist majority, who live in the central part of the nation, while the ethnic group of Christian majority lives in the mountainous side. If we adopt the threefold classification of Caucasoid, Negroid and Mongoloid, Myanmar belongs to the latter.[4] Myanmar has 60 million people, with 85%Buddhists, 6.2% Christians, 4% Muslims and Hindus and 4% Nat-worship.[5] Myanmar stands as the second largest nation in Southeast Asia, with a total area of 261,228 squares miles, bordered by China in the North, Laos in the East, Thailand in the Southeast, Bangladesh in the West and India in the Northeast.[6]

Religiously speaking, Myanmar is a Buddhist country. The first Christian missionaries who came to Myanmar were Europeans.[7] When Christianity was introduced to Myanmar by the early Catholic missionaries in the 16thcentury, Buddhism already existed as a local religion—the Buddha was a host when Jesus came to Myanmar as a visitor. These early missionaries withdrew from Myanmar due to many difficulties.[8]

---

[4]Saw Doh Say, "A Brief History and Development Factors of the Karen Baptist Church of Myanmar"(M.Th. Thesis, Fuller Theological Seminary, Pasadena, 1990), 6.

[5]The Burma Socialist Program Party, Union of Burma, *The System of Correlation of Man and His Environment: The Philosophy of the Burma Socialist Party* (Rangoon: Sarpay Beikman Press, 1964), 46.

[6]Terry Muck and Frances S. Adeney, *Christianity Encountering World Religions* (Grand Rapids, MI: Baker Academic, 2009), 9.

[7]Aleyamma Zachariah, *Modern Religious and Secular Movement in India* (Bangalore: Sevasadan Training Institute, 1994), 5.

[8]John C. England, "The Earliest Christian Communities in South East and North East Asia-An Outline of the Evidence Available in the Seven Centuries before A.D 1500,"*Asia Journal of Theology* 4, no. 1 (April 1990): 177.

As for the Protestant missions, Richard Mardon and James Chater of the British Baptists were the first missionaries who came from Bengal to Myanmar in 1807 to investigate the possibilities of Christian mission in Myanmar.[9] Though they were joined by Felix Carey, son of William Carey and they worked together for some years, the English Baptist mission work in Myanmar did not prove a conspicuous success.

But a more permanent Christian presence and successful mission was later inherited by Adoniram Judson of the American Baptist tradition who arrived in Myanmar on July 13, 1813 (by the way, Judson's bicentenary pilgrimage and mission to Myanmar will be celebrated soon). Eventually, most mainline churches arrived in the middle of the 19th century and established churches alongside the majority of Catholics and Baptists.[10] Thus, Myanmar is also known as "a perfect ethnological museum of religious-cultural hybrids in terms of the racial harmonies and religious pluralities."[11]

Social-Political Situations

Myanmar has experienced turbulent political rules throughout the monarchy period (pre-history-1885), colonial period (1885-1948), parliament democratic government (1948-1962), social military government (1962-1988), military regime (1988-2010) and the civilian government backed up by military regime (2010-to present). Myanmar was an isolated country living as a hermit nation for three decades (1962-1988). It was during this period, beginning on March 2, 1962, that the government took the power, expatriated foreign missionaries and made Buddhism national religion.[12] In spite of its attempt to be isolated from foreign influence, Myanmar could not totally segregate but established a relationship with the Chinese communist government in 1988.

In 1974, U Ne Win's "Burmese Way to Socialism" significantly led Myanmar to being one of the most impoverished countries in the world. Due to the severe social-economic and political conditions under U Ne Win, the government finally reached the climax of a massive pro-democracy protest in August 1988. As a champion for Myanmar's democracy, Daw Aung San Suu Kyi, a Noble Peace Laureate whose father was the father of Myanmar's independence, won the May 1990 polls by a landslide. But the military regime refused to relinquish power. As a result, the people protested peacefully against the military regime in 1988 and again in 2007. It is true that Myanmar is a country covered by clouds of social-political uncertainty and corruption.

---

[9]Brian Stanley, *The History of Baptist Missionary Society (1792-1992)*(Edinburgh: T&T Clark, 1992), 56.

[10]Alexander McLeish, *Christian Progress in Burma* (London: World Dominion Press, 1929), 21.

[11]Daw Sein Ko, *Burmese Sketches*, vol. 2 (Rangoon: British Burma Press, 1920), 332.

[12]Simon Pau Khan En, "Globalization and Inter-Religious Cooperation: A Myanmar Experience," *RAYS, MIT Journal of Theology* 7 (January 2006): 124.

As we look at Myanmar's religious-cultural existence throughout the 204 years of the Christian presence since Judson's mission in 1813, three significant phases can best be characterized: the first phase (led by foreign missionaries), the second (led by foreign missionary-trained local pastors), and the current third phase (in which the local churches need to be theologically rooted).[13] Taking the third phase as a serious concern for doing local theology in Myanmar, I here propose *Pyithu-Dukkha* to be one of the loci for doing a relevant theology in Myanmar at large, as defined below.

Pyithu-Dukkha Theology: A Definition

Pyithu-Dukkha is a combination of two Burmese words: *Pyithu* refers to the nation's 135 racial groups, or simply "people,"[14] while *Dukkha* indicates suffering, which is the Burmese sense of Buddhist character as derived from the Pali language. *Pyithu-Dukkha* therefore simply means "the suffering mass of people." The Buddhist perspective offers much insight about the cosmic *Dukkha* in developing the Asian-Burmese theology of divine suffering and human suffering. No single English phrase is equivalent to the word of *Dukkha* (*du,* bad, low; *kha,* empty, hollow).[15]

Chained in the circle of birth and death in the world of becoming (*samsara* in Sanskrit), all sentient living creatures suffer in all dimensions of life. *Dukkha* is central to both Buddhism and Christianity in Myanmar. *Dukkha* is the theme of Buddha's primary truth: Buddha said, "life is full of *Dukkha* in the sense that *Dukkha* is an essential part of human existence,"[16] while Christians believe that *Dukkha* is an essential part of the Messianic identity and Christian existence (Isa. 53; Lk. 24:26). A common basis for *Pyithu-Dukkha* theology thus lies in the dialectics of divine *Dukkha* and human *Dukkha*.

Pyithu-Dukkha theology is shaped by ontological dialogue with the interpretation of Christian theology of divine *Dukkha* and Buddhist notion of *Dukkha*. *Dukkha* is used by all Burmese to express the agony and pain rising out of unjust experiences. *Dukkha* is not just a physical sickness that can be cured by therapy, but it can be cured only when the total structure of the oppressed society is transformed. Myanmar has been free from western colonialism since 1948, yet other forms of neo-imperialism and militarism have taken over since 1962. Taking the social-religious pluralities and political-economic realities as vital

---

[13]Saw Hlai Bwa, *Our Theological Journey in Honor of Professor Dr. Simon Pau Khan En*, (Yangon: Myanmar Institute of Theology, 2012), iv. Reading the three phases as a serious concern for doing a contextual theology in Myanmar was articulated by Dr. Simon Pau Khan En, who is the pioneer of Burmese contextual theologian.

[14]For instance, *"Pyithu's Yin-pyin"* in Yangon, meaning "People's Park," which is a popular place to hold big festivals and other special music concerts.

[15]Heinrich Dumouln, *UnderstandingBuddhism Key Themes*, trans. Joseph S. O'Leary (New York: Weatherhill, 1994), 21-24.

[16]Bhikku Bodhi, *In The Buddha's Words: An Anthology of Discourses from the Pali Canon* (Boston, MA: Wisdom Publications, 2005), 17.

forces in Asia, Aloysius Pieris has articulated that the uniqueness of Asia embraces two realities: *"multifaceted religiousness* and *socio-economic suffering.*"[17]

As a nation in Asia, Myanmar is regarded as a suffering country with a Buddhist majority, and increasingly we see how political struggles, social injustices, racial alienations, ethnic conflicts and economic corruptions are running rampant in today's society. As the suffering people in Myanmar are the subjects of history, *Pyithu-Dukkha* theology needs to be interwoven with the drama of God's saving work. Melford E. Spiro, an American anthropologist, has remarked in relation to *Pyithu-Dukkha* that:

> *Dukkha* is the most frequently used term in the Burmese context; it is on everyone's lips at work, at school, in the house, on a trip. For the Burmese, as for the rest of humankind, the notion that life involves suffering is not an article of faith; it is a datum of everyday experience. But it is one thing to agree that life involves suffering and another to agree that life very form of life is *Dukkha*.[18]

The Buddhist Concept of *Dukkha*

Born in 563 BC, the Buddha was a contemporary of Confucius and a younger contemporary of Ezekiel the prophet.[19] For Buddha, the universe is subject to decay and in travail for deliverance. Man, as part of this creation, is in bondage to this decay. *Dukkha* in Pali is a compound of two words, *du* and *kha*. The prefix *du* is seen in the sense of vile, something bad, whereas the suffix *kha* signifies emptiness.[20] The Buddhist's idea of the universe lies in the doctrine of suffering (*Dukkha*), impermanence (*anicca*), and self-emptiness (*anatta*). Christianity has a similar concept: *suffering* is an essential part of human existence (Jn. 16:33); this planet is *temporary* (Rom. 8:18:30; 2Cor. 4:16-18); the *emptying* Christ is a Savior in a world of violence (Phil. 2:6-11).

These three anomalies are the basic teaching in Buddhism and *Dukkha* becomes a theme of Buddha's Four Noble Truths: (1) the truth of *Dukkha*; (2) the cause of *Dukkha*; (2) the cessation of *Dukkha*; and (4) the eightfold-path leading to end of *Dukkha*.[21] *Dukkha* embraces both physical and mental suffering—the former refers mainly to pain while the latter refers to sorrow which seems close to that of what Jesus said to His disciples, "My soul was very sorrowful even to

---

[17]Aloysius Pieris, *An Asian Theology of Liberation* (Maryknoll, NY: Orbis Books, 1988), 69.

[18]Melford E. Spiro, *Buddhism and Society, A Great Tradition and Its Burmese Vicissitudes* (Berkeley, CA: University of California Press, 1982), 74.

[19]Kenneth Scott Latourette, *Introducing Buddhism* (New York: Friendship Press, 1999), 5.

[20]M. V. Ram Kumar Ratnam, *Dukkha: Suffering in Early Buddhism* (New Delhi: Discovery Publishing House, 2003), 45.

[21]K. Sri Dhammananda, *What Buddhist Believes*, expanded and revised ed. (Kota Kinabalu: Laser Press Sdn. B.hd, 1999), 75. The Eightfold path is ethical-oriented: (1) right views, (2) right thought, (3) right speech, (4) right behavior, (5) right livelihood, (6) right moral effort, (7) right mindfulness and (8) right concentration.

death,"(Mk. 14:34). For the Buddha, *Dukkha* is related to even the moments of happiness since this is a world of *anicca*—similarly, Christians hold that a good condition is *Dukkha* in the sense that riches obstruct the rich from entering Kingdom and following Jesus (Matt. 19:16-22; Mk. 10:17-23).

Buddha diagnosed this situation and realized renunciation as the first step in searching for liberation. Self-emptiness is therefore the way to salvation. Ratnam said:

> *Dukkha* points to our ignorance concerning the meaning of life. *Dukkha* arising out of this type of ignorance is more intensive, acute, and paralyzing than physical and mental suffering of man. In fact, one can find remedies (immediate and remote) for the pain arising out of the physical and mental factors. Fever can be cured, enemies can be vanquished and desires can be fulfilled. The pain caused by the absence of wisdom concerning the true significance of life is more frustrating and acute because it is very difficult to find easy ways of overcoming it.[22]

Dukkha is associated with the problem of self-centeredness. The ignorance of self-ness divides *Dukkha* into three aspects: (1) *Dukkha* as ordinary *Dukkha* (*Dukkha-Dukkha*), (2) *Dukkha* as produced by one's ignorance of falsehood (*viparinama-Dukkha*), and (3) *Dukkha* as conditioned states (*samkhara-Dukkha*).[23]

The second one is relevant to Myanmar's current situation, for it tends to be a kind of suffering caused by human evils.

One has to understand the effect of self-importance/self-centeredness as the main cause of all evils that creates sufferings and then take refuge in three Jewels: (1) Buddha [liberator],[24] (2) Sangha (order of monks), and (3) *Dhamma* (teaching). Buddha's noble teaching about taking refuge in the three Jewels is analogous to the Psalmist's lament: "God is our refuge and our strength, a very presence help in trouble" (Psalm 46:1)?

The Christian Concept of *Dukkha*

At the core of Christians faith lies the claim that *Dukkha* is an essential part of the universal and humanistic existence. Adoniram Judson (1788-1850), the most successful American Baptist missionary who worked in Myanmar for thirty-seven years (July 13, 1813-April 12, 1850), employed the Buddhist term *Dukkha* in his translation of the Burmese Bible. His translation of *Dukkha* is bountiful in meaning, embracing various kinds of suffering, for instance, "harming" in Genesis 15:20, "groaning" in Psalms 22:1-2, "sufferings," and "groaning" in Romans 8: 18-27; 12:12, "affliction" in Psalm 90:15, Job 30:27; 2Corinthians 4:17, "trouble" Job 14:1; Psalm 91: 15, "adversity" in Proverbs 17:17, "persecution" in John 16:33, 2 Timothy 3:12, Acts 14:22 and more.

---

[22]Ratnam, *Dukkha: Suffering in Early Buddhism,* 46-47.

[23]Walpola Sri Rahula, *What the Buddha Taught,* revised and expanded ed. (New York: Grove Press, 1979), 19.

[24]Buddha is understood by Theravada Buddhism as a "Saint," while he is seen by Mahayana Buddhism as a Savior. I would define him as a "liberator" in the context of suffering.

The Christian concept of suffering can be summarized in four kinds: first *physical suffering* (pain, violence, hunger); second *mental suffering* (failure, imprisonment and abuse); third *emotional suffering* (despair and loneliness); fourth *spiritual suffering* (separation from God). At times of suffering, Christian minds are flooded with two questions: "why is this happening to me?" and "where is God in my suffering?"[25] Two forms of *Dukkha* can further be noted: "individual *Dukkha*" and "collective *Dukkha*." The former tends to be the result of one's choice of good or evil, whereas the latter is more commonly understood as a result of social evil. For the individual suffering, consider Adam and Eve's free choice of eating the fruit which was prohibited (Gen. 3:1-24). I believe, however, individual suffering is related to social suffering in consequential ways.

The Book of Job is probably the greatest and most profound discussion of the subject of individual suffering ever written. However, Job's suffering should not be understood as a result of his own choice, rather Job accepted his *Dukkha* as an essential part of human existence and he said, "A mortal, born of woman, few of days and full of trouble/*Dukkha*" (Job 14:1). Harold Kushner eloquently takes note of three statements:

> First, God is all-powerful and causes everything that happens on planet is without His will; second God is just and stands for people getting what they deserve so that the good "prosper" and the wicked are "punished," third Job is a good person in a way that Job deserves what happens to him as he is a sinner.[26]

Even though his wife asked him to curse God and his friends are prepared to stop believing in God, Job remains steadfast in his faith. The moral of Job's innocent suffering is that when hard times befall us, they are not something to tempt us to give up our faith in God. God has reasons for what He is doing and if we hold on to our faith long enough, He will compensate us for our suffering.[27] The Psalmist and most of the NT writers see suffering as God's test of faith (Jn. 9:3; 2Cor.1:8-9; Rom. 8:18-39, 1Pet. 1:6; Heb. 12:7-11).Seen suffering from the positive side, we have much to learn from Job about his right relationship of faith and hope. He overcame his *Dukkha* by trusting God. In the end, God rewards him for his faithfulness, giving him a new home and many blessings.[28]

In talking about the communal *Dukkha*, the Bible draws our attention to the story of the exiled Israel in the OT and the *Ochlos* in the NT, which will be our focus in chapter two. Here I first tend to argue where or not God is present in suffering. We will use excerpts from Psalm 22:1-31—where is God in our suffering? The laments depict that God is absent or even cruel. Actually, laments allow our integrity, helping us keep the conversation with God open. Laments help us

---

[25] Daniel J. Simundson, *Where is God in My Suffering? Biblical Responses to Seven Searching Questions* (Minneapolis, MN: Augsburg Publishing House, 1983), 7.

[26] Harold S. Kushner, *When Bad Things Happen to Good People* (New York: Anchor Books, 2004), 42-43.

[27] Ibid., 38.

[28] Gustavo Gutierrez, *On Job: God-Talk and the Suffering of the Innocent*, translated by Matthew J. O'Connell (Maryknoll, NY: Orbis Books, 1997), 7.

remember the experience of God's people who cried to God for help in times of trial.[29] The Psalmist begins Psalm 22 with complaints but ends with praise of God, who is present in times of crisis. Christians must believe that the tears and prayers of the suffering arouses God's compassion.[30]

Christians introduced the world to the idea of an empathetic God who suffers in love and solidarity with the victims. The social suffering of the victims in our modern world, especially in the light of Holocaust, has impacted the contemporary understanding of God and His relationship to human suffering. I believe the pain we feel reflects God's compassion. But is God present in the suffering of non-Christians, too? My answer is "yes": God's saving action is all the more revealed to them through the vehicle of suffering. One of the last words of Jesus on the cross is a lament which proves His human way of feeling pain (Mk. 15:34). As Daniel Simundson has clearly said:

> In times of suffering and sorrow, the compassionate God not only invites our very human prayers but also knows what it is like to be in so much pain. God hears and God understands. God suffers with us. Our lament is certainly heard by Jesus who Himself has gone the valley of suffering through. It is a great comfort for a sufferer to experience the presence of an understanding and compassionate God.[31]

Kamma and Sin: Cause and Consequence of *Dukkha*

We will now compare the Buddhist concept of *kamma*[32] and Christian doctrine of sin. *Kamma* lies at the heart of Buddhism: *kamma* means the link between act and consequence. Everything happening in one's life is the cause and consequence of *kamma*—as one acts, so one will be after death. For example, if you steal corn, you will become a rat.[33] According to Buddhism, *Dukkha* is the consequence of *kamma*. Being ignorant of doing good things (*kudo*) and committed to bad things (*akudo*) in the past brings *Dukkha* to one's present life. Deeds return to doers. Such a notion of *kammic* action and result is similar to what Paul says, "One reaps what one sows" (Gal. 6:7-8).

From a Christian perspective, an evil doer is a sinner and sin is the result of *kamma*. "Sin came into the world through one man and death spreads to all because all have sinned" (Rom. 5:12). The root cause of sin is *Dukkha* and human beings become mortal as a result of sin (Rom. 6:23).[34] Buddhists define all kinds of *Dukkha* as the result of *kamma*, while Christians believe that sin causes suffering but not all suffering is due to *kamma*. Consider the story of Jesus and the man

---

[29] Simundson, *Where is God in My Suffering?* 25-27.
[30] Ibid., 28.
[31] Ibid., 29.
[32] *Kamma* in Pali or *Kan* in Burmese is synonymous to *Karma* in Sanskrit.
[33] Jürgen Moltmann, *Ethics of Hope*, trans. Margaret Kohl (Minneapolis, MN: Fortress Press, 2012), 172.
[34] Terence E. Fretheim, "Divine Judgment and Warming of The World: An Old Testament Perspective," *Word and World* 4, Supplement Series (April 2000): 24, 27.

born blind, which demonstrates that the man's blindness is neither the result of his parents' sin nor the sin of the man himself (Jn. 9:1-3). This has nothing to do with the result of man's sin, but indicates God's glory.

It remains a lively question whether the root cause of the *Pyithu*'s *Dukkha* is a cause of *kamma*. Some Buddhists see *Pyithu*'s *Dukkha* to be the result of their demerit of *kamma* in the past, whereas some Christians consider *Pyithu*'s suffering to be a consequence of God's punishment. *Pyithu*'s *Dukkha* is neither a result caused by God's curse nor a result of *kamma*,[35] but a result caused by the military regime. In my judgment, the Buddhists are confusing their notion of *kamma* with rebirth. A Christian should introduce *kamma* to Buddhists in terms of this life and the life to come rather than the life in the past as Christ has restored all sinners to God (Jn. 12:31). Thus, *Pyithu*'s experience of *Dukkha* is not determined by their past actions, but rather, as a result of social evil.[36]

Pyithu-Dukkha as Asian Theology: Asian Theology's Genesis and Telos

Contextual approaches to theological concepts date all the way back to the New Testament and can be found in the period of Jesus' ministry in Galilee and Paul's spreading of good news among the Gentiles in the Greco-Roman world.[37] The Word became flesh in the Jewish culture (Jn. 1:1), thus Jesus had to observe Jewish culture. As Christianity was embedded with Jewish culture, the center of that period was Jerusalem. When Paul and other evangelists introduced mission to the gentiles, the center of Jewish Christianity shifted from Jerusalem to the Athens of the Hellenistic Christianity.[38]

At the infancy of Christianity, there was a tension between the Gentile Christians and Jewish Christians, who imposed Jewish cultural hegemony over gentile Christians. To solve this cultural conflict, the first Christian Conference was held in Jerusalem (Acts 15) and a compromise was made in order for the Gentiles not to be forced to observe the Jewish culture because the gospel can be transcended to all and any particular cultures.[39]

Consequently, the Epistle to the Galatians was written by Paul as the *Magna Carta* of Christian liberty from cultural imposition. The best example is Galatians

---

[35]People's suffering in Myanmar is not comparable to God's punishment over the environment disaster of Sodom and Gomorrah for human sin and rebellion God.

[36]K. M. Y. Khawsiama, "Toward A Theology of *Dukkha*: A Christian-Buddhist View on the Suffering of Ludu in Myanmar," *Asia Journal of Theology* 26, no. 2 (October 2012): 119-121.

[37]Gerald A. Arbuckle, "Inculturation and Evangelization: Realism or Romanticism?," in *Missionaries, Anthropologists, and Cultural Changes: Studies in Third World Societies*, ed. Vinson H. Sutlive, Nathan Altshuler, Mario D. Zamora, and Virginia Kerns (Williamsburg, VA: College of William and Mary, 1983), 171.

[38]Roberts J. Deotis, *A Philosophical Introduction to Theology* (London: SCM Press, 1991), 78.

[39]Ibid., 79.

3:28, which indicates *everyone* is one in Christ.[40] Throughout the history of world Christianity, the encounter of Gospel and culture is an issue.[41] The shift of the center of the gospel as a result of missionary enterprise—from the monocentric model to polycentric (from Jerusalem to Antioch, Athens, Alexandria, Roman, Eastern and World church).Thus Christianity shift can be termed as a World Religion in various nomenclatures as below:

> Jewish Christianity (Gospel in Jewish culture); Hellenistic Christianity (Gospel in Greek culture); Latin Christianity (Gospel in Roman culture); Western Christianity (Gospel in Euro-American culture); Asian Christianity (Gospel in Asian culture).[42]

In Asia, the genesis of contextual theological reflection can be said to have begun with the efforts of the 17th century Jesuits (Matteo Ricci in China, 1552-1610, widely known as the "wise man from the West" and Roberto de Nobii in India), who made the Gospel relevant to the local cultures.[43] More contextual efforts began in the early 20th century. After WW II and significantly since the 1970s, efforts at formulating contextual Asian theologies emerged with two major types of challenges: *ethnographical approaches* and *liberation approaches* in the Asian's context.[44]

Contextual theology in Asia emerged when Asian theologians began to be aware of their theological responsibilities and launched a movement for theological construction from their own context. Asian theology takes contexts and social reality as resources for theological reflection and faith confession.[45] Many non-Asian theologians suspect that Asian theology is analogous to Latin American theology of liberation. Yes, Asian theology shares a theological theme of liberation with Latin American theology, but the former is different from the latter in terms of "religiosity." In addition, most of the poor in Asia are non-Christians, whereas most of the poor in Latin America are Christians.[46]

Then, is Asian theology distinctive from Western theology? Yes, primarily because Asian theology emerges from the context of "poverty" and "religiosity." Yet "their difference should be regarded not as a source of conflict but as a basis for

---

[40]Simon Pau Khan En, "Gospel and Culture," *Engagement: Judson Research Center Bulletin* 7 (December 2006): 85.

[41]See also Richard H. Niebuhr, *Christ and Culture* (New York: Happer Torch Book, 1951).

[42]Pau Khan En, "Gospel and Culture," 85. See also Lamin Sanneh, *Whose Religion is Christianity? The Gospel Beyond the West* (Grand Rapids, MI: William B. Eerdmans Publishing Company, 2003).

[43]Stephen Neill, *A History of Christian Missions*, 2nd ed. (London: Penguin Books, 1986), 156.

[44]Hwa Yung, *Mangoes or Bananas? The Quest for an Authentic Asian Christian Theology* (Oxford: Regnum, 1997), 14.

[45]Huang Po Ho, *No Longer Stranger: Toward the Construction of Contextual Theologies* (Tiruvalla: Christava Sahitya Samithy, 2007), 25.

[46]Alfred T. Hennelly, *Liberation Theologies: The Global Pursuit of Justice* (Mystic, CT: Twenty-Third, 1995), 203.

mutual complement."[47] By that time when Asian theology was about to be born, the most influential western theologian was Karl Barth and some Asian Christian leaders requested Barth to contribute a theological article regarding the shaping of Asian theology. Contextual theology in Southeast Asia (S.E. Asia) in particular and Asia in general came to be born by the force of Barth's encouragement, as proven in his letter to the Southeast Asian Christians a few weeks before his death in 1968.

> Dear Christians in South East Asia (now S.E. Asia), can the theology, presented by me, be understandable and interesting to you—and how can you contribute in the direction which I believed I had to go, and at the place where I had to set a period and to what extent?...Now it is your task to be Christian theologians in your new, different and special situation with heart, head, with mouth and hands—I can only encourage you, yes, do that; say that which you have to say as Christians for God's sake, responsibly and concretely with your own words and thoughts, concepts and ways! The more responsibly and concretely you live, the better the more Christians. You truly do not need to become European, Western men, not to mention Barthians, in order to be good Christians and theologians. You may feel free to be S.E. Asian Christians. Be it! Be it neither arrogantly nor faintheartedly with regard to the religions around you and the dominant ideologies and realities in your lands! Be it all openness for the problems that are so burning in your regions and for your own, special and unique fellow men....[48]

In light of Barth's note, Christians in S.E. Asia in particular and Asia in general came to theologize Asian theology. "Asian theology" is used as a broader term to cover the Indian sub-continent through S.E. Asia to East Asia. Given Asia's diversity, Asian theology is used as a collective phrase for different varieties of Asian contexts.[49] Of many, *Minjung* theology from South Korea and *Dalit* theology from India served as the world's best known theologies rising from the Asian socio-political context.

To say that *Pyithu-Dukkha* has contributed to qualify itself as an Asian theology, it needs to be grasped by Minjung theology and Dalit theology from the ecumenical perspective. The term "ecumenical" is used in a generic sense, which denotes persons, associated with the ecumenical movement in the post-WW II period as represented by the World Council of Churches (WCC) and the Christian Conference of Asia (CCA). Together with WCC and CCA, the telos of Asian theology must be an engaged theology by which the community will be enabled to participate more fully in a holistic life.

---

[47] Jung Young Lee, *The Trinity in Asian Perspective* (Nashville, TN: Abingdon Press, 1996), 17.
[48] Kosuke Koyama, ed., *South East Asia Journal of Theology* 2 (Autumn 1969): 3-5. The original letter was written in German and translated into English by William Rader.
[49] Ibid.

Pyithu-Dukkha Theology in Conversation with *Minjung* Theology

The *Minjung* theology that rose out of the experiences of people in Korea during the 1970s was known to the West as the first Asian theology.[50] In opposition to President Park Chung Hee's dictatorship, the Student Christian Federation and National Council of Churches issued a Declaration of Korean Christians in May 1973, aiming at alleviating the suffering of people. Nam Dong Suh was the first person who began to use the term *Minjung* theology in February 1975.[51]*Minjung* theology is an articulation of theological experiences of farmers, students and all people.[52] A group of theologians developed *Minjung* as a contextual theology in Asia which was published by the CCA in 1981.[53]

First we need to define the term, *Minjung*. "*Minjung*" is a Korean combination of two Chinese characters, "*min*" and "*jung*," Min literally means the "people" while *jung* signifies the "mass." Combining the two words, *Minjung* means the "mass of people" or simply "people."[54]Second, *Minjung* theology is based on three biblical paradigms: (1) the exodus event in which God's liberative work is found; (2) the crucifixion-resurrection by which Jesus was condemned as a political offender and (3) Jesus' solidarity with the *Ochlos* (in Greek) and the *am ha aretz* (in Hebrew).[55]*Minjung* theology is shaped by the outcasts, those who do not possess political power, economic wealth or social status.[56]*Minjung* theologians proposed *Minjung* as the image of the *Ochlos,* whom Jesus treated as His friends, mothers and brothers in His inclusive community (Mk. 3:34-35).

Thus the main characteristics of *Minjung* theology are driven by three major subheadings: the theology of *Minjung* (people/*pyithu*), the theology of *han* (suffering/*Dukkha*), and the theology of *praxis* (action). I would stress that *han* is the most important element in the socio-political awareness of *Minjung* theology.

---

[50]Jürgen Moltmann, "Minjung Theology for the Ruling Classes," in *Asian Contextual Theology for the Third Millennium: Theology of Minjung in Fourth-Eye Formation,* eds. Paul S. Chung, Veli-Matti Karkkainen and Kim Kyoung Jae (Eugene, OR: Pickwick Publications, 2007), 69.

[51]Suh Nam-dong, *Theology at Turning Point* (Seoul: Korean Theological Study, 1976), 5.

[52]David Suh Kwang-sun, "A Biographical Sketch of an Asian Theological Consultation," in *Minjung Theology,* ed. Kim Yong-Bock (Singapore: The Christian Conference of Asia/CCA, 1981), 18.

[53]Na Young-Hwa, *A Critical Study of Korean Theology of Minjung in Comparison with Latin American Theology of Liberation* (St. Louis, MO: Covenant Theological Seminary, 1983), 3.

[54]The Commission on Theological Concerns of the Christian Conference of Asia, *Minjung Theology: People as the Subject of History* (Maryknoll, NY: Orbis Books, 1981), 16.

[55]Ahn Byung Mu, "Jesus and the Minjung in the Gospel of Mark," in *Minjung Theology: People as the Subjects of History,* ed. the Commission on Theological Concerns of the Christian Conference of Asia (Maryknoll, NY: Orbis Books, 1981), 138.

[56]Young-Hak Hyun, "Minjung Theology and the Religion of Han," *East Asia Journal of Theology,* The Commission on Theological Concerns (1985): 354.

Han in Korean may be defined as a collective feeling of agony and pain which is similar to *Dukkha*.

> *Han* is not just an individual feeling of sickness that can be cured by psychotherapy. This is a collective feeling of the oppressed and it can be cured only when a total structure of the oppressed society is changed—the feeling of *han* has a negative element. It is a repressed murmuring, unexpressed in words.[57]

The concept of *han* is found as an Asian expression for suffering: *upnaha* in India, *hen* in China, *horosul* in Mongolia, *krosocuka* in Manchuria, *oorami* in Japan and *Dukkha* in Myanmar.[58] Admittedly, a perfect translation of *han* is impossible in Korean. Thus, Koreans use stories and other forms of traditional and religious elements to articulate a better idea of *han*. They also express their feeling of *han* in a mask dance. The dancers create a new culture of hope in a mask of dance. They criticize the evil structure not by revolution but by non-violent dancing. If *han* is the cluster of *Minjung* theology, *dan* is the soteriology of *Minjung* theology.[59] In order to transform *han* into *dan*, Korean Christians attempt to practice what they believe in God.[60] The *Minjung* participate in their *Dukkha* not just as passivists, but as the active subjects of history.[61]

Coming to my conclusion, *Minjung* theology is both positive and negative toward applying as a model for the *Pyithu-Dukkha*. Positively, *Minjung* theology employs the experience of Jesus through its dynamic stories to make the perceptions of *Minjung* relevant to Christians and non-Christians. Yet in other sense, *Minjung* theology is seen by the Korean evangelical theologians as just a pro-Marxist theology or humanistic theology which emphasizes only social ethics, not evangelism and so on. With respect to this sense, *Minjung* theology is positively weak in evangelistic and pastoral concerns at large.

Despite its weakness and strength, I would argue that *Minjung* theology seem more relevant to Myanmar today than Korea because Korea was a Third World country when *Minjung* theology was born but is no longer. Having examined some representative examples of *Minjung* theology, we will draw some relevancies and provide more inclusive approaches to the ecumenical and evangelical theologies in Myanmar. We will now look at another representative version of Asian theology, Dalit theology.

---

[57] David Suh, "A Biographical Sketch of an Asian Theological Consultation," 27-28.

[58] Jea Hoon Lee, *The Exploration of the Inner Wounds-Han* (Atlanta, GA: Scholar Press, 1994), 2.

[59] Nam-Dong Suh, "Toward a Theology of *Han*," in *Minjung Theology*, ed. Kim Yong-Bock (Singapore: The Christian Conference of Asia/CCA, 1981), 155.

[60] Jung Young Lee, "Minjung Theology: A Critical Introduction," in *Emerging Theology in World Perspective: Commentary on Korean Minjung Theology*, ed. Jung Young Lee (Mystic, CT: Twenty-Third Publications, 1988), 11.

[61] Kim Yong-Bock, "Korean Christianity as a Messianic Movement of the People," in *Minjung Theology*, ed. Kim Yong-Bock (Singapore: Christian Conference of Asia/CCA, 1981), 77.

Pyithu-Dukkha Theology in Dialogue with *Dalit* Theology

The term *Dalit* is derived from a Sanskrit, meaning downtrodden or untouchable. The total population of *Dalits* are about 250 million.[62] According to Hinduism,[63] people are innately divided into four castes: Brahmin[64] (the priestly and highest caste who knows the *Vedas*/Hindu scriptures), *Kshatriya* (the warrior caste), *Vaishya* (the business caste), and Sudra (the workers who serve the three upper castes).

Considered unclean and lower in status than animals, *Dalits* do not belong to this pyramid of castes and are known as the "outcastes," who are forced to do work the upper castes consider unclean. It was within this context that *Dalit* theology emerged in the new Asian theological scene in the 1980s.[65] Exodus 3:7-8 and Luke 4:18-19 are taken as the theological paradigms. *Dalit* theologians criticize the Hindu Brahminic[66] dominance of Christians and propose liberation theology to reflect the struggles of *Dalits*.[67]

Dalit theologians view the Suffering Servant in Isaiah 53 as a *Dalit*-servant. The Word becoming flesh, living among humans, and taking on the form of a slave is seen as the One suffering with *Dalits* (Phil. 2:5-9).[68] They developed *Dalit* theology not only from the perspective of God's liberating work, but from the context of Jesus' breaking the frontiers and solidarity with religious outcastes.[69] Joseph D'Souza's notion of *Dalits* and Brahmins in comparison with Jesus' antithesis to the Pharisees plays a central role for dialoging the *Pyithu-Dukkha* theology with *Dalit* theology.[70] Six points will be noted.

First, Jesus refused to exclude anyone from access to God—for instance, the Samaritan, the polluted sinner was accepted by Jesus as one of His best friends. *Second*, while Pharisees and Sadducees dared not mix with polluted people, Jesus willingly mingled with the dregs of society, telling the sinners about the coming

---

[62] James Massey, *Indigenous People: Dalits, Dalit Issues in Today's Debates* (Bangalore: Indian Society for Promoting Christian Knowledge/ISPCK, 1994), 6.

[63] Hinduism began as an amalgamation of 3 religious traditions—Aryanism (the Aryans who worshipped Vishnu), Dravidianism (the Dravidians who worshipped Shiva), Animism (the tribal people who worshipped nature).

[64] *Brahmin* is not to be confused with *Brahman*, one of the gods of Hinduism.

[65] Arvind P. Nirmal and V. Devasahayam, *A Reader in Dalit Theology* (New Delhi: Indian Society for Promoting Christian Knowledge/ISPCK, 1990), 180

[66] Brahman is the name of Hinduism's god.

[67] V. Devasahayam, *Frontiers of Dalit Theology* (New Delhi: Indian Society for Promoting Christian Knowledge/ISPCK, 1997), 501.

[68] I. John Mohan Razu, "Being Dalits and Becoming a New Community in a Globalizing Context," in *Dalit-Minjung Theology: On Being A New Community and Ecclesia of Justice and Peace*, ed. James Massey and Noh Jong Sun (Bangalore: BTESSC, 2010), 141.

[69] Devasahayam, *Frontiers of Dalit Theology*, 501.

[70] Joseph D'Souza, *Dalit Freedom, Now and Forever: The Epic Struggle for Dalit Emancipation* (Greenwood Village, CO: Dalit Freedom Network, 2004), 90.

of God's Kingdom. *Third,* in contrast to the Pharisaic and Brahminic teachings, Jesus emphasized the concept of God as the Father of all, being created in His own image.

Fourth Jesus rejected the notion of our fate in this suffering life as pre-determined by our deeds (*karma*) and taught that all humans are equally sinners, and no matter whether Pharisee or Brahmin, they are as polluted as *Dalits* and need God's grace and forgiveness. *Fifth,* Jesus smashed the notion of human mediators between God and humans through the Pharisaic-Brahminic priestly way. *Dalits* do not need a priestly class to mediate between God and humankind. They can have direct accesses to God through Jesus. *Finally,* true religion is all about faith and work, in contrast to the Brahministic-Pharisaic work righteousness. "True religion exists in the practice of faith, caring for the orphans and widows in solidarity with the untouchables (*Dalits*)" (James 1:27).[71]

As Jesus challenged the Pharisees and Sadducees who held the superiority to dominate over the other, *dalit* theologians have been resisting the evils of Brahminism. The Brahmins and extremist Hindutva forces who killed Mahatma Gandhi seem strong, but Christians have been struggling for justice in cooperating with non-Christians.[72] The most significant non-Christian activist was Dr. B.R. Ambedkar, who was a Hindu-born but a Buddhist-adherent, the architect of India's constitution and the liberator of *Dalits*. He classified Hinduism as a religion of enslavement due to its pre-determining *Dalits'* birth and he finally chose Buddhism, primarily because it teaches compassion.[73]

To conclude, I am aware that first, *Dalit* theology wrestles with classism while *Pyithu-Dukkha* theology deals with political oppression and, second, *Dalits* belong to the Christianity majority, whereas the *Pyithu-Dukkha* belong to the Buddhist majority. Yet both share a theological theme of liberation and inclusion. As *Dalit* theologians take Jesus' inclusion of the outcastes as the central themes, Christians in Myanmar have to reinterpret salvation as *reconciliation,* which proposes the idea of *embrace* as a theological response to the problem of *exclusion* in the religious context and salvation as *holistic salvation* in response to the cries of *Pyithu-Dukkha* in the socio-political context.

---

[71] Ibid., 91-93.

[72] James Massey, *Another World is Possible: Dalit Perspective on Human, Globalization and Just Society*, CDS Pamphlet 6 (New Delhi: Indian Society for Promoting Christian Knowledge/ISPCK, 2004), 13-15.

[73] P. Mohan Larbeer, "Mission: Ambedkar's Perspective," in *Dalit-Minjung Theological Dialogue: On Being A New Community and Ecclesia of Justice and Peace*, ed. James Massey and Noh Jong Sun (Bangalore: BTESSC, 2010), 168.

Pyithu's Response to *Dukkha*: Social-Political and Religious-Cultural Perspectives

Social-Political Perspectives: The *Pyithu* as the Subject of History

Pyithu's response to *Dukkha* lies in two challenges: one is in response to external colonialism and the other is internal militarism. Since the era of monarchial rule (pre-history-1885), the *Pyithu* have been seen as the subjects of history under the rule of Kyansitha (1084-1112), claiming the right to possess the whole life of *Pyithu* even a single strand of hairs (*Thet Oo San Pai*). A group of *Pyithu*, led by university students made the strikes to achieve liberty from the Britishin the 1920s.In 1930s, a group of farmers led by Saya San led a revolt in response to exploitations by heavy taxes.[74]

At the beginning of WW II, a group of *Pyithu* went against the British and formed the Burma Independent Army. A national leader, Aung San and leaders of all ethnics formed the *Panlon Treaty* on February 12, 1947. Aung San proposed a statement on the *Panlon Treaty* that the equality of all racial groups: "a nation is a collective term applied to the *Pyithu*, irrespective of their ethnic origins, living in close contact with one another."[75] Sadly, Aung San was assassinated on July 19, 1947, before his vision had been fulfilled. As a result of his attempt, the *Pyithu* gained independence on January 4, 1948 and the decade from 1948 to 1958 was known as *Pyidaw Thar* (well-being).[76]

When U Nu and U Ne Win destructed the *PanlonTreaty* and established a modern military nation on March 2, 1962, a group of *Pyithu*, led by the ethnics protested, followed by the farmer's protest against the poverty, claiming that the peasants are like a people, who are thirsty for water while in the ocean.[77]In 1988, all classes of *Pyithu* joined the largest non-violent protest in the nation's history, calling for an end to the military regime. All universities were closed, thousands of *Pyithu's* students were killed and some were detained, while Aung San Su Kyi was put under house arrest.[78]

In 2007, a group of *Pyithu* led by Buddhist monks made the second largest protest, calling for liberty. A number of Buddhists were suppressed and killed. Another form of the military regime's exploitation over the *Pyithu* included forced labor among the ethnic groups. Thus, the ethnic groups took up guns to protect

---

[74]Stanley J. Tambiah, *The Buddhist Saints of the Forest, the Cult of Amulets* (New York: Cambridge University Press, 1984), 314-331.

[75]Maung Maung, *Aung San of Burma* (The Hague: Martinus Nijhoff, 1962), 27.

[76]Joel Tin Moe, "Korean Theology of Han and Its Relevance to Pyithu-Doukkha Theology of Myanmar" (M.Th. Thesis, Hanil University & Presbyterian Theological Seminary, Jeonbuk, 2000), 32.

[77]Alice Davies, "And the Harvest Shall be Plentiful," *Economic: Voice of Burma* 6, no. 7 (1996): 7.

[78]Ibid.

their homelands. Myanmar has recently experienced a nominal civilian government since 2010, and Su Kyi was released from house arrest and allowed to join parliament, but the country is still run by the military-backed government. The *Pyithu*'s response to *Dukkha* can be therefore defined by three phases: the first phase led by the *ordinary farmers*, the second led by the *University students* and the current third phase led by the *Buddhist monks*.[79]

Religious-Cultural Perspective

Nibbanic and *Kammic* Buddhism and Soteriological Reflections

Paul Tillich was right when he said, "religion is the substance of culture and culture is the form of religion."[80]There are two soteriological ideas of Theravada Buddhism: *Nibbanic* Buddhism and *Kammic* Buddhism.[81]*Nibbanic* Buddhism is a religion of radical salvation. *Nibbanic* Buddhism believes the source of *Dukkha* is desire and rejects everything within the world as a possible goal of salvation. As the origin of *Dukkha* is desire, one needs to eliminate desire by following the Eightfold Path.[82]

As *Nibbanic* Buddhism is soteriologically concerned with the transcendence of *Dukkha*, it seeks to achieve the goal of salvation only through wisdom (*pana*). The ultimate goal of *Nibbanic* Buddhism is meditation rather than deed for liberation.[83] Though meditation is known by all Burmese Buddhists as the royal road to *Nibban*, it is practiced only by a small number of true mediation practitioners. Soteriological action of *nibbanic* Buddhism is suitable only for the monks who can really meditate for liberation.

In contrast to *Nibbanic* Buddhism, *Kammic* Buddhism is seen as a religion of merit.The Buddhist belief in *karma* serves as a central work for salvation. Three kinds of *Kammic* Buddhism should be noted: charity (*tana*), morality (*sila*) and meditation (*bhavana*). *Kammic* Buddhism is primarily concerned with a better rebirth by improving *karma* and it is a religion of popular salvation, which is commonly practiced by a majority of Burmese Buddhists for the sake of liberation.

The difference between the *nibbanic* and *kammic* concepts of salvation is that the former sees salvation as a result of meditation while the latter understands salvation as the effect of action. *Kammic* Buddhism takes "deed" as the central theme toward its soteriological goal. Liberation is not to be actualized only in the last moment of one's life or only in the future, but it is anticipated. Because of

---

[79]Oh Jae Shik, "The People: Come of Age," in *Toward a Theology of People* (Tokyo: Christian Conference of Asia & Urban -Rural Mission, 1977), 51-52.

[80]Paul Tillich, *Theology of Culture* (New York: Oxford University Press, 1959), 42.

[81]Spiro, *Buddhism and Society, A Great Tradition and Its Burmese Vicissitudes*, 11.

[82]The Eightfold Path is moral-oriented and includes (1) Right View, (2) Right Thought, (3) Right Speech, (4) Right Behavior, (5) Right Livelihood, (6) Right Moral Effort, (7) Right Mindfulness and (8) Right Concentration.

[83]Ibid., 93.

this reason, *Kammic* Buddhists actively participate in liberative movements and engage in charitable works.[84]

Nat-Worship and Soteriological Reflections: A Buddhist Perspective

The word "*Nat*" is derived from the Sanskrit word "*nath*," which is adopted as an Anglicized form of the Burmese which means "spirit."[85] *Nat-worship* is tenaciously rooted not only in the hearts of Buddhists as a primal religion and but among the ethnic groups as a tribal religion.[86] One will see *Nat* shrines side-by-side with the Buddha shrines in a Buddhist house—Buddha and *Nats* are inseparable images for Buddhists. In Myanmar, Buddhists worship *Nats* for safety and liberation in their mundane life (*lokka*) while they worship the Buddha for the rebirth in their supra-mundane life (*lokkutara*).

The most basic belief in *Nat*-worship is that there are many spirits everywhere in both animate beings and inanimate beings—this is analogous to God's omnipresence. Buddhists live with many spirits, some benevolent and some malevolent. People and the spirits share one integral community life and *Nats* are believed to aid as major sources for liberation, security, and success.[87] *Nat*-worshippers allege their sickness and all means of *Dukkha* are caused by malevolent *Nats*. Thus, they solve their problems by worshipping *Nats*, who are able to help overcome *Dukkha* and bring good fortune.[88] There are two main reasons why Burmese Buddhists worship *Nats*. One is simply to please the *Nats* who are assumed to help people with their hardships and the other is primarily because they fear *Nats*. Failure to make sacrificial rites can bring misfortune to the people.[89]

Nat-Worship from the Tribal-Ethnic Perspective

I would like to look at only three ethnic groups, Karens, Kachins and Chins, who are the Christian majority. With regard to their worldviews, the ethnic *Nat*-worshippers have a three-tiered world: first (heaven), second (earth) and third (the underworld). As their folksongs address, heaven is supposed to be the abode of the Supreme Being, while the earth is designed as the place where the *Nats* live together with human beings.[90]

---

[84]Ibid., 68.

[85]Maung Htin Aung, *Folk Elements in Burmese Buddhism* (Oxford: Oxford University Press, 1962), 2.

[86]Simon Pau Khan En, "Nat-Worship: A Paradigm for Doing Ecumenical Theology in Myanmar," *Asia Journal of Theology* 8, no. 1 (April 1994): 45.

[87]Ibid. There are 37 spirits altogether.

[88]Benedicte brac de la Pirriere, "The Taungbyon Festival" in *Burma at the Turn of the 21st Century*, ed. Monique Skidmore (Honolulu, HI: University of Hawaii Press, 2005), 66.

[89]Nicholas Greenwood, ed., *Burmese Then and Now* (Bucks: Bradt, 1995), 59-63.

[90]Pau Khan En, "Nat-Worship," 46-47.

First, the Karens hold the belief in the existence of the Supreme Being, whom they call (*Ywa*). According to folklore, *Ywa* gave the book (the bible) to the Karens as an elder, but they neglected it. *Ywa* was angry for their negligence and took it back from the elder and gave it to the younger brother (white man). Historically, there was a hope among the Karens that one day the younger brother would bring the book back to them. This age-long expectation was fulfilled when the American Baptist missionary Adoniram Judson came to Myanmar in 1813. As Judson preached the Gospel to them, they readily accepted him as their white younger brother who had brought back the lost book.[91] The concept of *Ywa* in *Nat*-worship paved the way for the Karens to accept the Gospel when Judson preached about the Supreme Being and so the Karens were the first ethnic groups who accepted the Gospel and a group of Christian majority in Myanmar.[92]

Secondly, the Kachins have a concept of a Supreme Being. There are two types of *Nats*: one is the minor *Nats* living with humans on earth and the other is the major *Nats*, residing somewhere up heaven. The major *Nats* are understood as creators while the minor *Nats* are treated as the indwellers in the world.[93] The major *Nat* or *Karai Kasang* is believed to be a benevolent being while the minor *Nats*, or *Lamu Madu Aga Madu* are malevolent beings. The Kachins worship the major *Nats* for the sake of liberation. This shows that the Kachins see the Supreme Being as deity of good not of evil. This concept of the Supreme Deity enabled the Kachins to easily accept Jesus as their liberator and they even took over *Karai Kasang* for naming God when they became Christians.[94]

Like the Karens and the Kachins, the Chins (my tribe) also have a concept of a supreme deity, whom they call by several names, including *Pasian, Pathian, Khawzing, Pu Vana, Pangcim* and *Khanpughi*. The name *Pathian* or *Pasian* is derived from two Chin words: *Pa* means "Father" and *thian* or *sian* means "Holy." *Pathian* therefore means "Holy Father."[95] For the Chins, the Supreme Being is a benevolent being, while the *Nat* is malevolent. Unlike the two preceding ethnics and the Barma Buddhists, the Chins have a concept of blood sacrifice in favor of appeasing the malevolent *Nat*. The object of ritual rite is not to praise but to appease the *Nats* who are living with humans.

Even though the Chins believe in the existence of the Supreme Being, they never bother to propitiate him with ritual sacrifice because they conceive of the Supreme Deity as a transcendent being while the *Nats* are treated as the immanent being on earth. The Chins seek the help of the *Nats* in their sufferings by plighting blood sacrifice. This blood sacrifice paved the way for the Gospel among Chins

---

[91] Donald Mackenzie Smeaton, *The Loyal Karens of Burma* (London: Kegan Paul Trech & Co., 1887), 185.

[92] A. R. McMahon, *The Karens of the Golden Chersonese* (London: Paall Mall, 1876), 120.

[93] C. Gilhodes, *The Kachins-Religions and Customs* (Calcutta: Catholic Orphan Press, 1922), 100.

[94] Ibid., 101.

[95] Sing Khaw Khai, *The Theological Concept of the Zo in the Chin Tradition and Culture* (Yangon: Myanmar Institute of Theology, 1984), 125.

accepting Jesus' atonement, when Arthur E. Carson (an American Baptist missionary), preached the gospel in 1899.

In sum, what we can say about the Supreme Being and *Nat*-Worship is that God's liberative work among the ancestors offers us two major themes: first belief in the *mysterious work* of God in the practice of Buddhists and Ethnic groups was present even before they had heard of the Gospel; second the *continual work* of the Spirit is revealed among the ancestors after they become Christians—the former work is *secret* while the latter is more *open*. It is to be realized that the Burmese ancestors (both Buddhists and Ethnic groups) sought liberation outside the work of Jesus. As the Bible says,

> Long ago God spoke to our ancestors (*Nat*-Worshipers) in many and various ways by the prophets, but in these last days He (God) has spoken to us by Jesus the Son, whom He appointed heir of all things, through whom He also created the worlds (Hebrew 1:1-3). From this, I will proceed to God's revelation to humans as the creator and redeemer in the biblical world.

Chapter 2

A Biblical Concept Of Divine and Human *Dukkha*

The Bible as the Paradigmatic Record of God-Human Encounter

"God is the Story of Jesus and Jesus is the Story of the crucified people."[1]

The bible is the paradigmatic record of the divine-human encounter in a dialectical way—"God speaks and people hear that a dialogue between the divine and human is possible."[2] The first book of the Old Testament, Genesis, begins with the story of God's creation while the first book of the New Testament, Matthew, begins with the genesis of God's people through Jesus. The biblical witness is all about God's dialectical dealings with people. God's liberation of Israel in Egypt, God's covenant with the Israel, the rights of the liberated people, God's judgment and justice toward the wicked and the righteous are the basic contents of the biblical witness of the Old Testament.

According to the New Testament, Christian theology reflects God's liberation from sin, law, death through the sacrifice and resurrection of Jesus. Liberation through Jesus' vicarious death, the new covenant in His blood, the new rights and duties of new fellowship of all nations, embracing both Jews and Gentiles, slaves and freemen, men and women, adults and children (Gal. 3:28) are the basic witness of the New Testament.[3]

---

[1] C. S. Song, *Jesus and The Reign of God* (Minneapolis, MN: Fortress Press, 1993), 308.

[2] Terence E. Fretheim, *The Suffering of God: An Old Testament Perspective* (Philadelphia, PA: Fortress Press, 1984), 34.

[3] Jürgen Moltmann, "A Definitive Study Paper: A Christian Declaration of Human Rights," in *A Christian Declaration on Human Rights: Theological Studied of the World Alliance of Reformed Churches*, ed. Allen O. Miller (Grand Rapids, MI: William B. Eerdmans Publishing Company, 1977), 130.

As the turn to the climax of the tide of evil began with Adam and Eve's sinning against God by choosing to believe a lie, the result was lots of divine intimacy. From that moment, we are spiritually dead in God's eyes.[1] No matter how sinful we are, God still loves because we are His children. God was angry, of course, for a moment, not forever (Gen.6:12). The memory of God is not a memory of hate forever. Paul's exhortations to the Ephesians says it best: "if you are angry, do not let it lead you into sin; do not let the sun go down on your anger, and do not make any room for the devil" (Eph. 4:26-27).

Though every aspect of human life has been corrupted by sin, God forgives and continues to use sinful humans in making a covenant, such as Noah in general and Abraham in particular, through whom the new promise was restored for all nations (Gen. 12:1-3). The fall of humanity is followed by the bondage of Israel as the drama of God's deliverance. The social biography of the slave is paradigmatic. The culmination of God's redeeming action is the delivery of the slaves from the bondage of the Egyptian, Babylonian, and Greco-Roman empire and the establishment of a new community.[2]

The social-biography of the crucified people of God needs to be interwoven with the story of the crucified Jesus through whom we came to know the invisible God (Col. 1:15) and His relationship to human *Dukkha* and that God Himself suffers in solidarity with those who suffer in the OT and the NT. We cannot fully understand the story of Jesus outside the context of the social biography of God's crucified people in the Bible. In order to know Jesus, the incarnate, crucified and resurrected Word in the NT, we must know the crucified people first, the objects of God's compassion in the OT.

A Theology of Divine-*Dukkha* in the Old Testament

The Exodus Paradigm: The *Pyithu* as Objects of God's Deliverance

> God said, "I have observed the misery of my people who are in Egypt; I have heard their cry on account of their taskmasters. I have come down to deliver them from the Egyptians and to bring them out of that land to a good and broad land, a land flowing with milk and honey to the country of the Canaanites, the Hittites and Amorites, the Perizzites, the Hivites and the Jebusites."

(Exo.3:7-8)

A prominent OT scholar, Fretheim offers three reasons for the divine suffering in relation to human suffering: (1) God suffers *with* the people of Israel through

---

[1]Christopher J. H. Wright, *Knowing the Holy Spirit Through the Old Testament* (Downers, IL: InterVarsity Press, 2006), 19.

[2]Kim Yong-Bock, *Messiah and Minjung: Christ's Solidarity with the People for New Life* (Hong Kong: The Christian Conference of Asia/CCA, 1992), 8.

experience of suffering—*Exodus experience,* (2) God suffers *because* of the people's rejection of God as Lord—*divine covenant and broken relationship,* and (3) God suffers *for* the restoration of self-giving—*Messianic Suffering unto Death.*³ In line with Fretheim, I would argue that the Messianic suffering (Christology) would not exist in the NT without God's *Dukkha* in the OT.⁴ God's suffering in the form of Israel should be understood as a prototype of Jesus' *Dukkha* and a paradigm of *Pyithu-Dukkha* because "God's suffering is the heavenly counterpart to the suffering of the earthly servants/people of God."⁵

According to Fretheim, "The Book of Exodus is all about the beginnings of Israel as the people of God."⁶ Historically, the story began with the Exodus and this historical event is the pivotal point for the salvation of Israel. When God heard Israel's groaning, He could not keep silent. He remembered His covenant with Abraham (Gen. 12) and He took heed of the plight of Israel (Exo. 2:24-25). God took Israel's history in hand and gave His people a divine future.⁷ God's saving action becomes the biblical basis for a covenant with the people that was formulated at Mt. Sinai and codified as the covenant.

Thus, the word "exodus" (ἔξοδος) in Greek should be interpreted not only as the departures of the Israelites from Egypt but also as the consequential event of the law-giving to indicate Israel as God's covenantal partners.⁸ This interpretation employs Israel as the *am ha' aretz* in Hebrew in the OT, and the *Ochlos* in Greek in the NT, who are socially outcast, politically enslaved and religiously suppressed people. The Israel in Egypt were regarded by G.E Mendenhall as *Apiru,* a group of people living as slaves who stood outside the system of the law without legal protection under the rule of Pharaoh.⁹

Seeing Israel as the outsiders from the community even though they belong to the Jewish tribes, it is relevant to depict the *Pyithu-Dukkha* as the same picture of the captives who struggle for their national identity.¹⁰ The pattern of slavery experienced by Israel in Egypt reflects the fact that they were totally subjected

---

³Terence E. Fretheim, *The Suffering of God: An Old Testament Perspective* (Philadelphia, PA: Fortress Press, 1984), 108. Italics mine.

⁴Terence E. Fretheim, "Christology and the Old Testament," in *Who Do You Say That I Am? Essay on Christology,* ed. Mark Allen Powell and David R. Bauer (Louisville, KY: John Knox Press, 1999), 201.

⁵Fretheim, *The Suffering of God,* 148.

⁶Terence E. Fretheim, *Exodus—Interpretation: A Bible Commentary for Teaching and Preaching* (Louisville, KY: John Knox Press, 1991), vii.

⁷James H. Cone, *God of the Oppressed,* new revised ed. (Maryknoll, NY: Orbis Books, 1997), 58.

⁸Ralph, W. Klein, *Israel in Exile, A Theological Interpretation* (Philadelphia, PA: Fortress Press, 1979), 12

⁹George E. Mendenhall, *Ancient Israel's Faith and History: An Introduction to the Bible in Context* (Louisville, KY: John Knox Press, 2001), 2.

¹⁰Chris H. Moon, "An Old Testament Understanding of Minjung," in *Minjung Theology,* ed. Kim Yong-Bock (Singapore: The Christian Conference of Asia/CCA, 1981), 124-125.

in the Egyptian system. One of the best examples is that all the land in Egypt belonged to Pharaoh, but the people who cultivated it also belonged to Pharaoh (Gen. 47:13-26). Similarly, the Burmese farmers are economically exploited by the military. The paradigm can be stated as below:

> A changeable political climate and the brutal treatment of humans as machines: since Israel are God's people, the descendants of Abraham, they become the objects of God's salvation history and their welfare becomes God's concern and the Bible declares that they should be liberated by God from the Egyptians.[11]

When God heard the cries of Israel, God called Moses "through the revelation of the bush" to deliver them from the bondage of Egyptians (Exo.3:1-12). The word for the bush (*seneh*) is a verbal link to Sinai as the sign of God's covenant. The divine word out of bush from God and from *within* the world comes in order for God to take initiative through dialogue with Moses.[12] This shows that God was anthropomorphically revealed by acts through Moses as the agent on behalf of the suffering Israel.[13]

The Exodus is the point of departure of Israel's existence and the basis of their peoplehood established at Sinai (Exo. 20:2-3). The covenant is an invitation to Israel to enter into a responsible relationship with God wherein God is Israel's God and Israelis God's possession.[14] In the Exodus-Sinai, God is disclosed as the God of history whose revelation is identical with divine power to liberate the *Pyithu-Dukkha*. God's contest with Pharaoh shows that the *Pyithu*'s liberation can come only by God's power. God's presence continues to sustain the people through the wilderness to the Promised Land.

When Israel saw the great power which the Lord had put forth against Pharaoh, they put their faith in God, responding with a song: "I will sing to the Lord, for He has triumphed gloriously; horse and rider He has thrown into the sea—the Lord is my strength, my might and my salvation" (Exo. 15:1). Yet living in the wilderness for forty years is another challenge for Israel. God's act of liberation is not simply moving from oppression but it is also a gift of a land filled with blessings. God will not leave Israel in a halfway house in a wilderness because deliverance for God is not *from* something, it is *to* something, enabling the people to move from redemption to new creation.[15]

---

[11]Moon Hee-Suk Cyris, "An Old Testament Understanding of Minjung," in *Minjung Theology: Minjung as the Subjects of History*, ed. the Commission on Theological Concerns of the Christian Conference of Asia/CCA (Maryknoll, NY: Orbis Books, 1983), 124-125.

[12]Fretheim, *Exodus*, 55-56. Fretheim argues that God's revelation to Moses through the bush is a kind of divine condescension: "God made His presence lowly in order for humankind to enter into a genuine conversation."

[13]Fretheim, *The Suffering of God*, 128.

[14]Cone, *God of the Oppressed*, 59.

[15]Fretheim, *Exodus*, 59.

The Wilderness: The Carrying God and the Crying People

> The Lord your God, who goes before you is the One who will fight for you, just as He did for you in Egypt before your very eyes and in the wilderness, where you saw how the Lord your God *carried* you, just as one carries a child all the way that you traveled until you reach this place. (Deut. 1:30-31)

The wilderness is all about the carrying God and the crying people. The Bible reveals that carrying is a key dimension of God's saving act. According to Moses, God brought Israelites out of Egypt by carrying them, as parent carries a child. God carries not only as parent but as mother and nurse (Num. 11:12) and eagle (Exo. 19:4). The Exodus-wilderness tradition of God's job as a carrier for the crying people is developed by Deutero-Isaiah as a New Exodus—the old exodus was a dry way in the sea while the new exodus will be a wet way in the dessert (Isa. 43:16-19). Wilderness is a place where the crying people are face to face with danger and promise.[16] When danger and promise come together to the people of Israel, *Dukkha* or crisis takes place in the wilderness.

As a consequence of covenant, God wanted to teach Israel in the wilderness that humanity does not live by bread alone but by everything that proceeds from the mouth of God. God's people must learn about bread and the word of God. The Bible does not simply speak of promise without crisis. Otherwise, the biblical faith would be reduced only to a happy-ending-religion. The faith should also be a "protection-from-crisis religion" as the Bible speaks about a crisis situation and the co-existence of danger and promise. In the desert, God trained His people to be patient and put their trust in God.

The people of Israel thought God's deliverance from Egypt as a "happen-end story" but God wanted them to know "a trust-end" through the desert.[17] Walking in the wilderness for forty years was all about the speed of God's love and the test of Israel's trust. This was an important lesson for them to understand before they entered into Canaan. Forty years of national migration in the wilderness was such a long time. How slow and costly! We are finding today how experientially important this lesson is in time of crisis and suffering. This exodus event is still real in the context of *Pyithu-Dukkha*.

Speaking from the Burmese context, God entered our history and carried us all the way from our genesis. The love of God to *Pyithu-Dukkha* is ultimately revealed. Though the world in which we live today is efficient and speedy, God does not abandon the *Pyithu-Dukkha*, but walks with them throughout the wil-

---

[16] Kosuke Koyama, *Three Mile an Hour God: Biblical Reflections* (Maryknoll, NY: Orbis Books, 1980). 4. Koyama talks about "Three Mile an Hour God" from an Asian perspective in the sense that Asians walk three miles in one hour. The term *three mile* summaries Koyama's understanding of God's deliberate and patient love for His walking people in the wilderness.

[17] Ibid.

derness of *Dukkha*. If God is not Love, He would have gone much faster and left them behind. It is slow, yet it is the Lord over all speeds. As God's love has its speed, it goes in the depths of *Dukkha* with the promise of hope. Israel, which was taught the truth of bread (manna) and the word of God (mercy) in the wilderness as they walked three miles an hour by the speed of love, appear as the prototype of Jesus, who experienced all the wilderness paradigms of *Dukkha*.

Ultimately, Jesus walked toward the cross. There, He lost His mobility and He was not even moving at three mile an hour as humans walk. At this point of Jesus' immobility,[18] God seems powerless, yet Jesus was resurrected by the power of God (Jn. 12:27-28). The powerful God who has destroyed the enslaving power of Pharaoh is the living God, walking with the *Pyithu* in their struggle. History changes constantly and God's word is proclaimed in different ways. Yet the fact which does not change is that God acts transcendently in history as He sovereigns over the whole of history.[19]

The Prophetic Response to *Dukkha*: The *Pyithu* as Bearer of Messianic Image

It was on the foundation of the Exodus that the prophets constructed their theology and ethics.[20] My interest lies in the prophetic voices, primarily because they are not just the foretellers but the advocates through whom God sustains His covenant and partly because Christians ought to be prophetic advocates. The covenant is twofold: (1) placing Israel as God's liberated people in obedience to divine will (Exo. 20:2-3) and (2) as God's people responsibility taking care of the oppressed and the poor and the like.

The covenant between God and Israel was essential to protect the oppressed and the poor.[21] God, through Moses' legislation and the prophetic movements sought justice for the poor (Deu.10:17-18; Isa. 25:4). Yet Israel failed its side of the covenant by pursuing after foreign gods. How did God feel when they turned away from Him? The God who tearfully allowed judgment to fall does not leave those in a lurch who suffer as a result. God's grace was not destroyed by Israel's obedience. According to Isaiah,

> For a brief moment, I abandoned you, but with great compassion I will gather you. In overflowing wrath for a moment I hid my face from you but with everlasting love I will have compassion on you, says the Lord. (Isa. 54:7-8)

The conflict between *grace* and *obedience* was escalated when Israel became a monarchy, for the rulers forgot the Exodus experience and the function of the King in Israel as the protector of the oppressed. It was in this context that the

---

[18]Ibid., 7.

[19]George T. Montague, *The Holy Spirit: Growth of a Biblical Tradition-A Commentary on the Principal Texts of the Old and New Testaments* (New York: Paulist Press, 1970), 6.

[20]God often referred to the Exodus event whenever He spoke to other prophets in relation to redemptive activity, for example Jer. 2:6; Hos. 11:1-2, Isa. 19:1-10, Ezek. 20:10.

[21]Cone, *God of the Oppressed*, 59.

prophets arose as God's messengers. The core of prophets was to bring God's Word to the people, proclaiming Yahweh's future activity of judgment and renewal that was about to burst into the present. As the words they spoke came from God, the prophets began declaring, "Thus Says the Lord."[22] This became increasingly apparent to Israel. God is seen to be present not only in what the prophets have to say, but in the word as embodied in the prophets' lives. The prophets' lives were reflective of divine life. Thus to hear and to see the prophets was to hear and see God, who was suffering on behalf of the people.[23]

Taking truth and justice as the essence of God's character (Isa. 5:16), the prophetic works dealt with the compulsion to speak the truth and the courage to stand for justice.[24] Therefore Israel's disobedience of the first commandment at Sinai has consequences in the social life that they began to oppress the poor. Amos said, "The Lord has sworn by His holiness but you forgot Him, your time is now coming and you trample on the needy and plunder the humble" (Amos 4:2; 8:4). Hosea also remarked in this way:

> Even though Yahweh cared for you (Israel) in the wilderness, in a land of drought, as if you were in a pasture, you forgot Him and becoming an oppressor trampling on justice, doggedly pursuing what is worthless. (Hos. 5:11; 13:5-6)

Drawn from the statement of Micah (735-700 BC), "to be filled with power and authority of the Spirit means to be filled with justice and passion for the just cause of the exploited" (Mic. 3:8).[25] Micah singles out two terms in particular: "my people" and "this people." "My people" stands for prophets and the victims while "this people" implies the side of the ruling class who lived in Jerusalem (Mic.1:9; 2:9-11; 3:3-5).[26] As Micah said, "the oppressors eat the flesh of my people and strip their skin off them and, built Zion at the cost of bloodshed, Jerusalem by means of violence" (3:3-10). Living in a context of corruption, Micah courageously denounced social injustices and sought justices (3:2).

Similarly, Amos's time (722-721 BC) can be understood as one of *chaotic* moments in the history of Israel. The people who created chaotic moments were the *power-holders* and *wealth-possessors*. The rich bought the poor and sold them for a pair of shoes (Amos 2:6-7). As the nation is covered by clouds of corruption, Amos called for the people to turn to God, hate evil, love good and establish justice (5:4, 15).[27] The paradigms of political and moral corruption in Amos' time comes similar to Myanmar's context, in which all Chris-

---

[22] For instance, Jeremiah's inaugural vision, in which God said, "I put my words in your mouth and I am watching to fulfill my word to the end of your prophetic ministry" (Jeremiah 1:9; 1:12; 28:12).

[23] Fretheim, *The Suffering of God,* 149.

[24] Bernhard W. Anderson, *Understanding the Old Testament* (Englewood Cliffs, NJ: Princeton Hall, 1957), 289.

[25] Ibid.

[26] Ibid., 290.

[27] Jeff Haynes, *Politics in the Developing World: A Concise Introduction* (Oxford: Blackwell Publishing, 2000), 160.

tians are called to be prophetic in engagement with the *Pyithu*'s liberative movements regardless of social religious diversities (5:24). *Pyithu*'s well-being can only be achieved through a prophetic participation of all Burmese.[28]

We will now turn to Jeremiah ("weeping prophet" from 550BC) whom God called to be a prophet to the nations of the world (Jer. 1:5).[29] The experience of the Babylonian exile (597-587 BC) was a shattering event for Israel and Jeremiah pictured himself as a victim and a gentle lamb being led to a slaughter. This means Jeremiah was a vicarious sufferer in solidarity with the victims (11:19).Let us look at what God has said to Jeremiah: "indeed, I listened; Ephraim was in grief (31:18a): is Ephraim my dear son, is he the child I delight in? (31:20)—listen to a cry from Babylon" (51:54a).

The God who speaks at the creation is the God who listens to the cries of *Dukkha*. The God who turns deaf ears to our prayers and cries of the *Pyithu* does not deserve our worship. Of course, we cannot take advantage of the God who listens and weary God with our petty thoughts—this is why Jesus warned His disciples "not to deal with a babbling prayer" (Matt. 6:5). A sincere prayer that wells out of our heart and that cries out of the depth of our agony only touches the heart of the compassionate God.

What does the "new covenant" indicated in Jeremiah (Jer.31:31-34) mean?[30] Although this covenant will have admitted continuity with the Sinai covenant, it will be a new covenant, because it will be written in the heart of people, in contrast to the Sinai covenant, which was written on tablets of stones (Exo.24:12), and it will be grounded in a new act of grace and new heart filled by the spirit (Ezek. 36:25-28).[31] This is what James Muilenburgh calls "a relationship of grace, fulfilled in the new coming age of Christ."[32]

In light of this new covenant, justice for the poor is present also in time of Isaiah for whom David's reign is the major act of deliverance. Deutero-Isaiah (40-55) prophesies the deliverance of Israel from the Babylonians.[33] A central theme in Second Isaiah is New Exodus, the return from Babylon to Jerusalem. The land between Egypt and Canaan in the first Exodus was a wilderness (Deu.8:15), but in this new Exodus, the land between Babylon and Jerusalem will be transformed into a paradise, where the mountains will be lowered and the valleys raised to create a level road (Isa. 40:4). This Isaiah's prophetic vision is adopted by John in the

---

[28] Samuel Ngun Ling, *Theological Themes for Our Times: Reflections on Selected Themes of the Myanmar Institute of Theology* (Yangon: Judson Research Center, 2007), 165-166.

[29] Jack J. Lundbom, *Jeremiah Among The Prophets* (Eugene, OR: Cascade Books, 2012), 1-2.

[30] Joshua N. Moon, *Jeremiah's New Covenant* (Winona Lake, IN: Eisenbruans, 2011).

[31] Lundbom, *JeremiahAmong the Prophets*, 116-117. See also Jack Lundbom, *Jeremiah 21-36*,Anchor Bible 21B (New York: Doubleday, 2004).

[32] James Muilenburg, "The Office of the Prophet in Ancient Israel," in *The Bible in Modern Scholarship*, ed. J. Philip Hyatt (Nashville, TN: Abingdon Press, 1965), 74.

[33] Michael D. Coogan, *A Brief Introduction to the Old Testament* (New York: Oxford University Press, 2009), 333.

NT, saying "I am the voice of one crying out in the wilderness, make straight the way of the Lord" (Jn. 1:23).

It was during Isaiah's rule that Israel expected the Kingdom to be established by the Messiah.[34] Israel viewed God's reign as lasting from everlasting (Ps. 96:13). Empirically, they realized that in their situations in which God's reign is not always visible. Human rebellion continued to challenge God's rule. Thus, they envision that one day, Yahweh will reign from Zion and all nations will pay homage to Him (Isa.24:23). The people of Israel looks forward to that day of Messianic reign in line with David (Dan.7:18).[35] The Servant of the Lord (Isa.42:1-7) is embodied as the Servant of God(Isa. 53). The utterances of *Dukkha*, especially of Psalm 22, accompany Christ's path.

The Messiah ushered on the Lord's Day on which God is revealed for all nations (Isa.11:1-8). This Messianic coming in the form of the Servant is more than anything hitherto known and the history-changing event. This longing for the coming Servant is called the eschatological vision of the OT (Isa.42:1-7). As Messiah and His anointing occupied a major role for Israel throughout the captivity, so the coming Messiah ordained by the Spirit is not a kind of what the Israel has ever expected. As Fretheim stated,

> There is no suffering of the servant without the suffering of God. The Messianic Suffering is the heavenly counterpart to the suffering of the earthly servant of God. The Suffering Servant is viewed in vocational terms, willingly takes upon Himself the divine suffering and does what is finally necessary for the forces of evil in this world to be overcome (suffering unto death), for the sake not only of Israel but of the whole world. The suffering of people is reflective of the suffering of God, in the giving up of the servant for the world. As the Servant is the vehicle for divine immanence, so God experienced what the people suffered.[36]

Summary

The *Pyithu* and Israel on an Exilic Journey of *Dukkha*

As we compare the *Pyithu*'s exilic journey of *Dukkha* with the people of Israel, three similar stages are noticed. In the first stage, the *Pyithu* suffered as the victims of British until 1947 and gained independence in 1948 just as Israel suffered for 400 years and gained liberty from Egyptians.[37] As in the second exilic stage after independence, the *Pyithu* suffered from neo-colonization of U Ne Win's Burmese way to socialism begun in 1962 when U Ne Win took the power.

---

[34]Gerhard von Rad, *Old Testament Theology*, trans. D. M. G. Stalker, vol. 1 (New York: Harper & Row, 1962), 41.

[35]Hans-Joachim Kraus, *Psalms 1-59: A Continental Commentary* (Minneapolis, MN: Augsburg Publishing House, 1989), 131.

[36]Fretheim, *The Suffering of God*, 148.

[37]Samuel Ngun Ling, "In the Midst of the Stupas: Revitalization the Christian Presence in Myanmar," in *RAYS, MIT Journal of Theology* 3 (January 2003): 113.

This second stage of the *Pyithu*'s *Dukkha* is similar to the story of Israel's crying for their homeland while being exiled in Babylon.

During this period, U Ne Win brutally treated the *Pyithu* and expatriated foreign missionaries to their home countries. The most popular slogan that Ne Win promoted in this second stage was that *Amyo* (one race, Bamar), *Barthar* (one language, Burmese) and *Thatharna* (one religion, Buddhism). As a result, Buddhism is now a national religion and Burmese a national language. As in the third stage, the current military regime tries to make Burma a country of *Burmanization* or *Buddhistization* through totalitarianism. Our ethnic identities are assimilated into the religion and cultures of Buddhism.

Ethnic languages are denied as being part of Burmese. Christianity becomes an un-favored religion while Buddhism remains a favored religion. In terms of cultural assimilation, Christians face a situation similar to Israel's being assimilated to the Canaanites' culture when they entered into Canaan (for example, Canaanization occupied through inter-marriage and giving Canaanite names to Israelite children).[38]

Paradigmatically, the *Pyithu* are: (1) victims of the oppressors, yet they are objects of God's redemption; (2) captives of empires, yet they are the bearers of Messianic images. Using the *Pyithu*'s laments as the guidelines for determining God's laments, the correlation is that *Pyithu*'s cry becomes God's cry; God takes up the *Pyithu*'s cry and makes it His own. Though God did not permit the triumph of evil, evil become more and more prominent, causing three categories: God's being rejected by Israel becomes more and more pervasive; Israel experiences more and more suffering, and their future becomes more and more problematic.[39] It was within this foundation of the Messianic hope that an eschatology of the OT and a genesis of the NT are erected.

A Theology of Messianic *Dukkha* in the New Testament

Messiah in Solidarity with the *Ochlos-Pyithu-Dukkha*

The Word became flesh and lived among us.

(Jn. 1:14a)

As John said, "In the beginning" was the Word, and the Word was with God and the Word was God (Jn. 1:1). Instead of using the Hebraic term for the Messiah, John used the Greek term, *Logos* (the Word) which was more familiar to the Greek audiences he addressed. Messiah which John refers to the Word comes and lives among us as three Words: (1) the Word of incarnation (Christmas), (2) the Word of the cross (Good Friday) and (3) the Word of resurrection (Easter). Thus, the incarnate Messiah is the crucified Messiah and the crucified Messiah is the

---

[38] Ibid., 114.
[39] Ibid., 109.

risen Messiah. We cannot divorce the incarnate Messiah from the crucified Messiah, the crucified Messiah from the risen Messiah.[40]

The Messianic incarnation is the very essence of Christian faith and the final form of divine revelation. Thus, let us start with the incarnate Messiah who is in solidarity with the *Ochlos-Pyithu*.[41] To make sense of Jesus' solidarity with the outcasts, I would argue that incarnation should be understood as a positive syncretism combination of Jesus' divinity and humanity. The reason is that syncretism is at the heart of Jesus' incarnation. The word *syncretism* comes from the Greek word, *synkretizein*, meaning "to make two parties join against a third."[42] Theologically speaking, Christianity cannot be separated from those called outcasts (*Pyithu-Dukkha*).

Incarnation should not be regarded as the transformation of divine into human but as the participation of the divine in the form of servant (Phil. 2:9-11). The Word becoming flesh does not mean that *Logos* changes into man. The Word becoming flesh and dwelling amon us implies the coming of God into human existence in a perfect form of humiliation with sinful humans.[43] Jesus spoke of His coming: "I came not to call the righteous but the public sinners (*Pyithu-Dukkha*) (Mk. 2:17b).[44] As Wolfhart Pannenberg said, "the Messianic coming is not the ascent of human to God but the descent of God to human to be in a compassionate solidarity with the outcasts and sinful human beings."[45]

From the perspective of Jesus' solidarity with the *Ochlos-Pyithu-Dukkha*, it is certain in the NT that Mark is the first Gospel author to introduce the term *ochlos* in connection with the OT's use of *am ha' aretz*, which was interpreted as the "marginalized"(Mk. 1:22; 2:13).[46] In contrast to the term *Laos*, who are those within religious sphere as defined by Pharisees, Mark applies the term *Ochlos* to the community of Jesus' inclusion as His friends and brothers and showed His compassion (Mk. 6:34).[47]

From the perspective of Jesus' compassion toward the *Ochlos*, it is appropriate to dialogue with the Buddhist as how Buddhists and Christians speak about compassion in the context of the *Pyithu-Dukkha*. Jewish community in Palestine in Jesus' time in the first century was similar to the social-religious situation of India at the time of Buddha in the sixth century, which is relevant to the Burmese

---

[40] Koyama, *Three Mile an Hour God*, 24.

[41] Kim Yong-Bock, "Reading the Bible from Below," in *World Christianity in the 20th Century*, ed. Noel Davies and Martin Conway (London: SCM Press, 2008), 40-41.

[42] Koyama, *Three Mile an Hour God*, 64. The term *"syncretism"* was first introduced by a Dutch humanist Erasmus of the sixteenth century into the meaning of an eclectic mixture in philosophical and theological doctrines.

[43] Karl Barth, *Credo* (New York: Charles Scribner's Sons, 1962), 66.

[44] Ibid.

[45] Wolfhart Pannenberg, *Jesus: God and Man*, trans. L.L. Wilkins and D.A. Priebe (Philadelphia, PA: The Westminster Press, 1968), 334.

[46] C.E.B. Franfield, *The Gospel According to Saint Mark* (Cambridge: Cambridge University, 1959), 410.

[47] Mu, "Jesus and the Minjung in the Gospel of Mark," 140-141.

context.⁴⁸ My appreciation of Buddhism lies in its view of personhood, which comes close to Jesus' solidarity with the crowd. Jesus' vow at the beginning of His mission has much to do with the Buddha's vow after his enlightenment/awakening as he met a beggar. Buddha's vow is this:

> Having myself crossed the ocean of *Dukkha*; I must help others to cross it. Freed myself, I must set others free. This is the vow, which I made in the past when I saw all that lives in distress and crisis.⁴⁹

Similarly, Jesus' vow at the beginning of His mission is: The Spirit of the Lord is upon me as He has anointed me; He has sent me to announce good news to the poor, to proclaim release for prisoners and recovery of sight for the blind; to let the broken Victims go free, to proclaim the year of the Lord's favor (Lk. 4:18-19).

Comparing Buddha's vow with Jesus' vow regarding liberation, Buddha is, of course fundamentally different from Christ as Buddha was a self-appointed herald of the good news from the context of *Dukkha*, which does not claim any relationship with the Spirit, while Jesus was appointed by God and anointed by the Spirit. Yet I am struck that the main tenets of their vows are primarily filled with concern for the political conditions that victimize the oppressed.⁵⁰Placing Buddha as humanistic liberator and Christ as holistic savior in solidarity with the *Pyithu-Dukkha*, I am drawn into their *Karuna* for the people in their vow and the way they toiled unselfishly for emancipation from *Dukkha*.

The *Pyithu-Dukkha* are not only the objects of mercy, but the people who hold affection in the eyes of God to represent God's justice on earth. Jesus' solidarity with the *Ochlos* signifies the real presence of God's Kingdom in which He struggles together with the *Pyithu-Dukkha* and promises them the future of the Kingdom (Mk. 3:23-34). Jesus' ministry reflects the very nature of God's compassion or *Karuna*, which starts at *the lowest level* of incarnational solidarity and ends with the *highest point* of sacrifice for others on the cross. Solidarity is the counterpart of Jesus' ultimate sacrifice for the sinful and tortured *Pyithu-Dukkha* in struggle for God's justification and justice.

The Wounded Jesus: The Carrying and Saving Lamb of God

Behold the Lamb of God who takes away the sin of the world. (John 1:29)

The words, "carrying," "bearing," "taking away" are the key dimension of God's saving work from the Exodus event to God's redemption in Jesus' event. My great interest in a carrying God traces back to the Exodus-wilderness and

---

⁴⁸Mircea Eliade, *Images and Symbols: Studies in Religious Symbols*, trans. Philip Mairet (New York: Sheed & Ward, 1952), 12.

⁴⁹Edward Conze, *Buddhist Scriptures* (Baltimore, MD: Penguin Books, 1959), 54.

⁵⁰C. S. Song, *Third-Eye Theology: Theology in Formation in Asian Settings* (Maryknoll, NY: Orbis Books, 1979), 116.

Babylonian deliverance, in which God appeared as the carrying savior. The second Isaiah (40-60) in particular[51] helps us understand the portrayal of a carrying God in line with the carrying Lamb in John 1:29. By correlating the crucifixion of Jesus with the Passover sacrifice in the Exodus event (Exo. 12:27), John appropriates Jesus as the carrying Lamb through whom the wounded people are healed and the broken world is reconciled.[52]

Jesus as a sacrificial Lamb is not exactly the same as the Passover lamb slaughtered as a sign of God's deliverance from the Egyptians—the latter is nothing more than a sign for God to pass over Israel. By referring to the bread as Jesus' body and the wine as His blood, such words are not found in the Exodus-Passover lamb. Yet the word, "lamb" makes us aware that God's salvation could never be done without the wounds of Jesus (Isa. 53: 5; 1Pet. 2:24). Jesus' carrying away the sin of the world and carrying the cross (Jn. 19:17) points to His perfect obedience to God's commands.[53]

Carrying is the work of the slaves and servants in a manner in which God allows Himself to accept the role of servant. Jesus chose to serve, even to the point of washing His disciples' feet as a sign of removal of sin (Jn. 13:1).[54]Jesus' death involves cleansing power of sin and love—Jesus cleans us from all sin (1Jn. 1:7). Thus, Jesus is called the *hilasmos* not for us only, but for the sins of the whole world. The term *hilasmos* can be translated "expiation," or it may be rendered "at-one-ment"[55] (Jesus died once and for all, 1Pet. 3:18) as its effect is to reconcile with God and people. Jesus' sacrificial obedience to death is to meet the demands of God's justice and to bring about reconciliation.[56]

If we take the oppressed (*Pyithu-Dukkha*) as the objects of God's deliverance drawn from the exodus, God's divine is a "solo act." But when Jesus enters into the drama of God's saving work as the Lamb, the salvation drama has changed from a "solo act" to "dual act," played by God and Jesus. Because of Jesus' obedience to God who sent and commitment to sake of the people and the world (Jn. 3:16), the body of the Lamb, was broken and its blood was shed for many.[57]Thus it may be useful to consider what the wounded Jesus means for Him to die "for" or "on behalf of" (*hyper*) "many."

---

[51]Frederick J. Gaiser, "I Will Carry and Will Save: The Carrying God of Isaiah 40:66," *Word and World* 5, Supplement Series (April 2006): 94.

[52]Craig R. Koester, *Symbolism in The Fourth Gospel: Meaning, Mystery, Community*, 2nd ed. (Minneapolis, MN: Fortress Press, 2003), 220-221.

[53]Ibid., 222.

[54]Richard J. Clifford, *Fair Spoken and Persuading: An Interpretation of Second Isaiah* (New York: Paulist, 1984), 131.

[55]The "atonement," was translated from "at-one-ment" by William Tyndale when he translated the Bible from Latin into English in 1526. "Atonement" is synonymous to "reconciliation."

[56]Kathryn Tanner, *Christ the Key* (New York: Cambridge University Press, 2010), 248.

[57]C. S. Song, *Jesus,The Crucified People* (Minneapolis, MN: Fortress Press, 1996), 213-215.

The Greek word, *hyper* is used in an inclusive sense, not in an exclusive sense.[58] *Hyper* also implies "being in the company of," or "in solidarity with."[59] The wounded Jesus uttered the cryptic remarks: "I, when I am lifted up from the earth, will draw *all* people to myself" (Jn. 12:32) and "it is better for you to have one man (Jesus) die for the people in order that the whole nation shall not parish" (Jn. 11:50). *Hyper* implies Jesus' inclusion of the 135 racial groups of *Pyithu* whom Jesus restored unto God. Bonhoeffer also argues that "Jesus in the flesh is the inclusive Savior who carries all of humanity."[60]

The God-as-Lamb image makes God's incarnation all the more inclusive to deliver all sinful people, taking upon Himself sins. Laying down His life for many [*hyper*] to carry the sins is the supreme manifestation of sacrificial love. As God sends Jesus in the flesh as the Lamb so that He may save and carry all of humanity. In the wounded Jesus we behold the wounded people. In the wounded Jesus, we experience the loving and suffering God. Gaiser portrayed the carrying God in different images:

> God is the God who carries—the Shepherd who carries us in His arm (Isa. 40:10-11; Ps. 91:3); the Eagle who carries us on its wings (Exo.19:4; Isa. 40:31); the Ass who carries us along life's way; the Mother who carries us on her arm (Isa. 46:3; 66:12-13); the Servant who carries our diseases (Isa. 42:1; 53:4); the Savior who carries our sins and the Redeemer who carries us through death to eternal joy (I Pet. 2:24); and the Lamb who carries the sin of the world(Jn. 1:29).[61]

The Crucified Messiah and The Dying Buddha in *Dukkha*: The Cross and Lotus

The Messiah was crucified in weakness but lives by the power of God!

(2Cor. 13:4a)

The phrase, "Jesus was crucified in weakness" can also be translated: "He was crucified as a weakling."[62] The suffering Messiah on the cross serves as the soteriological means by which justification is built. The cross is the locus where we experience the supreme manifestation of God's sacrificial love. By correlating the cross event with the exodus event, the God who is revealed to Moses through the "burning bush" (Exo. 3:1-4) is now fully revealed to everyone (Jews and Gentiles) in the crucified Jesus on the cross.

---

[58] Joachim Jeremias, *New Testament Theology: The Proclamation of Jesus*, trans. John Bowden (New York: Charles Scribner's Sons, 1971), 291.

[59] Terence J. Forestell, *The Word of the Cross: Salvation as Revelation in the Fourth Gospel* (Rome: Biblical Institute Press, 1974), 193.

[60] Dietrich Bonhoeffer, *Discipleship*, trans. Barbara Green and Reinhard Krauss (Minneapolis, MN: Fortress Press, 2003), 90.

[61] Gaiser, "I Will Carry and Will Save," 102.

[62] Rudolf Bultmann, *The Second Letter to the Corinthians*, trans. Roy A. Harrisville (Minneapolis, MN: Augsburg Publishing House, 1985), 243.

Yet, the crucified Messiah is a "stumbling block" to Jews who demand signs and "foolishness" to Greeks who seek wisdom (1Cor. 1:22-23). For the former group, the crucified Christ is a stumbling block as He arrived in powerless. For the latter group, the crucified Messiah is foolishness as He cannot be accommodated to scheme.[1] In the midst of those doubts, the crucified Christ is both "wisdom and power" for Jews and Greeks. As Edward Young eloquently makes the portrayals of the crucified Christ,

> People were looking for a king in the Messiah, but He came as a Servant, people were looking for a powerful leader in the Messiah, but He came as an ordinary Citizen; people were looking for a warrior in the Messiah, but He willingly became a Prisoner; people were looking for a deliverer in the Messiah, but He offered Himself as a Sacrifice.[2]

As Jesus came in weakness while the people looked for a powerful Messiah to deliver them, a charge was placed above His head on the Cross, INRI, which says "This is the Messiah, King of Jews" (Matt. 27:37). Together with Paul, Christians claim that the cross is the foundation of Christian belief: "I never boast of anything except the cross of the crucified Christ" (Gal. 6:14). In Myanmar, the question to ask is whether or not the Buddhists see the crucified Christ as their liberator. I would like to engage the two pictures in dialogue with *Dukkha*:(1) the crucified Christ and the dying Buddha (2) the Cross in the rose and the Lotus on which the Buddha sits or stands.[3] Where do the suffering Christ and the compassionate Buddha converge and diverge from each other?

Just as the cross is a stumbling block to Jews and foolishness to Gentiles, so it is a dreadful image to Buddhists, because of Jesus' blood. The teaching of Buddhism is to kill not any living beings. Soteriologically speaking, Buddhism and Christianity stand in direct oppositions, the former believes in self-salvation, whereas the latter believes that salvation is by grace. In addition, the lotus and the cross are contradictory to each other. The Lotus is the symbol of natural beauty, appealing to our aesthetics, whereas the cross is the symbol of harsh and painful natures, revolting to the eyes of the beholder. Yet I appropriate Jesus 'self-emptiness in dialogue with Buddha's *anatta* and the beauty of Lotus in dialogue with the beauty of new creation after the resurrection of Jesus.

The God we encounter in Jesus on the cross is powerless and helpless. Jesus saved the sick and the poor from humiliation but He Himself went to the depths of humiliation. Jesus moved toward the periphery of the cross, finally being crucified outside Jerusalem city (Heb.13:12). There He could not move as He was nailed down. This is the extreme periphery where the crucified Christ challenges human powers.[4]

---

[1] Charles B. Cousar, *A Theology of the Cross: The Death of Jesus In The Pauline Letters* (Minneapolis, MN: Augsburg Publishing House, 1990), 28-29.

[2] Edward Young, *The Book of Isaiah*, vol. 2 (Grand Rapids, MI: William B. Eerdmans Publishing Company, 1972), 341.

[3] Song, *Third-Eye Theology*, 109.

[4] Song, *Jesus, The Crucified People*, 112.

Jesus suffered torture of His body, wore a crown of thorns, which I mean by the cross in the rose, and was nailed to and died on a Roman cross. He was persecuted by the Romans, abandoned by His Father and betrayed by His disciples. Christ died in loneliness with only women keeping an eye on Him from afar. On the deepest level, He related to God whom He Abba.[5] Jesus died with the cry: "my God, my God, why have you forsaken me?" (Mk. 15:34). Interestingly, the speaking God at the time of creation and the listening God at the time of prophetic voices is now the "mute God." There is no voice from heaven, like "you are my beloved son" in the baptismal event (Mk. 1:11).

This is what Moltmann calls, "the experience of hell."[6] What occurred on the cross between God the Father and Jesus the Son embraces the cosmic *Dukkha* and opens up the hell of torture. From this uttermost point of periphery, Jesus established His authority. Moltmann is most impressed with Jesus' cry of dereliction and he stated,

> God's forsakenness of Jesus in the context of a threefold account of crucifixion: (1) between Jesus and the Jewish law—in relation to Jewish Law, Jesus died as a *blasphemer* (Deu. 21:22-23); (2) between Jesus and Roman authority—in relation to Roman authority, Jesus died as a *rebel*; and (3) between Jesus and Father—in relation to the Father, Jesus died as a *forsaken victim*."[7] Jesus' death abandoned by God is at the core of divine *Dukkha* and it is the open secret of the Trinity. Jesus' death leads to the experience of death *in* God but not the death *of* God."[8]

I am driven by two images: the innocent Christ crying out to God and the sacrificial Lamb offered Himself for the gift of forgiveness.[9] The former is paradigmized as the victim (*Pyithu-Dukkha*), crying for justice in the context of human power (military regime). Though Jesus was innocent, not all *Pyithu* who suffer violence are innocent. But Jesus and the *Pyithu* share the same *Dukkha*: as Jesus suffered under the Roman Empire, so the *Pyithu* suffered under the Burmese military regime. I am struggling between the command to bring about justice for the victims and the call to embrace the perpetrators.

By and large, violence starts and ends with the drama of Jesus' saving work on the cross. Without violence, the central act of salvation is unthinkable. Thus below I will indicate three major ways in which the crucified Christ challenges human powers.

First, by suffering violence as an innocent victim, Jesus took upon Himself the aggression of the perpetrators and broke the vicious circle of violence. Hanging on the cross, Jesus provided the ultimate example of His command to replace a principle of retaliation ("eye for an eye and tooth for tooth" Exo.21:24) with

---

[5] Paul S. Chung, *Martin Luther and Buddhism: Aesthetics of Suffering*, 2nd ed. (Eugene, OR: Pickwick Publications, 2008), ix. See forward by Jürgen Moltmann, ix-xi.

[6] Ibid., x.

[7] Jürgen Moltmann, *The Crucified God: The Cross of Christ as the Foundation and Criticism of Christian Theology* (Minneapolis, MN: Fortress Press, 1993), 126-153.

[8] Ibid., 207.

[9] Volf, *Exclusion and Embrace*, 9.

a principle of non-resistance ("if anyone strikes you on the right cheek, turn the other also" Matt. 5:38-42).

Second, the cross is a predictable end to the life of Jesus' struggle for God's justice in a violent world. If Jesus had done nothing but only suffered violence, we would have forgotten Him as we have forgotten so many other innocent victims today.[10] In opposition to the kingdom of deception, Jesus transformed non-violence from barren negativity into a creative possibility, from quicksand into a foundation of a new world.[11]

Third, the cross is a divine embrace of the deceitful.[12] In taking upon Himself the sin of the world, God told the truth about the deceitful world and enthroned justice in an unjust world. When God was made sinful in Christ (2Cor. 5:21), the world of injustice was set aright (2Cor. 5:21); the cry of innocent blood was attended to. The truth about the world is told and reconciliation was done as Jesus said His last word on the cross, "it is finished" (Jn.19:30), *tetelestai* in Greek, meaning "paid in full" for sins." Or else, innocent Christ would eternally cry out to heaven and the world would remain awry.

Since a new world has become reality in the crucified-risen Christ (2Cor. 5:17), it is possible to live the new world in the midst of the old in an act of gratuitous forgiveness without giving up the struggle for justice. We can embrace perpetrators in forgiveness since God has embraced them in forgiveness through Jesus.[13] If the Jesus on the cross who said, "Father forgive them, for they do not know what they are doing" (Lk.23:34) will be our model, we ought to be able to embrace even our perpetrators in forgiveness.

Self-giving love is the first step of Jesus' embrace of the deceitful and sinners. God's giving His Son up to the point of death on the cross is in order not to give up on sinners. Jesus' self-denial (Phil.2:5-11) is appropriate for dialogue with the Buddhist's *anatta* and Jesus' nonresistance toward violators in engagement with Buddhist's notion of *ahimsa*. What we perceive in the crucified Christ and the dying Buddha is compassion and kenotic way of struggling with the *Pyithu* for their emancipation from *Dukkha*.

Buddha gave his own perfection up in order to help the oppressed who are not yet enlightened. With compassion, Buddha actively took part in suffering and showed his way of completeness to overcome the cosmic *Dukkha*.[14] But the dying Buddha did not cry: he died in a beautiful manner on his way to salvation. Rather, the Buddha statues show forth the world-transcending peace. The graceful Lotus on which Buddha sits is a primordial symbol of world genesis. The flower of the Lotus is aesthetic beauty.[15]

---

[10] Ibid., 293.
[11] Ibid.
[12] Ibid.
[13] Ibid., 294.
[14] Chung, *Martin Luther and Buddhism*, x.
[15] Ibid., In India, Brahman created the world by sitting and ruling on the Lotus.

In contrast to Buddha's beauty of the Lotus, the suffering Jesus on the cross has "no image of beauty" (Isa.53). Yet, this image of the crucified does not stand for Himself alone, as His background is always drawn in the shining color of the twilight of the resurrection. The cross was resurrected by God into a new creation, having been represented by the symbol of the rose since the medieval period.[16] The crucified Christ embraced by the leaves of the rose also points to the beauty of God's new creation.

As the Buddha sits and stands on the lotus blossom of world genesis, so Jesus who is crucified for the world is set on the petals of the cross of the resurrection of the world. The cross is the epitome of human brutality and is designed to demonstrate its powerlessness in front of powers. Yet God's glory is revealed most in the powerless death of Jesus(Jn.12:27). The lotus and the cross are two essentially different answers to some basic questions about life and death, seeking to unravel *Dukkha* that besets us in our lives. They point to the fulfillment of human destiny in the blissful presence of divine and concerned with the day-to-day struggles in the harsh reality of life. Thus, the place for the lotus and the cross to intercommunicate is the people, who struggle for justice and truth.

The Fellowship of the Messianic *Dukkha* and Human-*Dukkha*

> For to this you have been called, because Christ also suffered for you, leaving you an example, so that you should follow in His steps. (1 Peter 2:21

As the empathetic God has participated in our suffering, we become the objects of His suffering.[17] As a result, our suffering can be regarded as the fellowship of Christ's suffering. Participating in divine suffering means we have to be willing to suffer together with the sufferers.[18] The reason is that God's invitation is extended to us in the fellowship of bearing the cross (Mk. 8:34), sharing the bitter cup (Mk. 10:38) and being crucified with Christ (Gal.2:20). To participate in divine suffering means accepting this invitation to be in the fellowship of suffering. As Dietrich Bonhoeffer has illustrated well,

> We throw ourselves in God's arms and participate in divine suffering in the world and watch with Christ in Gethsemane. That is faith that is *Metancia*, and that is what makes a man a Christian. How can success make us arrogant or failure lead us astray, when we participate in the sufferings of God by living in this world?[19]

---

[16] For example, Luther's shield image of "Wappenbild."

[17] Karl Barth, *Church Dogmatics*, ed. G.W. Bromiley and T.F. Torrance, 4 vol. in 13 (Edinburgh: T. & T. Clark, 1936-1969), II/1:373.

[18] H. Wheeler Robinson, *The Cross in the Old Testament* (London: SCM Press, 1955), 192.

[19] Dietrich Bonhoeffer, *Prisoner for God: Letters and Papers from Prison,* trans. Reginald H. Fuller (New York: The Macmillan Company, 1954), 169.

The cross is the symbol of divine invitation for us to participate in His suffering by "taking up the cross and following Him" (Matt. 24:16). In faith, our suffering and the Messianic suffering are united together. The former is embraced by the latter.[20] Our suffering is enfolded by divine suffering. Faith in God sustains us to overcome suffering while suffering through the Holy Spirit trains an unquenchable faith. In faith, we who are subjects become the objects of God's suffering. This transition from the subjects (involuntary suffering) to the objects (voluntary) of God's *Dukkha* implies our participation in divine *Dukkha*.[21] In the process of this transition, Karl Barth has said,

> Man is brought to himself and becomes a real man not just a pietist (Christian), being so situated in God's presence as Jesus is, that is to be the bearer of God's wrath in solidarity with His Brother suffering for him.[22]

Participation in the fellowship of God's *Dukkha* is expressed in the broken Body of Christ and the fellowship of the cross.[23] That is why Paul calls the church as the fellowship of *Dukkha* to carry in the body the death of Jesus (2Cor. 4:8-10). Paul's use of carrying the death of Jesus implies our participating in Christ's suffering. Christ has left a residue of suffering for the benefit of His church and those who share in the suffering of Jesus' life. Christians' fellowship with Christ takes the form of mutual indwelling. Our participation in the fellowship of Messianic suffering is possible only because of the empathetic God who comes first into the world to share suffering with us on the cross.[24]

---

[20] Emil Brunner, *The Christian Doctrine of Creation and Redemption: Dogmatics II*, trans. Olive Wyon (Philadelphia, PA: The Westminster Press, 1952), 182.

[21] Jung Young Lee, *God Suffers For Us: A Systematic Inquiry into a Concept of Divine Passibility* (The Hague: Martinus Nijhoff, 1974), 81.

[22] Karl Barth, *Dogmatics Outline* (London: SCM Press, 1949), 107.

[23] Dietrich Bonhoeffer, *The Cost of Discipleship*, ed. and trans. Reginald H. Fuller (New York: The Macmillan Company, 1959), 20.

[24] George Hunsinger, *Disruptive Grace: Studies in the Theology of Karl Barth* (Grand Rapids, MI: William B. Eerdmans Publishing Company, 2000), 39.

Chapter 3
A Theological Concept of Divine-Human *Dukkha* in the Global Context: Theology between West and East

Pyithu-Dukkha in Dialogue with Martin Luther's Theology of the Cross

"A theology of the cross is a principle of Luther's entire theology."
Walther Loewenich[1]

Following the Chalcedonian formula of two natures of Jesus within the Alexandrian tradition,[2] Luther (1483-1546) spoke of Christology from the context of *communicatio idiomatum* (communication between two natures in Jesus).[3] Though Luther did not live in a world of Buddhism, his theology of the cross based on a dialectical aspect of Jesus' *Dukkha* and *Karuna* in the struggle for the liberation of the victims is a basis for dialoging with an Asian theology of *Pyithu-Dukkha*.

Taking the crucified Christ as the ontological image through whom God's saving work is revealed, a theology of the cross can be expressed in three ways: the cross is where (1) Jesus' humiliating act of suffering is manifested; (2) God's essence as ultimate love is reflected and (3) the distinction between the revealed God and the hidden God on the cross. The third one opens up God's mystery in the context of the *Pyithu*'s *Dukkha*.[4]

---

[1]Walther V. Loewenich, *Luther's Theology of the Cross*, trans. Herbert J. A. Bouman (Minneapolis, MN: Augsburg Publishing House, 1976), 13.
[2]Regarding the Christological argument, the Alexandrian tradition accepted *Logos-sarx* (word-flesh), whereas the Antioch tradition adopted *Logos-anthropos* (word-humans).
[3]Dennis Ngien, *The Suffering of God: According to Martin Luther's Theologia Crucis* (Eugene, OR: Wipf and Stock Publishers, 2001), 88.
[4]Ibid., 88.

The striking aspect of God's appearance on the cross is His compassion and pain for the sake of sinners. This point leads us to think about Luther's notion of "happy exchange" in which Jesus takes the *Pyithu*'s sinful forms and gives them divine form.[5] Jesus' descent into the hell of *Dukkha* paves the way for the *Pyithu*'s ascent into the gift of liberation. Jesus' act of *Dukkha* is integrated to the essence of God's compassion toward the *Pyithu-Dukkha*. As God's co-suffering with the crucified Christ is *hidden* from our eyes, so His solidarity with the *Pyithu* seems hidden. Yet God's presence with Christ and the *Pyithu* is *revealed* from the side of immanent trinity and the eyes of faith.

Luther's Christology is rooted not in glory but in humiliation. This concept makes Christology possible to begin from below in solidarity with humanity. Christ according to humanity is creature in *Dukkha* and Christ according to His divinity is God in *Karuna*; so *Dukkha* and *Karuna* are conjoined that one person in two natures of Christ.[6] By descending to the world in flesh, Christ's presence among humanity is dynamic.

In this regard, Asian *Pyithu* prefer to see Jesus as the ontological sacrament and example, who struggled for God's justice and liberation in Asia. God in the crucified Christ is immanently present with the *Pyithu-Dukkha* as their liberator. Rather than seeing the cross as an arbitrary design on God's part, we should view it as the outcome of God's primordial option to be identified with the *Pyithu-Dukkha*.[7] Christ's descent into hell of cosmic *Dukkha* can be reread in an Asian context as (1) struggle for the *Pyithu*'s liberation in social-political sense; (2) recognition of Christ's cosmic presence with the *Pyithu*, who suffer and (3) affirmation of Christ's *Karuna* toward all religious outsiders.[8]

A combination of Luther's *theologia crucis* (God's love) and *theologia verbis* (God's freedom) provides a dynamic basis for engaging not only with the praxis of soteriology, but dialogue with people of other faiths in Asia so that the full meaning of salvation will be manifested in Christ's work of restoration of all things (Col. 1:20). God's objective is cosmic-anthropological salvation to the ends of earth for all time to come (Isa.52:10).[9] Asian Christians should confess God's *karuna* in Jesus' *Dukkha* on the cross as the principle of Jesus' triumphal over the world of suffering and deception.[10]

---

[5] Marc Lienhard, *Luther: Witness to Jesus Christ*, trans. J. A. Bouman (Minneapolis, MN: Augsburg Publishing House, 1982), 174. Here, Luther echoes Augustine's phase "fortunate exchange."

[6] Norman E. Nagel, "Martinus: Heresy, Doctor Luther, Heresy! The Person and Work of Christ," in *Seven-Headed Luther, Essays in Commemoration of a Quincentenary 1483-1983*, ed. Peter Newman Books (Oxford: Clarendon Press, 1983), 46.

[7] Jon Sobrino, *Christology at the Crossroads: A Latin American Approach*, trans. John Drury (Maryknoll, NY: Orbis Books, 1978), 201.

[8] Chung, *Luther and Buddhism*, 409.

[9] Terence E. Fretheim, *God and World in The Old Testament: A Relational Theology of Creation* (Nashville, TN: Abingdon Press, 2005), 190.

[10] Regin Prenter, *Luther's Theology of the Cross* (Philadelphia, PA: Fortress Press, 1971), 3-4.

Pyithu-Dukkha in Dialogue with Karl Barth's Dialectical Theology

Due to his overemphasis on divine revelation and claiming religion as humans' creation against God, Karl Barth (1886-1968), in his earlier life was misunderstood by Asian theologians as an irrelevant theologian. Barth later became known in Asia through Katsumi Takizawa's work on *Barth's Urfaktum Immanuel* and *Buddhism's True Self*[11] as a theologian, who stood both in faithful commitment to biblical faith and in openness to other religions. Lay theologian, Madathilparampil M. Thomas (M.M. Thomas) of India developed more significantly Barth's theology of cosmic Christology in Asia.[12]

Taking God's self-communication with humans as a dialectical truth, Barth defined the counterpart of God and humanity as "theoanthropology."[13] In this study, Barth's theology of cosmic Christ will play a central role in our dialogue with an Asian theology of *Pyithu-Dukkha*. Interestingly, Barth described the triune Word (Father, Son, and Spirit) as "revealer, revelation and revealedness."[14] For Barth, God as "Wholly Other" is known only through the incarnate Jesus, who opens universal reconciliation.

Barth developed a universal character of Christology through a typology of Adam and Christ in Romans 5: not only Jews but Gentiles are included in the realm of Christ's reconciling work.[15] What Christ's divinity is to a theology of revelation and Christ's humanity is to a natural theology of reconciliation. In Jesus, not one race but all humans are posited and exalted as such to unity with God.[16] Based on Jesus' reconciling work, "God says His gracious YES to all His creatures in His continual work" (Rom. 1:20).[17]

In the world reconciled with God in Jesus, social-political and religious orientation became integral to Barth's notion of the cosmic Christology in Asia. Barth's dialectical theology of divine suffering and human suffering are rediscovered as the counterparts for Asian theology of "reconciliation" and "liberation." How do we reinterpret reconciliation in partnership with salvation? I contend that salvation comes not only as we are reconciled to God, and not only as we have to live

---

[11] Paul S. Chung, "Karl Barth and Religious Pluralism: A Conflict?" in *Theology Between East and West: Essays in Honor of Jan Milic Lochman*, ed. Frank D. Macchia and Paul S. Chung (Eugene, OR: Cascade Books, 2002), 44.

[12] See M. M. Thomas, "Christ-Centered Syncretism," *Religion and Society* 26, no. 1 (March 1979), 26-41.

[13] Karl Barth, *The Humanity of God*, trans. J. Thomas and T. Wieser (London: Collins, 1960), 9.

[14] Barth, *Church Dogmatics*, I/1:132.

[15] Hermann Diem, "Karl Barth as Socialist: Controversy over a New Attempt to Understand Him," in *Karl Barth and Radical Politics*, ed. and trans. George Hunsinger (Philadelphia, PA: The Westminster Press, 1976), 129.

[16] Barth, *Church Dogmatics*, IV/2:49.

[17] Jürgen Moltmann, *Experiences in Theology: Ways and Forms of Christian Theology*, trans. Margaret Kohl (Minneapolis, MN: Fortress Press, 2000), 80.

with one another within our narrow circle, but as we have to take the costly step of opening ourselves to religious outsiders (the *Pyithu-Dukkha*) with the same embrace of God through Jesus' atonement.

In the context of religiosity and suffering, God's reconciliation needs to be extended in recognition of religious outsiders as brothers and sisters. In the realm of Lordship, Barth claimed that nothing can be separated from God. Following in the footsteps of Barth, Moltmann insisted that a natural theology in the Barthian sense lies in his notion of Christ's universal reconciliation and inclusive nature of holistic salvation. The restorations of all things are possible in Jesus' descent into the sinful world.[18]

Within the framework of cosmic Christology, Barth developed prophetic Christology in warning the churches not to be the dumb dogs in service to the ruling powers, but to undertake the cause of *Dukkha* at its social roots.[19] Yet, in the cross, a place of violence, Jesus did not meet His enemies with retaliation, but with suffering love. Jesus not only treated His enemies with restraint, but offered Himself to save them all from sin. Barth's notion of the politics of Jesus is revealed to Asia as the politics of non-violent resistance toward the oppressors while in solidarity with the *Pyithu-Dukkha*.

Barth has something in common with both the reconciler seeking peace among God's creatures and with the liberationists combating injustices. Reconciliation seen through the work of Christ entails justice for the victimized/*Pyithu-Dukkha* and at the same time the possibility of forgiveness for the victimizers. Participating in the ministry of reconciliation, Christians in Asia have to take the costly step of reconciliation with all religious outsiders without giving up the struggle for justice of the oppressed.[20]

The Significance of Barth's Political Theology in the Context of *Pyithu-Dukkha:* Barmen, *Kairos*, Burmese in Dialogue

Barth was the principal author of Barmen Declaration against Nazism in Germany. In the Barmen Declaration against Nazism, Barth's aim was to redefine a new understanding of the Lordship of Christ by proposing the relation between Christ and the world Christologically, church and state politically, and faith and work ethically.[21] In this section, I have threefold aim. First, I will explore the Barmen Declaration of 1934. Second, I will dialogue the Barmen Declaration with the *Kairos* Document of 1985/6 prepared by the South African theologians against

---

[18]Ibid., 75-76. Moltmann defends that "Barth's earlier confrontation with Emil Brunner is not due to the natural side of natural theology but mainly to political realities of the pro-Nazi German Christians."

[19]Barth, *Church Dogmatics*, IV/3.2:275.

[20]Karl Barth, *Against the Stream* (London: SCM Press, 1954), 117. See also George Hunsinger, *Disruptive Grace: Studies in the Theology of Karl Barth*,58.

[21]Karl Barth, *Fragments Grave and Gay* (London: Collins Fontana, 1971), 72.

apartheid. Both documents are what John Gruchy called "liberating symbols for the global Christian reaction to oppression."[22] Third, I will ask whether or not the two documents are significant for Myanmar.[23]

First, the Barmen Declaration consisted of six articles.[24] The political implications of the first article are spelled out, directly and indirectly by the rest of the Declaration. Article I claimed the assumption that in Christ, God fully and finally revealed Himself in the world, and that therefore, there are no other sources of revelation for the church.[25] Article II concluded that Jesus is Lord over the universe and over all powers. There are no areas in which Christian must hear other powers and law alongside the voice of Christ. No area of life can be said outside the Lordship. This theological position can be found in his three occasioned publications[26] written during the church conflict against Nazism.

Article III claimed that no church should be subordinated to the unjust lordship of state, i.e. Nazism. In other words, whereas article II implied that theology and politics may not be separated, article III implied that they may not be confused when the state misuses its power. Article IV implied rejection of any imposition on the church from an alien form of polity. Article V interpreted the two-kingdoms theory in a Christocentric way, so that our hierarchy of loyalty is clear in subordination to God.[27] Finally, Article VI rejected any arbitrary chosen desires and plans, while affirming the message of God's free grace. This implies that all political activity engaged in by church will carry the basic status of a political witness to grace.[28] In George Hunsinger's reading of Barth's Barmen Declaration, "two are most important: Barmen's re-interpretation of the two-kingdoms doctrine and Barmen's suggestion that theology and politics stand in a pattern of unity."[29]

Two kingdoms theory causes not only the separation between church and state but also the silence of Christians in the face of Nazism. Luther said, "God ordained two regiments—one is ruled through faith and the other is ruled through

---

[22]John de Gruchy, *Bonheoffer and South Africa: Theology in Dialogue* (Grand Rapids, MI: Eerdmans, 1984), 130.

[23]For a full account of Barth's political theology for the politics of Myanmar, see my forthcoming article David Thang Moe, "The Significance of Karl Barth's Political Theology for the Politics of Myanmar," in *International Journal of Public Theology* (2017).

[24]Clifford Green, ed, *Karl Barth: Theologian of Freedom* (Minneapolis, MN: Fortress, 1991), 148-150.

[25]Moltmann, *Political Theology and Ethics*, 83.

[26]They include "Gospel and Law" (1935); "Justification and Justice" (1938), "Christian Community and Civil Community" (1948). These three publications can be found in Karl Barth, *Community, State and Church: Three Essays* (Garden City, NY: Anchor Books, 1960), 71-100, 101-148, 149-189. In this edition, the second essay "Justification and Justice" is entitled "Church and State." For the third essay "the Christian Community and the Civil Community," see also, Karl Barth, *Against the Stream: Shorter Post-War Writings 1946-1952* (London: SCM Press, 1954), 15-50.

[27]Hunsinger, *Disruptive Grace*, 80-81.

[28]Ibid.

[29]Ibid., 81.

law."[30] Article 16 of the Augsburg Confession declared, "One should obey the state and its law."[31] This became a justification for those who welcomed the fascist law and order of Hitler. On the other hand, the negative result of two kingdoms theory provided no basis for those who wanted to resist Hitler's pervasion of the state power. Two kingdoms theory holds that to obey the state, even unjust state, is to render obedience to God.[32] By contrast, the Barmen distinguished obedience to the just God and obedience to the unjust state.[33] This became the political question of Christian faith—whether Hitler or Jesus was Lord. Barth uttered an absolute No to Hitler. By referring to what Peter and other apostles said in the book of Acts 5:29, "we must obey God rather than human beings," Barth insisted that obedience to Christ's Lordship of justice means to disobey and resist an unjust lordship of Nazism.[34]

In sum, the Barmen Declaration can be read in two ways: one way is that there is a dialectical relationship between church and state, of which Christ is the center. Barth, unlike Luther, described church and state not as two kingdoms, but as two communities, with church as the inner circle of faith community, and state as the outer circle of civil community. In their identities, they contradict one another. One is a foretaste of God's kingdom, the other is a parable of God's kingdom. But in their vocations, both are God's servants. In Rom. 13:4, Paul sees the state as God's servant.[35] Barmen V implied that the state and the church exist by divine authority, each with the divine mandate. The state is to care for justice by the use of law in this world.[36] Since both communities have the same centers in one Lord, their common goals is to strive for political justice. By virtue of their vocations, church and state are identical, and their enemies are the same cosmic powers, which twist God's kingdom of justice. The task of church is not to Christianize the state but to see itself as partner of the state for a common good of both.[37]

On the other hand, the Barmen provided a conflict between church and state. The conflict emerges when state becomes the oppressor of church. Barth said, "When the state fails to apply just law and order, the church must stand for a prophetic witness against the state."[38] The Barmen Declaration must be understood as a critical corrective against Nazism and as the call of the church for protesting against Nazism. This leads me to dialogue with the Barmen Declaration with the *Kairos* Document against apartheid.

---

[30]Brandt, *Luther's Works*, 91-92.

[31]Ibid., see also, Moltmann, *Political Theology and Ethics*, 77.

[32]William J. Wright, *Martin Luther's Understanding of God's Two Kingdoms* (Grand Rapids, MI: Baker Academic, 2010), 19.

[33]Hunsinger, *Disruptive Grace*, 81.

[34]Gerald A. Butler, "Karl Barth and Political Theology," in *Scottish Journal of Theology*, Vol. 27. Issue 4 (November 1974): 441-456.

[35]Barth, *Community, State and Church*, 150, 157.

[36]Barth, *Against the Stream*, 26.

[37]Ibid., 23.

[38]Barth, *Community, State and Church*, 34.

Reading both documents through the political lens of Myanmar's socio-political experience of *Pyithu-Dukkha*, I am aware of their similarities and differences. I will focus on the former without excluding the latter. My aim is to look into the relationship between confession and politics, which is at stake in both documents.[39] Having emerged from the confessing movements, both documents can be understood as situative confessions. Confession, theologically, is the unity of faith in and obedience to the Lord (Barmen III); and the unity of word and deed in reaction to unjust political lordship.[40]

In my view, the Barmen Declaration was a doctrinal character of church confession, whereas the *Kairos* Document was a practical profile of political analysis. For instance, Barmen I, as noted, started with a strong theological declaration of Christological Lordship and declared its rejection of any false doctrine of the church which embraces a blind obedience to Hitler. Although the *DLURV* Document does not focus on doctrinal confession, its critique of "church theology" was similar to the aim of the Barmen Declaration. The church's blind obedience to the unjust regime is what the *Kairos* Document called "church theology."[41] However, what they have in common is that both Documents were grounded in a Christological basis. While the Barmen Declaration takes Christ's Lordship or kingly rule as a center, the *Kairos* Document takes Christ's prophetic role. The former employs Christ as Lord and the Church as the body of Christ, whereas the latter employs Christ as the exemplary prophet and the Church as a prophetic community in an unjust world.

The *Kairos* Document takes Jesus' prophetic role against domination as a model for the prophetic Church's resistance to what it calls "state theology." State theology is a theological justification of the status quo with its oppression. State theology canonizes the will of the oppressive rulers and reduces the oppressed to passivity and blind obedience. The *Kairos* Document contends that the misuse of Rom. 13:1-7 is a basis for the creation of state theology.[42] State theology assumes that in this text Paul urges Christians to obey to the state. But what is missing is a theological distinction between obedience to God and obedience to the unjust state. What is missing in the *Kairos* Document is found in the Barmen Declaration. The Barmen distinguishes obedience to God and obedience to the state so that there will be no confusion between two obedience.

I will now determine whether or not the Barmen and *Kairos* Confessions contribute any significance to the politics of Myanmar. I am fully convinced that that both Documents play a significant role in making the relationship between confession and politics in Myanmar. The strength of the Barmen Declaration is a

---

[39]Wolfgang Huber, "The Barmen Declaration and the *Kairos* Documents: On The Relationship between Confession and Politics," in *Journal of Theology for Southern Africa*, Vol. 27 (June 1991):48-60.

[40]Ibid., 50. Note that confession and witness are identical.

[41]*Kairos* Theologians, *Kairos Documents: Challenge to the Church, A Theological Comment on a Political Crisis in South Africa* (Grand Rapids, MI: Eerdmans, 1986), 8-14.

[42]Ibid., 3.

proposal of a dialectical relation between church and state as well as a conflict between the two with regard to Christ as the center. But what is missing is an aspect of church's eccentricity for the voiceless. The strength of the *Kairos* Document is a clear profile of a prophetic relation between Christ and Church with regard to the vocation of church as the preferential and prophetic voice for *Pyithu-Dukkha*.[43] We must see the political aims of both documents as critical corrective against Nazi and apartheid regimes and as corrective against any privatization and quietism of faith. This will be taken up later in the next chapter.

Pyithu-Dukkha in Dialogue with Dietrich Bonhoeffer's Prophetic Christ

Experiencing himself as a prisoner, Dietrich Bonhoeffer (1906-1945) argued that the suffering God is encountered as One who suffered in love with the sufferers/ *Pyithu-Dukkha*. The suffering in the world in light of the Holocaust has a profound impact on our contemporary notion of God's relationship to human D*ukkha* in the sense that God Himself suffers in love with the *Pyithu-Dukkha*.[44] If there is one theological center in Bonhoeffer's thought, it would be the prophetic Christology and ecclesiology in which he wrote his doctoral thesis and he described "Christ existing as church community."[45]

Bonhoeffer's uniqueness lies in his notion of Christology from below in solidarity with the oppressed. Bonhoeffer portrayed Christology as threefold: (1) the historical Christ—the Christ who was at the center of *human history* as Lord of history; (2) the contemporary Christ—the Christ who is at the center of *human existence* as the mediator between God and humanity; (3) the eternal Christ—the Christ who is the center between *God* and *nature*, working for the transformation of new creation.[46] This threefold Christology will play a central role in dialogue with an Asian theology of *Pyithu-Dukkha*.

Reflecting on Jesus' cry of abandonment (Mk. 15:34), Bonhoeffer commented that God allowed Himself to be edged out of the world on to the cross. Jesus' powerlessness allows Him to be humiliated with the powerless *Pyithu*. He famously says, "The Bible directs humans to God's powerlessness and suffering that "only a suffering God can help,"[47] the suffering people/*Pyithu*. In his letter from prison written in December 1943, Bonhoeffer also spoke of the suffering God as the

---

[43] Huber, "The Barmen Declaration and *DLURV* Document," 56-59.

[44] Thomas G. Weinandy, *Does God Suffer?* (Edinburgh: T&T Clark, 2000), 314.

[45] Geffrey B. Kelly, *Reading Bonhoeffer: A Guide to Spiritual Classics and Selected Writing on Peace* (Eugene, OR: Cascade Books, 2008), 3.

[46] Charles Marsh, *Reclaiming Dietrich Bonhoeffer: The Promise of His Theology* (New York: Oxford University Press, 1994), 93.

[47] Dietrich Bonhoeffer, *Letters and Papers from Prison*, ed. Eberhard Bethge, trans. Reginald H. Fuller (New York: Macmillan Publishing Company, 1953), 361.

helper in solidarity with all the suffering humanity, who bear the messianic image in their own way.[48]

For Bonhoeffer, suffering is the extension of action and the perfection of emancipation. As Jesus died for others, so we served God through engaging in services to the *Pyithu-Dukkha*.[49] Dying for us to bear our burden of sin, Christ's *Dukkha* calls us to be burden bearers of one another: "Christian worthy of the name is the cross: when Christ calls a man, He bids Him come and die."[50] The cross is not the end of a happy life but the beginning of new life in suffering with Christ. Suffering with Christ calls for obedience to take up our cross and follow Him in the struggle with the *Pyithu* (Matt. 16:24).

Following Jesus is not a matter of religious life in a sacred church, but in a secular world because "Jesus called men not to a new religion but to new life in solidarity with others."[51] Christ took us from the bondage of sin and turned us around to face the world. When a majority of German Christians did not resist the evils of Hitler, Bonhoeffer said "cheap grace is the deadly enemy of the church, our struggle is for the costly grace."

> Cheap grace means grace without cost of life; cheap grace means paying lip service to the doctrine of salvation without solidarity with the fellow sufferers. Cheap grace means preaching forgiveness without practicing forgiveness; it is Baptism without commitment; it is the Lord's Supper without confession of sin.[52] In sharp contrast to cheap grace, costly grace means to follow Jesus in a fallen world. Grace is costly as it costs Jesus' life. Grace is costly because it condemns sins and justifies sinners; it is costly because it costs people their lives; grace is costly because it compels us to the yoke of Christ and follows Him.[53]

Bonhoeffer asserted that all suffering people, both Christians and pagans, go to God in need. Apparently, in his letter written in February 1928, Bonhoeffer indicated his interest in the Buddhist's way of peace through *ahimsa* (non-violence) in reminiscent of Gandhi's pacific tactics.[54] In the context of *Pyithu-Dukkha*, Asian churches need to live out Jesus' teaching on *ahimsa* in opposition to forces of evil. As reconciliation does not come cheaply, but costs the life of Jesus on the cross, churches in Asia have to witness the prophetic Christ to the world of violence and

---

[48]Ibid., 118.

[49]Geffrey B. Kelly and F. Burton Nelson, *The Cost of Moral Leadership: The Scripture of Dietrich Bonhoeffer* (Grand Rapids, MI: William B. Eerdmans Publishing Company, 2003), 238.

[50]Dietrich Bonhoeffer, *The Cost of Discipleship*, ed. and trans. Reginald H. Fuller (New York: Macmillan Publishing Company, 1963), 47.

[51]Ibid., 86.

[52]Dietrich Bonhoeffer, *A Testament to Freedom: The Essential Writings of Dietrich Bonhoeffer*, ed. Geffrey B. Kelly & F. Burton Nelson (San Francisco, CA: A Division of Harper Collins Publishers, 1990), 307.

[53]Ibid., 308.

[54]Don S. Browning, *A Fundamental Practical Theology: Descriptive and Strategic Proposals* (Minneapolis, MN: Fortress Press, 1991), 47.

unjust in non-violent resistance to evils by standing with the *Pyithu-Dukkha*, who are in the face of death and life.[55]

Pyithu-Dukkha in Dialogue with Jürgen Moltmann's Crucified God

Jürgen Moltmann (1926-) appeared on the world theological scene with his book of *Theology of Hope* (1964).[56] Human *Dukkha* in terms of the Auschwitz, Hiroshima and Vietnam wars are the most profound basis for Moltmann's theology.[57] Experiencing as a prisoner in WW II, Moltmann accented the version of theodicy in dialogue with suffering of all religions, saying that "*Dukkha* is the central problem in all religions in the world."[58]

Moltmann is interested in the more existential question of *where* is God in our suffering than *why* this suffering happens to us. Human history after the death of Jesus Christ is a theodicy process and God is on trial throughout the history of suffering.[59] The question of why we suffer in this world of *anicca* is the salient issue of our time, but this question cannot be answered in this life based on the limited capacity of original sin.[60]

Rooted in his account of Calvary, the crucified God illuminates God's solidarity with the oppressed and God's vulnerability to the scourge of suffering within creation.[61] Moltmann was struck by the Psalmist's lament with plaintive prayers in Psalm 39:2-3 and Jesus' cry of abandonment (Mk. 15:34).[62] Together with Moltmann, when we read Jesus' cry, we know that Jesus was our divine brother in *Dukkha* who took us on His way to resurrection. Jesus' cry showed us *where* God is and where He *would* be in the future.[63] Moltmann's understanding of the "very visible crying Jesus and the hidden God" on the cross plays a central role in dialogue with an Asian theology of *Pyithu-Dukkha*.

---

[55] Heinz Eduard Todt, *Authentic Faith: Bonhoeffer's Theological Ethics in Context*, ed. Ernst-Albert Scharffenorth, trans. David Stassen and Ilse Todt (Grand Rapids, MI: William B. Eerdmans Publishing Company, 2007), 104.

[56] Miroslav Volf, Carmen Krieg and Thomas Kucharz, eds., *The Future of Theology: Essays in Honor of Jürgen Moltmann's 70th Birthday* (Grand Rapids, MI: William B. Eerdmans Publishing Company, 1996).

[57] Moltmann, *The Crucified God*, 220.

[58] Jürgen Moltmann, *The Church in the Power of the Spirit: A Contribution to Messianic Eschatology*, trans. Margaret Kohl (New York: Harper & Row, 1977), 161.

[59] Jürgen Moltmann, *The Way of Jesus Christ: Christology in Messianic Dimensions*, trans. Margaret Kohl (San Francisco, CA: Harper & Row, 1990), 183.

[60] Jürgen Moltmann, *The Trinity and the Kingdom: The Doctrine of God*, trans. Margaret Kohl (San Francisco, CA: Harper & Row, 1981), 51.

[61] Jürgen Moltmann, *The Source of Life: The Holy Spirit and the Theology of Life*, trans. Margaret Kohl (Minneapolis, MN: Fortress Press, 1997), 1.

[62] Jürgen Moltmann, *Passion for God: Theology in Two Voices* (Louisville, KY: Westminster John Knox Press, 2003), 76.

[63] Moltmann, *The Source of Life*, 5.

In his famous book *The Crucified God*, Moltmann is critical of the Greek notion of divine impassibility, which claims God cannot suffer and die. For Moltmann, Christ's suffering on the cross is not a single chapter in theology, but the key significance for all Christian theology.[64] The God revealed in the crucified Christ is the God to whom the *Pyithu-Dukkha* can relate and in whom they can rediscover their hope. David Tracy criticizes, "Moltmann's theology of the cross is shaped by dialectical rather than analogical thinking."[65] In line with Tracy's judgment, it seems to me that Moltmann's theology of the crucified God is achieved by a dialectical suffering of Jesus' divinity and humanity on the cross. God in the crucified Christ is present with the *Pyithu-Dukkha*.

The key to grasping the meaning of the cross is found in Jesus' cry of abandonment.[66] Jesus' cry can be classified into three aspects: liberation from the compulsion of sin, liberation from the idols of power, and liberation from God-forsakenness. In developing the third aspect, Moltmann adopts *paradidonia* in Greek, which designates that God *gave* His Son *up* to the cross in order *not* to give up on sinful *Pyithu* (Rom. 8:32). On the cross, the Father suffered grief and the Son suffered Father-forsakenness. This God who shares His grief with His Son is the same God who is in compassion with the *Pyithu-Dukkha,* who bears the image of the crucified Jesus.[67]

When we describe our experience of divine suffering and companionship drawn from the Johannine concept of "mutual being" (1Jn.4:17) and Paul's phrase of "*in* Christ," it is possible for God to suffer in love with the *Pyithu-Dukkha*. This kind of experience is what Moltmann calls the "realistic *divinization* in which the suffering *Pyithu* lives *in* God and *with* God."[68] Moltmann's crucified God from the pit is affected by the suffering of creation and God's struggle to bring a life of hope out of *Dukkha*.

Moltmann's theology of theodicy culminates with the "presence and promise": first the crucified God is a source of strength and "present" in love with the *Pyithu-Dukkha*, and second eschatologically the *Pyithu*'s *Dukkha* will finally be transformed into joy based on what God has "promised" in the resurrection of Jesus Christ. Therefore, the future of God's glory is inextricably linked with the redemption of our contemporary *Dukkha* in the groaning world we struggle for the hope of transformation (Rom.8:18).

---

[64] Moltmann, *The Crucified God*, 72.

[65] David Tracy, *The Analogical Imagination: Christian Theology and Culture of Pluralism* (New York: Crossroad, 1981), 408. Tracy argues that *analogy* is the language of ordered relations articulating *similarity* within *differences*.

[66] Moltmann, *The Crucified God*, 192.

[67] Ibid., 191, 222.

[68] Ibid., 277.

Pyithu-Dukkha in Dialogue with Miroslav Volf's Embracive Messiah

Having received two advanced degrees under the famed German theologian Jürgen Moltmann, Miroslav Volf (1956-) is a unique theologian of the bridge in our day, wrestling with boundaries between exclusion and embrace and peace and violence. Volf is perhaps best known for his award-winning book, *Exclusion and Embrace*.[69] Reaching back to the New Testament metaphor of salvation as reconciliation, "while we were enemies, we were reconciled to God through Jesus' atonement" (Rom. 5:10), Volf proposes the idea of "embrace" as a theological response to the problem of "exclusion."

Volf's theology is, by and large, motivated by the *innocent Jesus* crying out to the Father (Mk. 15:34) and the *Lamb* offering as the gift of forgiveness (Jn.1:29). Volf felt caught between the demand to bring about justice for the victims and the call to embrace the ultimate other. Below is Volf's response to his professor, Moltmann's question,

> After I finished my lecture, professor Moltmann stood up and asked one of his typical questions: but can you embrace a *cetik*? It took me a while to answer though I immediately knew what I wanted to say. No, I cannot—but as a follower of Christ, I think I should be able to.[70]

Centik used in Volf's book can be applied in Myanmar as the concept of all religious outsiders and ultimate evil. Volf's concept of embrace is rooted in God's unconditional embrace of everyone in Jesus. He said, "Forgiveness sums up much of the significance of the cross."[71] Treating embrace as God's unilateral act, a Christian's embrace of the other is unconditionally accepted. A true embrace is reciprocal and healing for both. Volf mused that a violent Cain could be "healed and embraced by Christ who laid down His life for us *only* if he set out to walk in Christ's footsteps" (1Jn.3:11-17). Volf argues that God did not abandon Cain to the circle of exclusions even though "he set away from the presence of the Lord" (Gen. 4:16).[72]

Moving from violence against the other to embrace, Volf proposed the need for forgiveness, repentance and making space in oneself for the other. Jesus' passion is the agony of a tortured soul and wrecked body offered as a prayer for the forgiveness of the torturers—"Father forgive them; for they do not know what they are doing (Lk. 23:34).[73] I believe the Bible narrates how God has necessarily used the *sacrificial mechanism* to remark the world in which we need to sacrifice for others and embrace the ultimate other.[74] Through the risen Jesus, it is possible

---

[69] Volf, *Exclusion and Embrace*.
[70] Ibid., 9.
[71] Ibid., 125.
[72] Ibid., 98.
[73] Ibid., 123.
[74] James G. Williams, *The Bible, Violence, and the Sacred: Liberation from the Myth of Sanctioned Violence* (Valley Forge, PA: Trinity Press International, 1991), 224.

to live a new world in the midst of the old in an act of gratuitous forgiveness without giving up the struggle for justice (2 Cor. 5:17).

The consequence of the cross states God's desire to break the power of human enmity without violence and receive enemy into divine communion. The arms of Christ are open and a sign of a space in God's self and invitation for the enemy to come in.[75] As Bonhoeffer also said, "Forgiveness itself is a form of *Dukkha*; when I forgave, I not only suffered a violation but suppressed the rightful claims of strict restitutive justice."[76]

In seeking the possibility for forgiveness, we must pay attention to the well-known story of Joseph, who was ready to undertake the tough journey of reconciliation with his brothers who sold him into slavery. God made Joseph forget all his hardship and all his father's house (Gen. 41:51). Joseph was able to forgive and embrace his brothers, the betrayers, and became their savior (45:14-15; 46:1ff.). Joseph's forgiving of his brothers' sins becomes our forgiving of the ultimate other. Yet the memory of the victims must be kept alive as long as it is needed for the perpetrators' repentance.[77] While I am writing this paper, the image of military regime's killing their own innocent citizens in my country is flooding my mind. It seems impossible for me to embrace the perpetrators with my bloody hands as it seems impossible for the Jews to embrace the Nazis.[78]

Following the crucified Christ, our question will no longer be how dare God forgives even evildoers, but rather, how God, without forgetting the victims, can help heal their memories. According to Volf, "There can be no justice without the will to embrace the other."[79] Seeking justice and embracing the other is what we need in Myanmar. Without the will to embrace, each party will insist on the justness of their own cause and strife will continue. Without giving up the struggle for justice, to accuse evildoers by offering our forgiveness is to invite them to admit guilt and repent slowly.[80]

In sum, the embracive Christ demands us to make space in ourselves to embrace the perpetrators with forgiveness and the *Pyithu-Dukkha* with compassion for whom Jesus was crucified—forgiveness is the boundary between violence and peace. Drawn from Volf's idea of the embracive Christ, it is possible to embrace religious outsiders and the oppressors in Myanmar. If there is one theological center in the strength of Volf, it would be a theology of "reconciliation" and he prioritizes it over liberation theology, which struggle against the oppressors. The church needs to correct this "imbalance" between reconciliation theology and liberation theology. I will argue this later.

---

[75] Volf, *Exclusion and Embrace*, 126.
[76] Bonhoeffer, *The Cost of Discipleship*, 100.
[77] Volf, *Exclusion and Embrace*, 136-137.
[78] Ibid., 138.
[79] Ibid., 220.
[80] Miroslav Volf, "Forgiveness, Reconciliation and Justice: A Christian Contribution to a More Peaceful Social Environment," in *Theology Between East and West*, eds. Paul S. Chung and Frank D. Macchia (Eugene, OR: Cascade Books, 2002), 286-187.

Pyithu-Dukkha in Dialogue with Kazoh Kitamori's Painful God

Kazoh Kitamori (1916-1998) is one of the pioneers in making known Luther's theology of the cross to the Asian world. Kitamori, a Japanese theologian, rose to international reputation primarily through his book *The Theology of the Pain of God*, published in Japanese in 1946,[81] one of the first contextual theologies from Asia to appear in English after (WW II) in 1958.[82] Living in a time of suffering from the terrible effects of two atomic bombs, Kitamori used the "analogy of pain" (*analogia doloris*) as the proper way to speak about the pain of God, who is in love with the people in pain.

Kitamori insisted that the pain of God is the fundamental theme of God's redemption.[83] He brought two Japanese words, *tsutsumu* and *tsurasa* together, using Jeremiah 31:20 and Isaiah 63:15 to construct his theology. These two verses share the Hebrew root *hamah*, which refers to "compassion and pain." Jeremiah 31:12 refers more to the "pain of God" whereas Isaiah 63:15 refers more to the "compassion of God." Kitamori explained that the Japanese word *tsutsumu* means to embrace while *tsurasa* signifies feeling pain in one's deep personal self for the sake of others.[84] When *tsusumu* is combined with *tsurasa*, the fusions of "passion and compassion" happen together.

The love rooted in the pain of God represents the God of *tsutsumu* and of *tsurasa*. Divine pain and human pain are qualitatively different but they share a common ground. Kitamori described God's pain in three orders of divine love: love of God; pain of God and the love rooted in the pain of God. The first order is God's immediate love of those who are worthy—this kind of love is directed toward Christ and mankind before the relation is affected by sin (Hos. 11:1, 4). The second order is that God feels pain and thus He sent His begotten Son to the world for the forgiveness of sin.[85] The third order is love rooted in the pain of God in the sense that God continues to love the justified sinners.

Thus, the *Pyithu*'s attribute of *Dukkha* can be applied to the pain of God in light of Jesus' suffering. Jesus as the truly divine and truly human becomes the ladder to God's love and pain. God's pain is primarily due to His love and wrath. The love of God is His primary work and the wrath of God is His secondary work. This means that God is revealed to the *Pyithu-Dukkha* as God in pain through Jesus.[86] Jesus' command to take up the cross serves as the example in God's relationship of pain with the *Pyithu-Dukkha*.

---

[81] Kazoh Kitamori, *The Theology of the Pain of God* (Richmond, VA: John Knox Press, 1958).

[82] Warren McWilliams, *The Passion of God: Divine Suffering in Contemporary Protestant Theology* (Macon, GA: Mercer University Press, 1985), 100.

[83] Kitamori, *The Theology of the Pain of God*, 19.

[84] Ibid., 151.

[85] Ibid., 120.

[86] Ibid., 111. Moltmann's book *Crucified God* is part of Kitamori's influence. See Moltmann's *Crucified God*, xi.

Taking the *Pyithu*'s pain as a witness to God's pain in a world of unjust and violence, Kitamori developed God's pain and human pain in terms of an ethical and eschatological attitude. The ethical result for Christians is to love God and love their neighbors, who are in pain. Reflecting on Luke 10:27, which indicates regarding loving God and loving neighbors, the tasks of Christians is to shoot one arrow at two targets at the same time. The Christian ethical concept of pain embraces a possible factor in dialogue with the Buddhist's notion of *Karuna/* compassion toward the *Pyithu-Dukkha*.[1]

In talking about suffering from an eschatological perspective, Kitamori emphasized the tension between *theological axiom* (the End has arrived in the person of Jesus) and *theological reality* (full redemption is yet to come). The End is conceived as a present reality while it is still pointing to the full redemption of suffering in the future. In line with Oscar Cullmann's view of "inaugurated eschatology," Kitamori noted suffering is an inherent part of human life until the Lord's return.[2] The God of *tsutsumu*/passion and *tsurasa*/compassion is dynamically revealed to the *Pyithu-Dukkha*. What heals the *Pyithu*'s wounds is the love rooted in the painful wounds of Jesus (Isa. 53:5; 1Pet. 2:24).

While I am moved by Kitamori's theology of the pain of God, I would like to criticize his hermeneutics on the reverse of the love and pain of God. He concludes his theological position on the pain of God with the following meditation.

> My prayer night and day is that the gospel of love rooted in the pain of God may become real to all humans. All human emptiness will be filled if this gospel is known to every creature.[3]

He is right in combining the pain and love of God. However, we must disagree with him when he regards the love being rooted in the pain of God, instead of the pain being rooted in the love of God.[4] This is not quite right from a biblical point of view. John 3:16-17 says, "God so loved the world that He sent His Son into the world not to condemn, but to save the world." This text reminds us that love is the root of pain, not that pain is the root of love. God's pain through Christ is rooted in His love through Christ. The pain of God flows from the love of God. Love is God's essence, and pain is His action. Even in our human experience, we feel pain for someone in trouble and show our compassion because we love that person. Thus, love must be the root of pain.

Pyithu-Dukkha in Dialogue with C.S. Song's Crucified People

We will turn now our attention to today's best known Taiwanese theologian, Cho-an Seng Song (1929-). Of all Asian theologians today, Song is the most widely

---
[1] Ibid., 26, 99.
[2] Ibid., 144.
[3] Kitamori, *The Theology of the Pain of God*, 150.
[4] For a critique of Kitamori, see Song, *Third-Eye Theology*, 67.

published, writing Christian theology steeped in Asian religious motifs through a simple whimsical style.[5] Seeing God's redemptive work in creation through all cultures, Song insists Asian theology be articulated from the womb of Asia.[6] Song's two major themes are: first a theology of incarnation—the gospel must be incarnated into Asia, and second a theology of emancipation, borrowing its methodology from Latin American liberation theology.[7] Song uses the word "transposition," as a key to understanding "incarnation," how the Gospel spread from place to another place. The world was transposed from Palestine to the Greco-Roman world and to the rest of Europe, the West and the East.

In light of the religious plurality and social-political suffering,[8] Song invites us to see the incarnated Jesus as the representative of the crucified *people* in Asia. If Jesus is the mediator between God and humanity and the second person of the Trinity, Song strongly argued that God must be the story of Jesus and Jesus must be the story of the crucified people in Asia. To talk about Jesus, we must talk about the crucified people simultaneously who are the oppressed, the exploited, and the marginalized with whom Jesus was associated during His ministry and ultimately crucified *for* and *with*.[9]

Song interprets Jesus' cry of abandonment, "my God, why have you forsaken me?" (Mk. 15:34) not as a theological trial between God and God, as Jesus was crucified not as a *divine* but as a *human*: Song contends, "If God is separated in an abandonment of the Son, how can we understand Jesus' sharing the same substance with His Father within the Trinity?" As applied in Asia, the crying Jesus is better paradigmized as the Asian-*Pyithu-Dukkha*. With this, we will see how immanent Trinity is more related to the social Trinity in line with Jesus' last cry, "Father, to your hand, I commit my Spirit" (Lk. 23:46).

This statement shows the relationship between the Father and the Son within the suffering context of the Trinity. The Father co-participates with the Son in a kenotic way. Song treats Jesus' cry on the cross as a way that God is a "vindictive Deity" but co-suffers in Spirit. Song takes Jesus' *Dukkha* as the starting point for understanding a theology of the cross and a cosmic Christ in solidarity with the *Pyithu-Dukkha*. If Jesus is a suffering humanity, there can be many *Jesus-es* not only of Jewish flesh, but of Burmese. For Song, "Jesus is experienced among the people in their life of *Dukkha* as their liberator."[10]

Song's theology of the cross turned a Christology from above into a Jesus-logy from below in a provocative way.[11] The analogy of the historical Jesus as the Passover Lamb in the exodus becomes the lamb who died with the *Pyithu-Dukkha* (Rom. 5:8; Gal. 2:20). The Jesus, who died 2,000 years ago can be discovered in

---

[5] Yung, *Mangoes or Bananas?* 168-169.
[6] C. S. Song, *Theology From The Womb of Asia* (Maryknoll, NY: Orbis Books, 1986)
[7] C. S. Song, *The Compassionate God* (Maryknoll, NY: Orbis Books, 1982), 10-11.
[8] Ibid., 5-6.
[9] Song, *Jesus, The Crucified People*, 211.
[10] Ibid., 120.
[11] Ibid., 229.

the midst of the crucified people today and tomorrow. The answer to Jesus' continuing presence is proved in His Eucharistic words: "this is my body and this is my blood, the blood of the covenant, shed "for many" (Mk. 14:22). The preposition, "for" (*hyper* in Greek) stands for "in behalf of" (Christ died *for* us, Rom. 5:8) while the word "many" (*polloi*) implies the inclusive sense of being "in solidarity with," or "in the company of the *Pyithu*.[12]

By people (*Pyithu*), I mean those men and women whose company Jesus enjoyed and with whom Jesus liked to eat and drink and to whom Jesus declared God's reign belongs. The crucified Jesus is in solidarity with the crucified *Pyithu*, who need to be healed of their ailments, who long to be liberated from their *Dukkha*, who needs to be given hope in the midst of *Dukkha*, and who seek the assurance of new life in the face of death.[13] Song's people-centered hermeneutic of incarnational theology can be summed up is this way: to know the crucified Jesus, we must know the crucified people at the same time—knowing the crucified people comes first followed by the crucified Jesus.

Pyithu-Dukkha in Dialogue with Kosuke Koyama's Water Buffalo Theology

Kosuke Koyama (1929-2009) is the second-most influential Asian theologian whose theology roots deeply in the biblical soil and flowers in the Asian fields. Experiencing the devastation brought by the American bombs in Hiroshima, Koyama's thought was reflected by the crucified Christ. Consequently he wrote his doctoral dissertation on Luther's *theologia crucis* at Princeton.[14] He was sent by the United Church of Christ in Japan as a missionary to Thailand in S. E. Asia from 1960-68.

Koyama's hermeneutic is people-centered and contextual, drawing from the smells, sights and sounds of daily life to illuminate the gospel in a profound way.[15] In his best known book, *Water Buffalo Theology*, Koyama was clear that he was sent not to Italy to speak about Thomas Aquinas's *Summa Theologiae* or to Switzerland to talk about Karl Barth's *Church Dogmatics*, but to Thailand to speak about Asian countryside theology among the suffering Buddhist-farmers who used water buffaloes at works.[16]

Taking suffering as the center for doing a "countryside theology," Koyama compared Thailand with the Israel, in which God's pathos and love was at work in Thailand as it was in Israel. Koyama set the Israel's experience of *suffering*, im-

---

[12]Ibid., 125.
[13]Ibid., 213-216.
[14]Kosuke Koyama, *Mount Fuji and Mount Sinai* (London: SCM, 1984), 3.
[15]Daniel J. Adams, *Cross-Cultural Theology: Western Reflections in Asia* (Atlanta, GA: John Knox Press, 1987), 56.
[16]Dale T. Irvin and Akintunde E. Akinade, eds., *The Agitated Mind of God: The Theology of Kosuke Koyama* (Maryknoll, NY: Orbis Books, 1996). See also Koyama, *Water Buffalo Theology*, vii.

permanence and *destruction* by rebelling against their God in conversation with the Buddhist teaching of *Dukkha* (unsatisfactoriness), *anicca* (transitoriness) and *anatta* (self-destruction).[17] Like Israel, Buddhists and (all humans) face *Dukkha*, *anicca* and *anatta* from the perspective of God's saying work. God does not reject *Dukkha*, *anicca* and *anatta*, but *historicize* them by His relationship to humans. This is a starting point for a theological response to God's saving work in dialogue with the Buddhist's *arhat* (saints).

In spite of Israel's suffering, transitoriness and rebellion against God, the compassionate God remains in a saving covenant with them and says, "turn to me and be saved, all the ends of the earth" (Isa. 45:22). In this sense of God's transcendence into history, the insight of the Buddha and the message of Israel encounter as a point of *historicization*. The three masks of humankind receive *new* meaning as Koyama noted:

> *Dukkha* signifies Israel's unsatisfactory devotion to God; *anicca* means Israel's breaking the covenant; *anatta* inspires one to eliminate "I," which rebels God. "Our concept of holistic salvation thus begins when we bring Israel's new experience of salvation into the Thai Buddhist context."[18]

The broken relationship between God and Israel and among creatures was restored only through the crucified Jesus. The crucified heart can only communicate the crucified Christ with the crucified people. The crucified heart is rooted not in self-centered love but self-denial (1Cor. 2:2; Matt. 16:24). Koyama argued that our Buddhist-farmers neighbors were less interested in Christology than neighborology, of how we put into practice Jesus 'self-giving love.[19] Our neighbors are more interested in neighborology than Christology but Christology shapes neighborology, too. Koyama's strength lies in Jesus' self-giving love as a bridge to connect different parties.[20]

Koyama's concern was to demonstrate Israel's saving history and the crucified Christ who saved others from humiliation. God initiated the salvation event of "dead-alive" and "lost-found" through the *Anatta* of Christ. *Anatta* is the invitation for Christ to be in *karuna* with the *Pyithu-Dukkha*. The crucified heart is a prism through which he looked at the work and presence of the crucified God among the *Pyithu-Dukkha*. God's involvement in love and pain throughout history comes to focus in *karuna* with the *Pyithu*. For Koyama, Jesus' cry of abandonment on the cross turned into an ontological redemption through the same man who said "I am not *alone*, for the Father is *with* me" (Jn. 16:32).[21] Therefore, this is the pattern to be followed by Christians, those who have the crucified heart in witness to God as "*Immanuel*" with the *Pyithu-Dukkha*.

---

[17]Ibid., 112-115.
[18]Ibid., 115.
[19]Ibid., 91.
[20]Kosuke Koyama, "The Crucified Christ Challenges Human Power," in *Asia Faces of Jesus*, ed. R. S. Sujirtharajah (Maryknoll, NY: Orbis Books, 1993), 75.
[21]Koyama, *Water Buffalo Theology*, 177.

If there is one theological center in Koyama's concept of God, it would be "a hot God."[22] For Koyama, God is not a cool God, but a hot God who feels compassionate for the suffering creatures. By a cool God, he means an apathetic God who is without passion.[23] An apathetic or cool God is free from the painful creatures. By contrast, he speaks of a hot God who feels compassionate for the suffering creatures, such as the *Pyithu-Dukkha*. Koyama's concept of the hot God is grounded on the cross. Building on a theology of the cross, he took Christology to be the center for his missiology in Asia. The cross of Christ was unique, because the "true knowledge of the hot God," he said comes from the suffering of Christ and this happens concretely when Jesus loves the strangers and the oppressed and took a solidarity with them.[24] More importantly, he emphasized the inseparability of Christology and soteriology (liberation, justice and reconciliation).

Finally, Koyama's priority of neighborology over Christology is both appreciative and debatable. It may be true that other faiths, Buddhists in the particular case of Koyama is more interested in neighborology than in Christology partly because the violent death of Christ is problematic to a Buddhist doctrine of *ahimsa* (nonviolence). According to Yung, what cannot be denied is that it is Christology that shapes neighborology.[25] I agree with Yung that we become neighbors to others or we should treat other faiths as our neighbors primarily on the basis of Christ's restoring us into a communion of self-giving love. So if we communicate the self-emptiness of Christ to the analogous concept of Buddhist doctrine of *anatta*, which eliminates "I" for the sake of others, Buddhists would be interested in seeing some convergences between the Christian doctrine of anatta, grounded in the hot God and the Buddhist *anatta*, grounded in the self-emptied Buddha.[26]

According to Koyama, a mutual exchange of religious enrichment is result from an inter-personal dialogue (people-centered dialogue). For this reason, he prioritized an interpersonal dialogue over an interreligious dialogue (religion-centered dialogue).[27] When we prioritize an interpersonal dialogue, we take our commonality as the bridge of humanity. When we prioritize an inter-religious dialogue, we compare and contrast the different religious doctrines and the conclusion of dialogue ends up as a mission of hostility. In order not to happen this, Koyama invites us to prioritize an inter-personal dialogue over an inter-religious dialogue. Though I am moved by his creative methodology, I wonder how we would envisage it in practice. The reason is when we dialogue with other faiths, they bring their religions because religions is their skins. The question we need to ask is: can we really separate a person from his/her religion in Asia?

---

[22] Ibid., 108.
[23] Ibid.
[24] Kosuke Koyama, "Extend Hospitality to Strangers: A Missiology of Theologia Crucis," in *Currents in Theology and Mission*, 20.3. (1993): 165-176 (especially p. 167).
[25] Yung, *Mangoes or Bananas?* 166-167.
[26] For a full account, see David Thang Moe, "The Crucified Mind: Kosuke Koyama's Missiology of Theology of the Cross," in *Exchange: Journal of Contemporary Christianities in Context*, 46/1. (2017): 5-28 (especially pp. 19-20).
[27] Koyama, *Water Buffalo Theology*, 93-95.

Koyama, unfortunately, did not provide a clear answer to this question. However, his methodological approach worth considering insofar as it implies the idea that Christians should prioritize an inter-personal dialogue (human-centered) over an inter-religious dialogue (religious doctrine-centered). The motivation and goal of such kind of dialogue will be a mission of hospitality rather than of hostility. In the context of *Pyithu-Dukkha*, it is imperative for the oppressed Christians and Buddhists to prioritize an inter-personal dialogue with a common hope of liberation from the socio-political oppressors. Since they share of the common experience of socio-political suffering, Christians and Buddhists should cooperate and resist their common enemies of military regime.[28]

Pyithu-Dukkha in Dialogue with Aloysius Pieris' Theology of Liberation

Aloysius Pieris (1934-), from Sri Lanka, is one of the leading Roman Catholic Asian theologians alive today. Since graduating from the Pontifical Theological Faculty in Nepals in 1966, he became the first Christian ever to be awarded a doctoral degree in Buddhist philosophy at the University of Sri Lanka in Colombo. Pieris has been a proponent of interreligious dialogue in struggle for the liberation of the poor. He is very close to colleagues among the liberation theologians in Latin America but different from them in his specific emphasis on Asians' "suffering and multifaceted religiosity."[29]

According to Pieris, one must take the tasks of liberation of the poor and inter-religious dialogue in the theological reflections and praxis of Asian churches. When suffering and religiosity meet each other in harmony, they both become a driving force for holistic liberation. Pieris' interest in an Asian liberation offers us twofold way: first Jesus' struggle *to* be poor in terms of His renunciation of the world (2Cor. 8:9)—*voluntary poverty* (Matt. 8:20), and second Jesus' struggle *for* the poor against Mammon's power that creates oppression (Matt. 25:31-46)—*forced poverty*.[30] The former comes closer to the Buddha's way of *interior liberation* in terms of renunciation of the worldly wealth, while the latter coincides with the Buddha's resistance to evils.

Jesus' kenotic way of salvation through agape-love complements the Buddha's *anatta* detachment from craving in the struggle for liberation. This principle of complementarity becomes meaningful in constructing an Asian theology of the *Pyithu*'s liberation.[31] Not only Christians, but other neighbors are following Jesus' way of poverty for liberation. Jesus' suffering at Calvary is discovered everywhere in the suffering life of the people. Given this fact, Pieris proposes twofold task: one is to witness to Jesus' humiliating life in humble service to all sufferers;

---

[28]Moe, "The Crucified Mind," 20.
[29]Pieris, *SQ Asian Theology of Liberation*, 69.
[30]Ibid., 15.
[31]Ibid., 15.

the other is to proclaim Jesus' uniqueness as the new covenant in solidarity with the sufferers and resist evil.[32]

What inspires Pieris in this direction comes from two biblical axioms: the *irreconcilable* antagonism between God and wealth and the *irrevocable* covenant between God and the oppressed, Jesus Himself being this covenant.[33] The option for Christ to be poor has a messianic and soteriological role in the history of God's salvation because God shaped the history via Jesus' kenotic way of self-denial. The biblical God shows special preference for slaves in the struggle against their oppressors.[34]

God's face in the crucified Jesus should be referred in an Asian perspective as a kenotic way of participating in the struggle for the *Pyithu*'s spiritual and physical emancipation. Redemption and creation stand not in a polar tension, but are understood as one reality of God. Therefore, God's universal presence in creational and redemptive acts need to be expressed not only in the institutional church, but also in the passionate solidarity with religious outsiders, who struggle for their own emancipation.

Seeing Christ as the cosmic savior who is dynamically present in the world through His creative powers and redemptive acts, Pieris uses a threefold way of core-to-core dialogue in a pluralistic context: they include (1) the historical-cultural bridge in terms of relativity (2) the theological-mystical bridge in terms of God's mystery, and (3) the ethical-practical bridge in the name of social justice and wholistic liberation. This threefold sense of relativity, mystery and justice is what relates God's ontological revelation and self-communication to human struggles in Myanmar.[35]

In response to co-experience of humanistic suffering and religiosity in an Asia's context, our task is to witness Jesus' inclusivity to non-Christians and to participate with the victims against evil. In this way, a theology of the cross becomes *liberative* in solidarity with the victims through the resurrected power and *inclusive* in recognition of religious outsiders through whom God's natural revelation is ontologically evident in Asia. Within a kenotic Christology, we have to witness to God's *liberative knowledge* and *redemptive love* for the *Pyithu-Dukkha* in dialogue with the Buddhist's *Karuna*.[36]

---

[32]Michael Amaladoss, *Life in Freedom: Liberation Theologies from Asia* (Maryknoll, NY: Orbis Books, 1997), 95.

[33]Ibid.

[34]Pieris, *An Asian Theology of Liberation*, 64-65.

[35]Aloysius Pieris, "The Buddha and the Christ: Mediators of Liberation," in *The Myth of Christian Uniqueness: Toward a Pluralistic Theology of Religions*, ed. John Hick and Paul F. Knitter (Maryknoll, NY: Orbis Books, 1987), 163.

[36]Aloysius Pieris, "Buddhism as a Challenge for Christians," in *Christianity Among World Religions*, ed. Jürgen Moltmann and Hans Küng (Edinburgh: T&T Clark, 1986), 65.

Pyithu-Dukkha in Dialogue with Jung Young Lee's Empathetic God

We now turn our attention to Jung Young Lee, one of the most creative Asian theologians, who plays a central role in bridging "western either-or thinking"[37] and "Asian both-and thinking" through *yin-yang* symbolic thinking. Lee proposed "both-and thinking" as a better context for interpreting Christian faith. Lee's interest lies in the dialectic of divine-human suffering between East/Asia and the West. Thus, he wrote his doctoral dissertation on the topic of *God Suffers for Us*,[38] in which he explored the concept of divine passibility in contrast to the Greek notion of divine impassibility.

From the perspective of *yin-yang* thinking, Lee viewed God as the Creator of "both-and:" heaven and earth, male and female and light and darkness, etc. *Yin* represents female, whereas *yang* represents male. *Yin* and *yang* are primarily opposed, but they fulfill each other in God's creation because they are dialectical symbols.[39] *Yin* cannot exist by itself without *yang*, just as *yang* cannot exist independently of *yin*. Likewise, male is not complete without female; male is complete in female and female in male. The complementary relationship of opposites is necessary for a whole and when the whole becomes a *primary* concern of its parts, the complementary paradox is possible.

Lee's hermeneutic of *yin-yang* relational symbolic thinking opens the window through which the dialectic of divine and human suffering is possible. Lee based his affirmation of divine *Dukkha* on God's nature as *Agape-love* (1Jn. 4:8) and divine empathy. *Agape* is the basis of divine empathy and empathy is a mode of *agape*. Lee distinguished sympathy from empathy: the former is often used as an emotional feeling, whereas the latter is God's actual participation based on His agape-love. God does not merely feel with (sympathy) the human situation, but He feels Himself into (empathy) the human situation and participates in it through the incarnational action in the world.[40]

When the empathetic God suffers for us, His inner tension is revealed as "holiness" and "love." God's love has two dimensions that are dialectically united: the transcendental (holiness and righteousness) and the immanental (grace and mercy)—holiness is the presupposition of love, while love is the fulfillment of holiness. Lee said "*Agape* is the paradoxical unity of holiness and love."[41] The empathetic God who relates Himself graciously to love the world is the greatest sufferer of all (Isa.52:13; Jn.3:16).

---

[37]Wilfred Cantwell Smith, *The Faith of Other Men* (New York: New American Library, 1963), 72. Smith stated "we in the West presume that an intelligent man must choose *either* this *or* that."

[38]Lee, *God Suffers For Us*.

[39]Lee, *Trinity in An Asian Perspective*, 31.

[40]Lee, *God Suffers for Us*, 9-10.

[41]Ibid., 15.

Lee proposed five-fold sense of divine passibility. First, he treated creation as the presupposition for redemption. Second, Lee saw the incarnation as the revelation of *Agape* and the perfect form of divine empathy—incarnation classifies the Empathetic God as "God of Emmanuel with us" (Matt. 1:23). Third, he pictured the cross as the model of God's empathy.[42] Fourth, he described the Spirit as the continuing presence of God's empathy—"The empathetic Spirit Himself intercedes for us with groaning too deep for words" (Rom.8:26-27) Fifth, he understood the Trinity as an archetype of divine empathy. The agape characterizes the relations among the Father, Son and Spirit. Given this fact, Lee interestingly depicted trinity as *change* (Father), *yang* (Son) and *yin* (Spirit) in their communal relation to the humanistic groaning of the *Pyithu-Dukkha*.[43]

Lee did not see Christ's suffering as simply God's response to human suffering, but rather, as God's entering into history with His suffering in the biblical world. *Dukkha* in this cosmos is universal because Christ Himself entered in the midst of this transitory world (2Cor. 5:17). Thus suffering should be understood as a manifestation of participation in the suffering of Christ. The fellowship of Christ's *Dukkha* (Phil.3:10) reaches and embraces the whole community of God's *Pyithu-Dukkha* in the world.[44]

The fellowship of *Dukkha* between Christ and humans produces three elements that help overcome the *Pyithu*'s *Dukkha*. First, this fellowship gives the meaning of significance to suffering—God works *against* suffering and God works *through* suffering as God has a plan and purpose in all suffering. Second, this fellowship demands churches' witness to Christ's *Dukkha* and compassion to all those suffer in society—the fellowship of *Dukkha* offers God's love as the strength to endure the *Pyithu*'s suffering, and third, this fellowship of divine suffering and human suffering gives us hope to anticipate the transformation of suffering into the joy of eternal life.[45]

Within his *yin-yang* relational concept, Lee did not divorce God's suffering from divine empathy or the present from the future, for joy of the future is latent in the present and a fuller joy awaits the final consummation of time.[46] Through the endurance of *Dukkha*, the *Pyithu* come to learn that they are limited and in need of the empathetic God, who co-suffers with them. Therefore, Lee's soteriological resolution to the problem of the *Pyithu-Dukkha* is not the elimination of *Dukkha*, but overcoming and transforming it into divine suffering through the empathetic dialectic of both divine and human experience.

In all, Lee's notion of "both-and *yin-yang* thinking" is helpful in dialogue between two different things, calling for the mutuality, complementariness and coexistence in the midst of much diversity. However, "both-and" thinking is limited in response to what Jesus told us not to serve two masters ("we cannot serve both

---

[42] Ibid., 58-60.
[43] Lee, *The Theology of Change*, 73.
[44] Lee, *God Suffers for Us*, 81.
[45] Ibid., 84.
[46] Ibid., 88-89.

God and money," Matt. 6:24). This biblical remind us to hate the one and love the other. Lee is positively weak that he never developed his *yin-yang* thinking from this dualistic perspective. In my judgment, *Lee's yin-yang* symbolic thinking sides with the paradoxes.

Chapter 4

Pyithu-Dukkha Theology for New Ecumenical and Evangelical Horizons

Missio Dei: God's Mission in the Context of *Pyithu-Dukkha*

Mission in the Bible: God as a Missionary God

Martin Kahler said, "Mission was the mother of all theology."[1] Theology, for Kahler, began as an accompanying manifestation of mission. In line with Kahler's metaphor, I argue that theology springs out of mission in the same way God uses the mother to give birth to children. All theology we do comes from God's Mission. Mission is rooted in the Bible and History—history is the arena of God's act of mission, whereas the bible is a missionary book. In chapter 2, we discussed how God becomes a missionary God.[2] The NT witnesses to Jesus as a missionary sent into the world (Jn. 3:16)—Jesus is seen as a global missionary. According to David Bosch, "Mission is not primarily the activity of the church but the attribute of the triune God. The Latin word, *missio dei* is translated as *apostello* for 'sending' in the NT and *salah* in the OT."[3]

Mission in the History: From Edinburgh to Asia

Historically, the first World Missionary Conference held in Edinburgh, June 14-23, 1910 is widely regarded as the culmination of nineteenth century Protestant Christian mission as well as the driving force for the beginning of the ecumenical movement, giving birth to the International Missionary Council (IMC)

---

[1] Martin Kahler, *Schriften zur Christologie und Mission* (Munich: Verlag, 1971), 190.

[2] Craig Ott, Stephen J. Strauss, and Timothy C. Tennent, *Encountering Theology of Mission: Biblical Foundations, Historical Developments, Contemporary Issues* (Grand Rapids, MI: Baker Academic 2010), 3.

[3] David J. Bosch, *Transforming Mission: Paradigm Shifts in Theology of Mission*, 20th anniversary ed. (Maryknoll, NY: Orbis Books, 2011), 389.

in 1921 and the World Council of Churches (WCC) in 1948.⁴ The conference was attended by fourteen hundred delegates. Delegations were especially strong from Asia and unusually weak from Africa. It was a Protestant conference—no Roman Catholics and East Orthodox missionary organizations were invited.⁵ Two goals were stated for the conference. The first was to deepen the church's sense of its missionary's obligation to the world beyond the West.

This leads to what Stephen Neill famously said, "The age of *missions* (the western missions of church) is at an end; the age of world *mission* has begun."⁶ The second goal was to identify the problems missionaries faced and to think outside the box when developing methods to reach the unreached.⁷ As the conference proposed, the mission task was to recognize the presence of God in the non-Christian worlds and to use the local religious cultures as points of contact for proclaiming the gospel and cultivating Christian faith. This is what came to be called "fulfillment theology"⁸ in the words of Terry Muck. While many delegates embraced fulfillment theology, others reacted against it. But either way, no one could ignore fulfillment theology, particularly in the context of interreligious communication of the gospel. Fulfillment theology sees other religions not as the mere objects for conversion, but as the neighbors to whom the moral religious insights must be both given and received for developing Christianity in local cultures.⁹

The world mission concept of fulfillment theology initiated at the Edinburgh mission conference was developed by the International Mission Conference held in Willingen, Germany 1952 as a famous concept of *missio* Dei (the mission of God).¹⁰ The mission of God first and foremost belongs to the mission of God rather than to the mission of the church. God is the originator of mission and the church is a participant in God's mission in terms of witnessing to Christ to all nations. Drawing upon the concept of *missio Dei* that emerged from the 1952 meeting of the IMC in Willingen, we can draw three critical insights¹¹ for developing a theology of mission in Asian Burmese context.

First, the concept of *missio Dei* holds that mission primarily belongs to and begins with God rather than to and with the church. In other words, God is the originator and source of mission and the church is the agent joining in God's world mission or economy of salvation. Second, the mission of God is fundamentally

---

⁴Daryl Balia and Kirsteen Kim, eds., *Edinburgh 2010 Witnessing to Christ Today*, vol. 2 (Eugene, OR: WIPF & STOCK, 2010), 1.

⁵Brian Stanley, *The World Missionary Conference, Edinburgh 1910* (Grand Rapids, MI: Eerdmans, 2009).

⁶Cited from Bosch, *Transforming Mission*, 391.

⁷Terry C. Muck, *Why Study Religion? Understanding Humanity's Pursuit of the Divine* (Grand Rapids, MI: Baker Academic, 2016), 98.

⁸Ibid., 99.

⁹Ibid., 99-100.

¹⁰George F. Vicedom, *The Mission of God: An Introduction to a Theology of Mission*, trans. Gilbert A. Thiele and Dennis Hilgendorf (St. Louis, MO: Concordia, 1965), 6.

¹¹Bosch, *Transforming Mission*, 398-402.

Trinitarian in nature. The Trinity and mission are inseparable. There is no mission without the Trinity; the Trinity is unknowable apart from God's economic act of mission. The triune God is involved in one economic mission of creation (creation out of nothing, Gen. 1) and of new creation or redemption or reconciliation (creation out of the old, John 3: 16; 2 Cor. 5: 17).[12] In order to redeem and reconcile the sinful world to God's own self, the Father sent the Son by the power of the Holy Spirit. *Missio Dei* is all about a Trinitarian movement of the Father's sending of the Son and the sending of the Spirit by the Father and the Son.[13] The third theme is the emphasis on the ongoing incarnate work of Christ and the cosmic presence of the Spirit in the created order, including the religiously pluralistic world.

The Protestant mission born in the Edinburgh and Willingen came to be in dialogue with the Roman Catholic in the Vatican II (1962-65). Both Edinburgh and Vatican II affirm that Christ is the light of all nations[14] and His revelation cannot be limited among other faiths. The statement from Mission and Evangelism Conference of the WCC held in San Antonio, Texas in 1989 sums it up well: "we cannot point to any other way than Jesus, at the same time, we cannot set limits to saving power of God."[15]

With the spirit of Edinburg and the Vatican, the Christian Conference of Asia (CCA) came to exist as an organ of cooperating among the ecumenical churches in 1959 under the theme "Witnessing Life Together." Within the umbrella of the WCC, the CCA believes that the purpose of God's mission in Asia is life together in a common obedience of witness to Christ in relationships with all peoples, including other faiths at large.[16]

Religious Plurality Challenges for Mission in Asia

Catholic theologian Alan Race's classic threefold typology—"exclusivism, inclusivism and pluralism"[17] stands at the forefront of missiological debates in Asia in general and Myanmar in particular. To summarize Race's threefold typology, exclusivism maintains the particularity of Christ (Jn. 14:6; Acts 4:1), the negative view of other religions as idolatrous, and the need of calling other faiths to Christ. Inclusivism holds the uniqueness and superiority of Christ to other religious figures, the universality of saving grace and the unnecessity of calling other faiths to

---

[12]For detailed discussion of a Trinitarian Missiology, see my article, David Thang Moe, 'The Word to the World: Johannine Trinitarian Missiology (John 20: 21-22)', *Journal of Pentecostal Theology,* 26.1. (2017): 68-85.

[13]Bosch, *Transforming Mission,* 400.

[14]Lesslie Newbigin: *The Open Secret: An Introduction to the Theology of Mission,* revised ed. (Grand Rapids, MI: William B. Eerdmans Publishing Company, 1995), 1.

[15]Fredrick R. Wilson, ed, *The San Antonio Report – Your Will be Done: Mission in Christ's Way* (Geneva: WCC, 1990), 32.

[16]Yung, *Mangoes or Bananas?* 147.

[17]Alan Race, *Christians and Religious Pluralism* (London: SCM Press, 1983).

Christ. Pluralism rejects the particularity of Christ and sees all religions as different paths leading to one mountain.[18]

In his book *Dissonant Voices*,[19] Harold Netland re-defines the trilogy in response to the relation between Christianity and other religions. *Exclusivism*: it claims Jesus as the final revelation of God, the sole source of salvation and Christianity as a religion of absolute truth. The central claim of Christianity is true in conflict with other religions.[20] Gavin D'Costa argued that exclusivism is primarily concerned with two central insights: first salvation comes from faith in Christ alone (*solus Christus*), and second, this salvation won by Christ is only available through faith in Christ, which comes from hearing the gospel preached (*fides ex auditu*), requiring true repentance and baptism.[21]

Inclusivism: although the inclusivist position claims that Christ is central in God's self-revelation or self-communication and His salvific plan for the world, it allows for God's ontological creation and salvific action through other religions.[22] The inclusivist position attempts to balance the principle of *solus Christus* (uniqueness of Christ) with the concept of the *universal salvific will of God* (cosmic Christ) in openness to God's revelation outside the church. Inclusivists do not attempt to call other religions to Christ with repentance because they think that is the work of the Spirit. The Edinburgh Conference and the Second Vatican Council were a point of departure for inclusivism, which has been widely adopted by most of the ecumenical Asian Christians.

Pluralism: it distinguishes itself from that of exclusivism and inclusivism by denying God's final revelation and salvific act in Jesus Christ alone. Pluralism goes beyond inclusivism in rejecting any idea as superior or normative regarding Christianity. The pluralist position stands together with all other religious faiths as one of the equal paths to God or the ultimate reality.[23] Which model should I employ in this paper? The answer is none. Many theologians of religions, such as Terry Muck complain that "Race's classic threefold typology is misleading among theologians of religion without a proper description of the meaning and methodology of a theology of religions."[24]

In order to overcome Race's classic threefold typology, I would like to employ a trinitarian theology of religions in the context of *missio Dei*. I find Gavin D'Costa's Trinitarian proposal of three theses helpful for overcoming Race's threefold typology and for developing a Trinitarian theology of religions in the Asian-Burmese context.

---

[18] 10-11.

[19] Harold A. Netland, *Dissonant Voices: Religious Pluralism and the Question of Truth* (Grand Rapids, MI: William B. Eerdmans Publishing Company, 1991).

[20] Ibid., 9.

[21] Gavin D'Costa, *Christianity and World Religions: Disputed Questions in the Theology of Religions* (Chichester: John Wiley & Sons, Ltd., 2009), 25.

[22] Netland, *Dissonant Voices*, 9. See also D'Costa, *Christianity and World Religions*, 9.

[23] Ibid., 9.

[24] Terry C. Muck, "Instrumentality, Complexity and Reason: A Christian Approach to Religious Diversity," in *Christian-Buddhist Studies*, 22 (2002): 115-121.

The first thesis is Christocentric Trinitarian that guards against exclusivism by dialectically relating the universal and the particular. Secondly, Pneumatocentric Trinity that allows the particularity of Christ to be related to the universal activity of God in all religions. Thirdly, if the Spirit is universally active in all creation, then God's universal revelation is possible through all religions and cultures.[25]

In line with D'Costa, I argue that a contemporary theology of mission in Myanmar should take the Trinitarian revelation as a basis for interrelating the incarnate work of Christ and the universal presence of the Spirit in the world, including other religions.[26] In His self-revelation to the world, the Father uses Jesus the Son and the Spirit as Iraneaus's typology of 'two inseparable hands.' If Jesus defines who God is in terms of both full divinity and fully humanity and what His saving purpose is, the Spirit expresses where God is both in the spheres of the church and Asia's religiously pluralistic world. In what follows, I ask: what does it mean to be Christians living among people of other faiths? How should we witness to the triune God among people of other faiths?

Mission as Dialogue with the *Pyithu-Dukkha*

Christians in Asia in general and Myanmar in particular have face two options: one is *escape* and the other is *engagement*. Escape means turning our backs on our nation, neighbors of other faiths in rejection, washing our hands and determining to harden our hearts against them. This is a result of misreading the church as being called out of the world to be a holy community without interacting with the world (1Pet. 2: 9). In sharp contrast to escape, engagement or dialogue means turning our faces toward our neighbors of the *Pyithu-Dukkha*, in compassion and respect, and getting our hands dirty and worn out in service for the well-being.[27] This paper chooses the latter as the Christian response to the divine commission. The church means both being called out of the world to be a gathered community of faith and being sent out to the world to be a scattered and public community to engage with people of other faiths for the well-being of the nations.

Many scholars, such as Moltmann argue that Christians must embody not only the immanent Trinity (the inner communion of the triune God) by way of doxology (this is doxological trinity), but also the economic or social trinity (God's external relation to the world) by way of dialogical engagement with people of

---

[25]Gavin D. Costa, "Christ, The Trinity and Religious Plurality," in *Christian Uniqueness Reconsidered: The Myth of Pluralistic Theology of Religions*, ed. Gavin D. Costa (Maryknoll, NY: Orbis, 1990): 16-29.

[26]For a full account, see my forthcoming article, David Thang Moe, "A Trinitarian Theology of Religions: Themes and Issues in Evangelical Approaches," in *Evangelical Review of Theology*, vol. 40.2. (July 2017).

[27]Cited in Richard Magnus, "The Christian Role in a Pluralistic Society, with Specific Reference to Singapore," in *Pilgrims and Citizens: Christian Social Engagement in East Asia*, edited by Michael Nai-Chiu Poon (Singapore: ATF Press, 2006): 169-178, especially 171-172.

other faiths, or *Pyithu-Dukkha* in public spheres.[28] Christian community must be grounded in this dialectical embodiment of the Trinity. If the former is a pious act of faith (worship, prayer and preaching), the latter is a prophetic practice of faith or communicating of faith. In the context of *Pyithu-Dukkha*, the paper emphasizes the latter without excluding the former. The question is no longer why Christians in Myanmar should be in dialogue with the *Pyithu-Dukkha*, especially the oppressed Buddhists, rather Christian engagement with the *Pyithu-Dukkha* should be re-considered as imaging the nature and the call of the relational God.

To be sure, Christian dialogical engagement with Buddhists in Myanmar can be demonstrated in two ways. One is Christian dialogical engagement with the oppressed Buddhists or *Pyithu-Dukkha* in the society and the other is Christian resistant engagement with the Buddhist oppressors in the state. The former is my focus here. I will study the latter below. As an embodiment of the dialogical God, I consider Christian dialogue with the oppressed Buddhists imperative for the purpose of religious peace and social justice. Moltmann reminds Christians not to lose their identity in an engagement with other faiths and he formed dialogue in this way: "from anathema to dialogue—from dialogue to co-existence—from co-existence to convivence—from convivence to cooperation."[29]

Likewise, Swiss theologian Hans Küng has argued over the years that world peace cannot be promoted without Christian dialogical engagement and cooperation with people of other faiths. He famously states this truism: "there can be no peace among nations without peace among the religions."[30] Küng strongly believes that religious peace and social justice in the world depend on the success of the inter-religious dialogue and cooperation.[31] Küng's statement is hard to ague against in part because the majority of the world's population is religious,[32] in part because the majority of Myanmar's population is religiously Buddhists. Thus, I argue that Christian mission in Myanmar is to be understood and practiced as dialogue with the oppressed Buddhists. Religious peace and social justice cannot be promoted against majority Buddhists, but only with them.

In reality, Christian minority cannot effectively promote religious peace and social justice in Myanmar. Religious peace and social justice can be promoted only through dialogue with the oppressed Buddhists who represent the country's highest percentage of religion. In dialogue with Buddhists, the goal is to share a mutual notion of ethics in response to the *Pyithu*'s suffering. I would argue that Christianity and Buddhism share a common ground of ethics in response to social-political *Dukkha*. Buddhism is grounded in the ethics of compassion (*karuna*) and non-violence (*ahimsa*) of the Buddha. Analogously, Christianity is grounded in the compassionate ministry and nonviolent death of Christ. *Pyithu-Dukkha* the-

---

[28] Moltmann, *The Trinity and the Kingdom*, 151-177.
[29] Moltmann, *Experiences in Theology*, 20-21.
[30] Hans Küng, *Global Responsibility: In Search of a New World Ethic* (New York: Continuum, 1993), 76.
[31] Ibid., 105.
[32] Cited in Volf, *Exclusion and Embrace*, 284.

ology needs to be interwoven with the drama of Christ's compassionate mission in dialogue with the Buddha's notion of compassion.

Jesus' vow at the beginning of His mission has much in analogous common with the Buddha's vow after his enlightenment as he met a suffering beggar. His vow is this;

> Having myself crossed the ocean of *Dukkha*, I must help others to cross it. Freed myself, I must set others free from the bondage of *Dukkha*. This is the vow, which I made in the past when I saw all that lives in distress and crisis.[33]

Jesus' vow at the beginning of His mission is;

> The Spirit of the Lord is upon me as He anointed me; He has sent me to announce good news to the poor, to proclaim release for prisoners and recovery of sight for the blind, to let the broken victims go free, to proclaim the year of the Lord's favor (Lk. 4:18-19).

Comparing the Buddha's vow with Jesus' vow regarding liberation, the Buddha is, of course, fundamentally from Christ, as the Buddha was a self-appointed herald of good news and does not claim any relationship with the Spirit, while Jesus was appointed by God and anointed by the Spirit. Yet, my interest is that the tenets of their vows are primarily filled with ethical concerns for the political conditions that victimize the oppressed, or *Pyithu-Dukkha*.[34] Jesus' compassion for the oppressed comes close to the Buddhist notion of compassion for the oppressed. *Karuna*, defined by Buddhists as compassion for the oppressed could be engaged with the gist of Jesus' solidarity with the *Pyithu-Dukkha*. Jesus' involvement in becoming a friend with the religious outsiders and the outcasts loudly calls for Christian engagement with the *Pyithu-Dukkha* in the public society (Matt. 11:19). Jesus' compassion toward the *Ochlos* shares the analogous theme as the Buddhist praxis of compassion toward the suffering of the oppressed.

From this perspective of Jesus' compassion toward the *Ochlos*, it is appropriate to engage with the Buddhist notion of compassionate liberation for the *Pyithu-Dukkha*. Placing Jesus as a holistic sense of liberator (both physical and spiritual liberation) and the Buddha as a partial sense of liberator (physical liberation) in solidarity with the *Pyithu-Dukkha*, I am drawn into Buddha's compassion for the oppressed in their vows and the way they toiled unselfishly for liberation from *Dukkh*a. The *Pyithu-Dukkha* calls for the relational compassion of Christ and the Buddha in their struggle for liberation of the oppressed. In light of liberation, Pieris suggests that one must take the issue of suffering and the task of interreligious dialogue into the ethical praxis of Asian churches.

Pieris' interest in an Asian theology of interfaith liberation offers us twofold way: first, Jesus' struggle to be poor in terms of His renunciation of the world (2Cor. 8:9—voluntary poverty (the seed of liberation) and second Jesus' struggle for the poor against mammon's power that creates socio-political oppression

---

[33]Edward Conze, *Buddhist Scriptures* (Baltimore, MD: Penguin Books, 1959), 54.
[34]Song, *Third-Eye Theology*, 116.

(Matt. 25:31-46)—forced poverty (the fruit of liberation). The former is close to the Buddha's path of interior liberation in terms of renunciation of the worldly wealth, while the latter coincides with the Buddha's external way of ethical resistance to the powers of evils in the world.[35]

In sum, Jesus' compassion for the outcasts and oppressed signifies the presence of God's kingdom in which He struggles together with the Pyithu-*Dukkha* and promises them the future of the kingdom (Mk. 3:23-34). Analogously, the Buddha showed the way for liberation of the poor and oppressed. From this analogous perspective, we may argue that the Buddha and Jesus are ethically (not eschatologically) meet each other at the point of the *Pyithu*'s suffering. So the Buddha comes into an ethical relationship with Jesus for the sake of *Pyithu-Dukkha's* liberation. Jesus' ministry reflects the nature of God's compassion, which starts at the lowest level of incarnational solidarity with the outcasts and ends with the highest points of sacrifice for all on the cross. Jesus's death on the cross is partly the consequence of His faithful solidarity with the oppressed and poor.[36]

Mission as Witness to Christ among the *Pyithu-Dukkha*

Jesus urges His disciples to be His witnesses (Acts 1:8). But Jesus is not explicit about witness. Let me comprehend what Jesus means by witness in the context of socio-political oppression and multi-culturality. By embodying Jesus as the witness of God, I consider Christian witness in Myanmar to be in terms of both *verbal* proclaiming about Christ and *visible* practicing Christian faith. As Leslie Newbigin rightly states, "the mission of Jesus was not only to proclaim (verbal witness), but also to embody the presence of God's kingdom in His person (visible witness).[37] Jesus is not merely the bearer of the gospel of salvation and of God's kingdom, but the embodiment of that gospel. Likewise, Christians in Myanmar must be both the proclaimers of the gospel of Christ (verbal witnesses) and the embodiments of the gospel (visible witnesses).

The verbal witness is more to do with the evangelistic work of proclaiming Christ's holistic salvation to *Pyithu-Dukkha*, while the visible witness is more to do with social work of nation-building. Both are interrelated. The point is not *either* the verbal witness of evangelism *or* the visible witness of practicing faith for social justice. Rather we must embrace both as the models of mission in Myanmar. However, the goal is different. If the verbal witness of evangelism calls people of other faiths or Buddhists (the majority of *Pyithu-Dukkha*) to Christ, the visible witness of dialogue brings about social justice. Both kinds of goal are evident in the life and ministry of Christ. Jesus calls people with repentance (Mk. 1:15) and liberate them from social injustice (Lk. 4:18-19).

---

[35]Pieris, *An Asian Theology of Liberation*, 15.

[36]For a full account, see David Thang Moe, "Being Church in the Midst of Pagodas: A Theology of 'Embrace' in Myanmar," in *Mission Studies: Journal of the International Association for Mission Studies*, vol. 31.1. (2014): 22-43.

[37]Lesslie Newbigin, *The Open Secret: An Introduction to the Theology of Mission*, rev. ed. (Grand Rapids, MI: Eerdmans, 1995), 40.

Unfortunately, some conservative Christians emphasize the death or atonement of Christ, while some liberal Christians emphasize social ministry of Christ. I must argue that the holistic gospel of Jesus' social ministry of solidarity for the oppressed and the poor and of His atonement for both the oppressed and oppressors are one. The result is God's holistic mission. God's holistic mission implies God in Christ is concerned with the whole person (body, spirit and soul) and the whole community of both the oppressed and the oppressors and natures (Col. 1:19-20).[38] Many Christians in Asia in general and Myanmar in particular concern only one aspect of either social ministry of Christ or atonement of Christ for either physical or spiritual salvation. This study argues that to follow the example of Christ, the church must witness to Christ by addressing the whole person of the *Pyithu-Dukkha* and the whole community of the oppressed and the oppressors in all their needs of healing the broken bodies and saving the lost souls.

In order to heal the broken bodies and the lost souls of the *Pyithu-Dukkha*, Christians in Myanmar must address the relational issues of sin and salvation. Some conservative Christians interpret sin in individual term and tell Buddhists that they need Jesus the Savior because they are sinners. But the hearers feel deeply offended and often reply that I did not kill someone and burn down anyone's house, how dare you call me a sinner? A Christian concept of sin as a state (Rom. 5:12-21) does not make sense to Buddhists.[39] On the other hand, some liberal Christians understand sin more being structural or a condition and struggle for healing the broken bodies and they fail to embrace the need of saving the lost of souls of *Pyithu-Dukkha*, Buddhists. In witnessing to Christ as a holistic liberator for the *Pyithu-Dukkha*, we must correct this imbalance.

I would suggest that Christians must address sin both as a state and a condition or an immoral act for the purpose of holistic salvation. When we interpret sin as a state, the mission task is to convince Buddhists that they need Jesus for the forgiveness of their sin (Rom. 5:12-21). Sin separates every human from communion with God. Only Jesus can restore a communion with God. Paul said, "God reconciles us to Himself through Christ" (2Cor. 5:18). In this respect, salvation for Buddhists—both the oppressed and oppressors has to do with the spiritual dimension of reconciliation, forgiveness and redemption. The mission goal is to convince Buddhists that they are sinners that they need Jesus. We must convince Buddhists not by way of imposition, but through persuasion. Imposition is what Koyama calls the "crusading mind that attempts to coerce other faiths."[40] This stands against the mind of Christ. The mind of Christ is the crucified mind (Phil. 2:5-7).

---

[38] Brian Woolnough and Wonsuk Ma, ed, *Holistic Mission: God's Plan for God's People* (Eugene, OR: Wipf & Stocks, 2010), see the back cover of the book.

[39] For a full account, see my article David Thang Moe, "Sin and Evil in Christian and Buddhist Perspectives: A Quest for Theodicy," in *Asia Journal of Theology*, vol. 29.1. (April 2015): 22-46.

[40] Koyama, *Three Mile an Hour God*, 54.

The crusading mind is a one-traffic witness of Christian mission and the crucified mind is a two-way traffic witness of Christian mission. According to Koyama, the one way mission of the crusading mind is rooted in imperialism, while the two-way mission of the crucified mind is rooted in the self-giving love and self-receiving love of Christ.[41] If one has to choose, I would strongly suggest that the latter must be preferred in the context of the *Pyithu-Dukkha* mainly because it embodies the mind of Christ. The crucified mind loves and sacrifices for the other in light of the claim that all are created equal. The crucified mind approaches mission with a humble and dialogical style, whereas the crusading mind approaches mission with an imperial and monological style. It is the crucified mind of Christ that provides the proper ground for the Christian mission model of witnessing to Christ the Savior among Buddhists in love and respect.[42]

On the other hand, Christians must understand sin as a condition or an immoral act. In this sense, Christians have much to in common with the Buddhist doctrine of the failure to uphold proprieties in personal relations.[43] In defining sin as a condition, the mutual task of the oppressed Christians and Buddhists – *Pyithu-Dukkha* in Myanmar is to struggle against the injustices of the oppressors. The goal is to heal the broken bodies of *Pyithu-Dukkha*. Defining sin as a state requires for the forgiveness of Jesus by way of His gracious act of saving the lost souls of the oppressed Buddhists and oppressor-Buddhists. This sort of salvation analogously relates to the Buddhist doctrine of liberation.

According to Buddhism, there are two different kinds of liberation, which are characterized in terms of the monkey metaphor and the kitten metaphor. When a baby monkey is in a difficult situation, from the start she is active to get out of danger. On the contrary, the baby kitten cries, waiting for her mother to deliver her. The baby kitten symbolizes the Christian understanding of salvation on the basis of total grace in the deliverance of other power, while the baby money symbolizes the Christian view of justice on the basis of dynamic acts. These two metaphors are helpful when thinking about salvation both as a forensic aspect of forgiveness and a transformative aspect.[44]

The baby kitten plays a symbolic role in God's justification through Christ as a free gift without any self-work (Eph. 2:8) (we remain *passive* in receiving grace). As Christ is united with us as a real presence in Word and Sacrament, we become co-workers of God to promote social justice in the context of the *Pyithu-Dukkha*.[45] The baby monkey plays a part in this social vocation (we become *active* in Christ's social vocation). The active monkey echoes James' word: "Faith without works is dead" (Jam.2:26). We are not saved by law or work, but

---

[41]Ibid., 54.

[42]Ibid., 53-54.

[43]Julia Ching and Hans Küng, *Christianity and Chinese Religions* (London: SCM Press, 1989), 73.

[44]Carl Braaten and Robert Jenson, eds., *Union with Christ: The New Finnish Interpretation of Luther* (Grand Rapids, MI: William B. Eerdmans Publishing Company, 1988), 68.

[45]Paul S. Chung, *Constructing Irregular Theology: Bamboo and Minjung in East Asia Perspective* (Leiden: Brill, 2009), 34.

we are saved by grace for good work (Eph. 2:9). We become the moral witnesses of Christ in addressing salvation and sin. I argue that sin needs to be defined in terms of both a state and a condition. The result is to witness to Christ as a holistic Savior for the whole person of the *Pyithu-Dukkha* and the whole community of the oppressed and the oppressor-Buddhists. The gospel of social ministry and the gospel of atonement are one and holistic. What God has joined together, Christians in Asia in general and Myanmar in particular must stop separating them.

Ecclesio Dei: God's Church in the Context of the *Pyithu-Dukkha*

The Church as the Participatory Image of the Triune God

In his book *The Household of God*,[46] Newbigin categorized Christian churches into three groups: first, Roman Catholic Church (110 AD) and Orthodox (1054); second, Protestant-Reformed Churches (1521); and third, Pentecostal Churches (1901). According to Newbigin, the first two groups emphasize the sacraments (the sacramental model) whereas the second group emphasize the Word (the pulpit model) and the third groups emphasizes the audience through music (the charismatic model).[47] More interestingly, Volf creatively develops a theological concept of the church as the image of the triune God in his widely-read book *The Church as the Image of Trinity*.[48]

Volf argues a Trinitarian ecclesiology in dialogue between Roman Catholics, Orthodox and Protestants (Free churches). Volf raises two correlated questions: first, what is the church? Second, where is the church? The Greek word for *ecclesia* can be understood as the "assembly of people" gathered by God (Deut. 4), the "household of God" (Eph. 2:21), "one Body of Christ" (Rom. 12:5) and the "community"[49] gathered in Jesus' name" (Matt. 18:20). The triune God constitutes an assembly into church from the people of Israel into the new covenant toward the eschatological new creation.

Second, where is the church? The church does not exist only through the narrow portals of ordained ministers, but through the life of the whole congregation. The Spirit does not constitute the church exclusively only through those who bear offices, but through all members who serve with their gifts (1Pet. 4:10-11).[50]The question where is the church?" cannot be answered without reference to Christ's presence. The church is characterized by the mutual personal indwelling of the

---

[46]Leslie Newbigin, *The Household of God, Lectures on the Natures of the Church* (London: SCM Press, 1953).

[47]Ibid., 12.

[48]Miroslav Volf, *After Our Likeness: The Church as the Image of the Trinity* (Grand Rapids, MI: William B. Eerdmans Publishing Company, 1998).

[49]See also Stanley J. Grenz, *Theology for the Community of God* (Grand Rapids, MI: William B. Eerdmans Publishing Company, 1994).

[50]Volf, *After Our Likeness*, 152.

triune God and the church comes into being through the mutual services of the whole congregation through its different gifts.[51] Our confession of faith can only mediate Christ's presence (Eph.4:5). God uses all the church member as the participatory agents in His continual work of mission.

The Eucharist and Doxology are central to the life of the church, which demonstrates the mutual relationship and personhood of Trinity. As we have noted above, Moltmann contends that in our praise of God in the Eucharistic form, the Father is the recipient of praise from His creatures and the Spirit is glorifying the Son.[52] In contrast, in the form of the Doxological Trinity,[53] our praises go to the triune God together. The Eucharistic Trinity turns into the Doxological Trinity by transforming thanksgiving into prayer. Doxological Trinitarian is the beginning of seeing God's being as the goal of salvation history. The church's doxology of the triune God is the purpose of the participator church (Ps. 67:3-4).[54] I find Jürgen Moltmann's use of doxological Trinity helpful for developing the relation between the immanent Trinity and Asian liturgical theology. The inner communion among the triune God with different functions is the model for the inner communion of Christians with different gifts (2Cor. 12; Eph. 4).

Taking communion as the identity of the immanent Trinity, Japanese theologian Nozamu Miyahira sees the need to rearticulate the Western concept of monotheism as communal-theism from an Asian perspective.[55] By communal-theism, Miyahira does not mean tri-theism. Rather he contextualizes the commu-nal personhood of the triune God (three persons in one substance) through the lens of Asian cultural identity of community. Miyahira explains communal-theism by saying that the self becomes aware of itself when it meets what is not itself. "This is because," he asserts, "in Asia in general and Japan in particular, the self is determined by its relationship with others."[56] I find Miyahira's contextual proposal of communal-theism helpful for renewing the church as a relational community of one faith with many gifts (Eph. 4:5). As a community of faith, our relation to fellow Christians in love is essential to embodying God who is in relation to us first.

Simon Chan rightly states in his book *Liturgical Theology*: "The church is not merely the agent to accomplish God's purpose, the church is the embodiment of God's ultimate purposes itself."[57] While the instrumental role of the church is important, what is often missed in Asia is the importance of the ontological identity of the church in her spiritual relation with God and with fellow Christians. The result is the failure to see worship as an act of mission. As central to Christian life as liturgy

---

[51] Ibid., 228-330.

[52] Jürgen Moltmann, *The Spirit of Life: A Universal Affirmation* (Minneapolis, MN: Fortress Press, 2001), 302.

[53] Moltmann, *The Trinity and the Kingdom*, 151.

[54] Ott, Strauss, and Tennent, *Encountering Theology of Mission*, 80-81.

[55] Nozamu Miyahira, *Towards a Theology of the Concord of God: A Japanese Perspective on the Trinity* (Carlisle: Paternoster, 2000), 124.

[56] Ibid., 117.

[57] Simon Chan, *Liturgical Theology: The Church as Worshiping Community*. (Downers, IL: IVP, 2006), 21.

is, it cannot be an end in itself. I argue that worship itself is an act of mission. Mission is not just from inside (church) to the world (outside), but also from outside to inside. By the latter, I mean bringing the issues of the world into liturgy and reflect them in our prayer and preaching.

What we understand mission is primarily about going outside the church and being involved in society. But in reality, not all church members are involved in society. However, by bringing the world issues into our liturgy, everyone is involved in.[58] To emphasize the liturgical community as an embodiment of the immanent Trinity, I would argue that mission does not merely come to us from God in terms of His economic relation, but mission may also go to God by way of our doxology. I am not talking about two kinds of mission. Mission is one and God is the originator and we are participating in that one mission. Rather I am talking about a mutual participation in one mission of God.

On the other hand, the economic or social Trinity (God's external relation to the world) provides Christians the paradigm of dialogical relation with others outside the church. Church's participating in the life of the triune God is not only a future hope of anticipation but a present experience (1Jn. 1:3). The church becomes the foretaste of Kingdom in which God's divine elements relate to each other (the immanent trinity) and to the world (the social or economic trinity). In light of the social trinity, the church must witness to God's salvific history in the Exodus and the cross in dialogue with the *Pyithu*'s liberation of economic poverty, political oppression and spiritual alienation. In the context of the *Pyithu-Dukkha*, God uses the church as His pious and prophetic image to pray and struggle for the liberation of the *Pyithu-Dukkha* by the power of the Spirit.[59]

Being the image of immanent Trinity and social Trinity, the church is called to glorify God on the one hand and to edify the *Pyithu-Dukkha* who are the messianic image on the other. The task of the church is to witness to the vertical mutuality of Trinity in horizontal dialogue and interpersonal relationship with each other in the world. To sum up, the triune God uses the church as His image to share the creative and redemptive process with others in transforming the world of individual and communal dimensions.

The Messianic Church as *Koinonia* and *Diakonia* for the *Pyithu-Dukkha*

We now see the messianic church as *koinonia* and *diakonia* in bearing Jesus' threefold office. Moltmann is the one who develops the messianic ecclesiology from the three offices of Christ as prophet (*diakonia*), priest (sacrifice) and king (resurrection/rule). In its prophetic task, the church participates in liberating ministry. In its priestly vocation, the church lives under the cross in solidarity with

---

[58]Thomas A. Schattauer, *Inside Out: Worship in an Age of Mission* (Minneapolis, MN: Fortress, 1999), 1-21.
[59]Moltmann, *The Trinity and the Kingdom*, 133.

Pyithu-Dukkha. As part of Christ's exaltation, the church lives as *koinonia* in the power of Spirit.[60]

The messianic church is bound together with the messianic history, messianic presence and messianic destiny.[61] Participating in the passion as the Body of Christ, *koinonia* and *diakonia* become central to the life and work of the church. The Greek word *koinonia* has a multitude of meaning. The first use of the Greek word for *koinonia* is found in Acts 2:42:47 as an apostolic communion, participation, and sharing.[62] A special application of *koinonia* is used to describe a communion that exists in the celebration of the Eucharist (1Cor.10:16). The Eucharistic *Koinonia* counts for the spiritual relationship with God and organic brethren bound in sharing joys and pains together.[63]

In sharing the common experiences of joys and pains, tears and fears, the Eucharistic *koinonia* or church is linked to action (orthopraxy), not just belief (orthodoxy). The church is called not only for being together, but for acting together. This is what I call *diakonia*. *Diakonia* is seen as service, yet I prefer to use it as a stronger sense as humble servanthood (*doulos*). In light of servanthood, *koinonia* creates a mutual bond and *diakonia* overrides each individual's pride and fulfills others' concerns with self-giving love. Jesus said, "I came not to be served but to serve others" (Mk.10:45).

Paul also claimed, "In humility look not to your own interest but to the interests of others" (Phil.2:3-4). Servants focus on others. We have to forget long enough to lend a helping lends to the *Pyithu-Dukkha*. When we stop focusing on our own needs, we become aware of the needs around us: "Jesus emptied Himself in the form of a servant for others" (2:3-5). Self-denial is the core of servanthood. True servants serve God with at least four attitudes: servants focus on others (Phil.2:4); servants base their identity in the Christ-centered life (Jn.13:3-4); servants think like stewards, not owners (1Cor. 4:1-2) and servants think of ministry as an opportunity, not an obligation(Heb. 6:10; Ps.100:2).

The Eucharistic *koinonia* characterizes the church not only as a fellowship but as a dutiful congregation in service to the *Pyithu*.[64]*Diakonia* starts in a companionate heart, as compassion is the motivating power of God's transforming mission.[65]Paul speaks of three forms of transformation (Rom. 12:1-2). First, there is external transformation, (*shema* in Greek), which means "to vary from one context to another;" second, there is internal transformation, (*morphe*), which implies an inward change by renewing of minds; once inward being has changed, a person

---

[60]Moltmann, *The Church in the Power of the Spirit*, 66. Moltmann borrows from Bultmann's typology of Jesus' threefold office (prophetic office, kingly-sacrificial office and kingly office).

[61]Ibid., 75.

[62]Lawrence O. Richards, *Expository Dictionary of Bible Words*(Grand Rapids, MI: Zondervan, 1985), 275-276.

[63]Ibid.

[64]Moltmann, *The Church in the Power of the Spirit*, 121.

[65]Arland J. Hultgren, *Paul's Gospel and Mission: The Outlook from His Letter to the Romans* (Philadelphia, PA: Fortress Press, 1986), 95.

is a new creation in Christ and this internal transformation led to the third transformation, that is interpersonal transformation in relationship with others. Thus, the church is *called* by God out of the world, *placed* in the world as *Koinonia* and *sent* into the world for the sake of social *diakonia*.¹

Church-State Relation: Reading Romans 13:1-7 as a *Hidden Transcript* in Myanmar

The Church's Public Vocation as Honoring *Good* and Resisting *Evil*

Placing Lordship over against Caesar (Rom.10:12), why would Paul say, "let every person be subjected to the secular authorities; for there is no authority except from God and those authorities that exist have been instituted by God" (13:1)? But are *all* authorities to be honored? Viewing Roman Christians as the surveillance of the imperial authorities, James Dunn elucidates on how Paul's rhetoric is counter-imperial and Paul's critique of state authority offers us two factors. First, Rome serves God rather than serving Jupiter, and so Roman authority comes from God. Second, Rome should exercise its power rightly, otherwise, its authority is not deemed to be designated by God.²

I concur with Dunn, but I think James Scott's more in-depth discussion on the social-political context of Romans helps us to better see Paul's counter-imperial motifs and how Romans 13 can speak to the Burmese context of the *Pyithu-Dukkha*. In his book *Domination and the Arts of Resistance*,³ James Scott provides both *public transcript* and *hidden transcript*, drawn from Romans 13 to show how competing ideologies between the dominating group (the regime) and subordinating groups (the *Pyithu*) interact.

According to Scott, *public transcript* is highly partisan and partial narrative, controlled by the powerful. The *public transcript* can be understood as the dominant elites who propagate their power over the *hidden transcript* of subordinated groups/the *Pyithu*.⁴ In contrast, *hidden transcript* is discourse and counter-ideology, which derives from resistance to domination.⁵ The *hidden transcript* is defended in the teeth of power and we can view it as a political domain striving to enforce against great odds, certain forms of resistance in relation with the domin-

---

¹Rick Warren, *The Purpose Driven Life: What On Earth Am I Here For?* (Grand Rapids, MI: Zondervan, 2002), 282.
²James D. G. Dunn, *Romans 9-16*, WBC (Waco: Word, 1988), 773.
³James C. Scott, *Domination and the Arts of Resistance: Hidden Transcripts* (New Haven, CT: Yale University Press, 1990).
⁴Richard A. Horsley, "Jesus, Paul and The Arts of Resistance: Leaves from the Notebook of James C. Scott," in *Hidden Transcripts And the Arts of Resistance, Applying the Work of James C. Scott to Jesus and Paul*, ed. Richard A. Horsley (Leiden: Brill, 2004), 3-4.
⁵Scott, *Domination and the Arts of Resistance*, 118.

nant: thus, it would be accurate to think of the *hidden transcript* as a condition of practical resistance rather than a substitute for it.[6]

The *hidden transcript* arises in resistance to the *public transcript* of the self-portrait dominant elites. It is in this sense that we should not see Paul as just a "passivist" but as a "carrier" and as an "active agent," who creates the *hidden transcripts*.[7] This inspires us to see how Paul's *hidden transcript* is subverting Rome's public transcript. We can also see how the religious dimensions are interconnected with the political dimensions. According to Richard Horsley, "the key to understanding the dynamics of political resistance by the subjected is rooted in the off-stage hidden transcript."[8]

Applying Scott's work to Myanmar, Roman 13 is to be read as a *hidden transcript* where the dominant elites rule the nation. Paul refers to the civil authorities as God's ministers for the common good of people.[9] In Myanmar, the civil authority has the four-fold slogan to rule the nation: "security, prosperity, peace and development." Sadly, the authorities fail to practice these factors and violate human rights. Thus, "Law and order" simply means the *Pyithu*'s absolute subjugation to the military regime, whereas "peace and stability" simply means silent submission to the total control of the regime.

Living in the midst of corruption, the church in Myanmar has been silent primarily because of its two basic theological grounds: the *separation* between church and state and the *subjugation* of church to the state.[10] Lap Yang Kung is right when he articulates; "one of the characteristics of the Myanmar Baptist tradition is the separation between religions and politics and it becomes an excuse for the church to refrain from politics."[11] In my view, the church's separation and escape from the state comes from the misinterpretation of Peter's language: "you are a chosen people, a royal priesthood, a holy nation, a people belonging to God that you may declare the praise of Him who called you out of darkness into His glorious light" (1Pet.2:9). In light of this text misinterpretation, Christians think of the church's intervention in politics as a dirty act. They think that Christians are not responsible for the dirty things of public issues.

Christians in Myanmar needs to see God's universal realm and socio-political concern in a larger framework. Barth provides a helpful image for a better notion of what the universal work and presence of Christ means for the relationship between church and state for a common good. According to Barth, Christ is the center of both two concentric circles. The smaller and inner circle is the Christian

---

[6]Ibid., 191.

[7]Ibid., 123.

[8]Horsley, "Jesus, Paul and the Arts of Resistance," 21.

[9]N. T. Wright, "The Letter to the Romans: Introduction, Commentary and Reflection," in *New Interpreter's Bible*, ed. Leander E. Keck, vol. 10 (Nashville, TN: Abingdon Press, 2002), 715.

[10]Pum Za Mang, "Separation of Church and State: A Case Study of Myanmar (Burma)," *Asia Journal of Theology* 25, no. 1 (April 2011): 43-44.

[11]Lap Yan Kung, "Love Your Enemies: A Theology for Aliens in Their Native Land: The Chin in Myanmar," *Studies in World Christianity* 15, no. 1(April 2009): 93.

community or church, which *knows* Christ as Lord through faith. The larger and outer circle is the civil community, which *has* Christ as its center and experiences Christ through its worldviews and cultures even though it may not know Him.[12] Barth's view of Christ's Lordship in the inner circle and outsider circle helps us to understand a clearer picture of how Christ uses both churches and state as His two-hand instruments for the well-being of Burmese society.

Since church and state are God's two-hand servants for the well-being (Rom. 13:4), they have common vocations within God's covenant. Max Stackhosue said;

> Covenant responds to the question of how we all humankinds are to form communities of mutual responsibility as we live out our vocations. People require one another to be whole, and persons in community require a shared framework of common moral obligations that provide principles by which to structure these relationships. God's universal covenant holds that God sets terms and mandates for our lives together. Christians must hold that God's covenant of our lives occur in a context that extends to all humanity, for we are created to be relational and are bounded together in a mutuality of existence not of our own construction.[13]

Against the demarcation between church and state and of the subjugation of the church to the state, the church must re-read Romans 13:1-7 as a hidden transcript that demands Paul's dialectical vision of church-state relation and conflict.[14] Since the state is the church's partner for promoting the well-being in resistance to their common enemy of evil, which combats God's kingdom, their public sense of vocational relationship is necessary. Unfortunately, the state fails to practice the well-being of the nation, instead she oppresses the church and other powerless people, *Pyithu-Dukkha*. In light of the latter, the church must necessarily resist in conflict against the evil of the state. The church must not be subject to the state if the state abuses the power and becomes the source of oppression. As a prophetic presence, the church should work with the government authorities for the common good. Yet, when secular structures claim to be absolute, the church must say "we must obey God rather than any human authority" (Acts 5:29).[15]

The phrase, "there is no authority except from God" should not be misinterpreted as all authorities being *sanctioned* by God, but rather as not being an authority if it is not of God. I agree that all authorities come from God the creator of heaven and earth and the sustainer of human history, but I am not sure if God *ordains* all authorities or not. For this major reason, I do not wish all authorities to be *honored* as we see the three sections of Rom 12:9-21; 13-17 and 13:10-14

---

[12]Karl Barth, "The Christian Community and Civil Community," in *Community, Church and State: Three Essays* (Eugene, OR: Wipf & Stock, 2004), 149-189.

[13]Max L. Stackhouse, *Public Theology and Political Economy: Christian Stewardship in Modern Society* (Lanham, MD: University Press of America, 1991), 26-27.

[14]For a full account, see my article David Thang Moe, "Reading Romans 13:1-7 as a Hidden Transcript of Postcolonial Theology in Myanmar," in *Journal of Theology for Southern Africa,* 157 (March 2017), 71-98.

[15]Ibid.

are linked by the contrast between "good" and "evil"—"respect to whom respect is due, honor to whom honor is due" (Rom. 13:7).[16]

Written right under Caesar's nose to Christians' living in the hostile environment of the empire, Romans 13 is subversive. It would better be placed in its political-literary-rhetorical text and be read as a *hidden transcript* so that we can *honor* the good and *resist* the evil. Rom. 13:1-7 is a text which, demands our obedience to what is just and never to what is unjust. I am aware of the struggle between *honoring* good and *resisting* evil in Myanmar[17] and I admit how difficult it is for me to be subject to the corrupt authorities.

I would like to conclude this section with the model of *Kairos Document*, prepared by the South African theologians and released in 1985, which I refer to the threefold manifestation of 1) state theology, 2) church theology, and 3) prophetic theology.[18] The first model canonizes the will of the oppressors in obedience to the governing authorities. The second stands as "neutralist" between oppressors and the oppressed. In contrast to these two models, the third model is "liberationist" in resistance to evil power (Jer. 8:11).[19] The third model was applied by the Christians in South Africa in their resistance to the 'Apartheid system' and they were successful. Similarly, Christians in Myanmar should apply the third model by reading Romans 13:1-7 as a hidden transcript in *honoring* good and *resisting* evil for the better society of shalom.

Regnum Dei: God's Kingdom in the Context of the *Pyithu-Dukkha*

Jesus as the Relational and Universal Reconciler of Two Kingdoms

My use of two kingdoms refers to "the kingdom of God on earth" and "the Messianic Kingdom in heaven" (Rev.12:15, Dan.7:13-14). This concept of two kingdoms allows us to see the Messiah as the relational God and the universal reconciler between heaven and earth, breaking down the walls of hostility between Jews and Gentiles and between Christians and non-Christians through the cross" (Eph.2:13-20).

---

[16]A. Katherine Grieb, *The Story of Romans: A Narrative Defense of God's Righteousness* (Louisville, KY: Westminster John Knox, 2002), 121. She associates the *inclusio* of Romans 12:17-21 with *evil.*

[17]Peng Kuo-Wei, *Hate the Evil, Hold Fast to the Good: Structuring Romans 12:1-15:13* (Bloomsbury: T&T Clark, 2006). 203-211.

[18]David J. Bosch, "God's Reign and the Rulers of this World: Missiological Reflections on Church-State Relationships," in *The Good News of the Kingdom*, ed. Charles Van Enen, Dean S. Gilliland, and Paul Pierson (Maryknoll, NY: Orbis Books, 1993), 90.

[19]Ibid., 91.

The Latin phrase for *regnum Dei* (or *basileia tou Theou* in Greek) is translated as "the Kingdom of God" or "Kingdom of Heaven." The term "the Kingdom of God" is used here as it tells us more about the transcendental Lordship in heaven and immanent Lordship on earth. The Kingdom used in the OT is a sense of kingship (1Chro. 29:10-12; Dan.4:3).[20] God's kingship is seen in terms of God's relationship with the world (Jer.23:24; Ps.65:12-13).[21] God is present and active wherever there is world. God does not create the world and leave it, but God creates the world and enters into it and lives within it (Jer.23:24).[22] Daniel mirrors Kingdom as the coming of the Messiah to universe (Dan.4:24), which will be characterized by mercy toward the oppressed.

Such concept of God's Kingdom of justice in the OT comes to fruition in the life and ministry of Jesus in the NT, while the "kingdom of heaven" is instead used in the Gospel of Matthew for the Jewish audiences imposed restrictions on the use of the name of God. The NT expresses God's Kingdom in a number of ways, sometimes paradoxical:

> It is in the world but not of it (Jn.18:36); it comes as a free gift but demands all that we have (Lk.12:30-33); it is God's very reign but works in hidden ways (Matt.13:33); it is already present (Lk.17:21) yet still coming in the future (Matt.6:10); it does not consist of talk (1Cor. 4:20) but is proclaimed (Lk.4:43).[23]

A theological debate over different interpretation of God's Kingdom has emerged among scholars. Of many, I will side with Oscar Cullmann, who describes God's kingdom as "inaugurated eschatology," which expresses the decisive action of God in Jesus and the eschatological fulfillment of God's purposes.[24] We not only hope for Jesus' future coming, but experience God's imminent rule in the present world. The Kingdom of God is inaugurated by Jesus and so the reign of God is the central theme of His ministry. The vision of God's reign marked the beginning of Jesus' ministry—"the time is fulfilled and the Kingdom of God has near, repent and believe in the good news" (Mk.1:15).

The reign of God in Jesus' proclaimed is not a territory. It is God's activity in the *whole* world, not just in the Christian sphere. Thus Jesus' proclaiming of God's Kingdom includes the pronouncement of the forgiveness of sins, welcoming the outcasts, social-political freedom and personal salvation. In words and

---

[20]Kevin J. Vanhoozer, Nicholas T. Wright, Daniel J. Treier, and Craig Bartholomew, eds., *Dictionary For Theological Interpretation of the Bible* (Grand Rapids, MI: Baker Academic, 2005), 420.

[21]Martin K. Hopkins, *God's Kingdom in The Old Testament* (Chicago, IL: Henry Regnery, 1964), 235.

[22]Fretheim, *God and World in the Old Testament,* 21.

[23]A. Scott Moreau, Gary R. Corwin, and Gary B. McGee, *Introducing World Missions: A Biblical, Historical and Practical Survey* (Grand Rapids, MI: Baker Academic, 2004), 81.

[24]Richard T. France, *Divine Government: God's Kingship in the Gospel of Mark* (Grand Rapids, MI: William B. Eerdmans Publishing Company, 2003), 1-3.

deeds, Jesus lived that vision of God's reign with people: "Jesus, above all, is the Proclaimer of God's reign on earth."[25]

Jesus has broken down the dividing walls between heaven and earth and restored all sinners to God through the cross—there is no boundary in God's reign.[26] After resurrection, the humiliated Jesus is exalted as Lord—Lord above all life (Phl.2:9-11).[27] In His last command to His disciples, Jesus claimed that "all authority in heaven and on earth has been given to me" (Matt.28:18b). Theologically, it is impossible not to assume God's direct relationship with the world. But how can we not be open to God's work outside the church in the midst of the *Pyithu-Dukkha* or even inside the church?

The work of the triune God's universal reign takes place in a two-fold way (inside the church) and (outside the church) for two reasons: universal reconciliation and continual creation (Col.1:20). The triune God is mysterious in both spheres, yet God's work in church seems more direct and open than the secular sphere.[28] God's kingdom is an inclusive realm in which He rules all 135 racial groups of the *Pyithu-Dukkha* with reconciling love. Paul's description of this inclusive realm is a powerful one: "there is no longer Jew nor Greek, no longer slave nor free, no longer male nor female." He could have also said, "for you are all (135 races) one in the reconciling Christ" (Gal.3: 28).[29]

The Kingdom as God's Theocracy: Kingdom of Shalom and Freedom

In his book *Models of the Kingdom*,[30] Howard Snyder helpfully provides us the eight models of the kingdom. He proposes the kingdom as;

> (1) The future hope; (2) the inner spiritual experience (interior kingdom); (3) the mystical communion (heavenly kingdom); (4) the institutional church (the ecclesiastical kingdom); (5) the counter system (subversive kingdom); (6) the political kingdom (theocratic kingdom); (7) the Christianized culture (the transforming kingdom); and (8) the earthly utopia (the utopia kingdom).[31]

These eight models are worthy to be studied. However, due to the space limit, I do not wish to study all. I find the sixth one—the kingdom as God's theocracy—most relevant and helpful for the context of the *Pyithu-Dukkha*. At the core of this

---

[25]Norman Perrin, *Rediscovering the Teaching of Jesus* (New York: Harper & Row Publishers, 1967), 54.

[26]Martin K. Hopkins, *God's Kingdom in the New Testament* (Chicago, IL: Henry Regnery, 1964), 3.

[27]Gunther Bornkamm, *Jesus of Nazareth*, trans. Fraser McLuskey and James M. Robinson (London: Hodder & Stoughton, 1960), 64.

[28]Walter Altmann, "Interpreting the Doctrine of the Two Kingdoms: God's Kingship in the Church and in Politics," *Word and World* 7 (Winter 1987): 47.

[29]Karl H. Hertz, ed., *Two Kingdoms and One World: A Sourcebook in Christian Social Ethics*(Minneapolis, MN: Augsburg Publishing House, 1976), 9.

[30]Howard A. Sydney, *Models of the Kingdom* (Nashville, TN: Abingdon, 1991).

[31]Ibid., 18.

study lies the claim that God's rule or theocracy embraces the whole 135 racial groups of Burmese (*Pyithu-Dukkha*) and the world. This demands that God's rule is not to be confined to the narrow ecclesiastical church (model 4). Indeed, God uses the church as both the foretaste of His kingdom of freedom and the instrument for witnessing to His shalom and freedom. By her identity, the church is the foretaste of God's kingdom, by her vocation, the church is God's agent for His kingdom of shalom and freedom. Both are interrelated.

As Moltmann convincingly puts, the Christian doctrine of the Trinity provides God's Lordship of shalom and freedom whereby to harmonize personality and sociality in the free and just community of men and women, without sacrificing one to the other.[32] The Christian doctrine of God's theocracy of shalom and freedom compels us to develop not only a religious Christian community of freedom and egalitarianism among men and women, but also a socio-political community of freedom and shalom among the Burmese people in Myanmar. God rules the world and Myanmar not by coercion, but by love.[33] As I mentioned above, Rom. 13:4 tells us that God appoints the governing authorities as the state rulers of their nation and fellow citizens for the common good—freedom and justice. In other words, the state rulers in Myanmar are the analogies of God the ruler.[34]

The question we should ask is: how can the Buddhist state rulers see themselves as the analogies of the ruling God? The answer is that they can know it through the ethics of their natural law or their eightfold path of threefold principle—morality, meditation and wisdom. It is God who tells humans as His image that they have natural knowledge of good and moral things.[35] By having natural knowledge of moral things, Buddhist state rulers may know God's universal will of justice and freedom. To imitate God's lordship or theocracy of shalom and freedom means not to lord over people by coercion, but to rule and lead people by love for the common good of justice and freedom in Myanmar. Since God's goal of human life is shalom in mutual relationship, lordship of humans over the other humans stands against God's theocracy of shalom and freedom in Myanmar.

Where the just Lord of the universe reigns, there should be no room for the humans to rule or lord over the other human beings. Any imperial lordship of humans over humans is not only inimical to God the ruler, but also sin—sin of oppression. Understanding this way provides a prophetic role of Christian community not only for witnessing to God's kingdom of freedom and shalom, but also for resisting against any imperial rulers. In light of this, we must see God not only as the universal ruler, but also as the ethical judge. God uses the church as the prophetic agent to judge the immoral state rulers who combat God's kingdom of shalom and freedom. Bruce Nicholls affirms that God's Kingdom provides the relational center for integrating our understanding of salvation and ethics of evan-

---

[32]Moltmann, *The Trinity and the Kingdom*, 199.
[33]Ibid., 199.
[34]Cited in Barth, *Community, Church and State: Three Essays*, 149-189.
[35]Cited in John Barton, *Understanding Old Testament Ethics: Approaches and Explorations* (Louisville, KY: John Knox Press, 2003), 47-49.

gelism to social justice.[36] As I mentioned above, such holistic vision of salvation is evident in Jesus' social ministry.[37] The content of Christ's kingdom mission of freedom is displayed in its reality among the suffering outcasts those who are the paradigms of the *Pyithu-Dukkha* in Myanmar. As Moltmann rightly puts;

> The kingdom of freedom and shalom consists of the liberating lordship of the crucified one; the fellowship of the first-born of many brothers and sisters. The Son liberates men and women from servitude to sin through His own servitude (Phil. 2). He frees men and women from death and fear through His own surrender of Himself to death. In this He leads people into the glorious liberty of God by making them alike Himself, in fellowship with Him.[38]

Moltmann's doctrine of the kingdom provides a better understanding of mutual and egalitarian communion with one another. Moltmann encourages us to interpret shalom and freedom in the mutual and equalitarian relationship between the state rulers and the ruled, not as subjects and objects; but as fellow humans.[39] God's kingdom is first of all the divine redemption manifested in the liberating work of Jesus and secondly the realm in which the life of shalom and freedom may be experienced in the world.[40] Therefore, the church must be the witness of the kingdom of shalom and freedom God offers to the world in Christ.[41] What the church must proclaim in the context of the *Pyithu-Dukkha* is what Paul calls the "kingdom of justice, peace and joy in the Holy Spirit" (Rom. 14:17). The kingdom of justice and peace refers to our experience of socio-political justice and internal peace with God and external peace with one another, while the kingdom of joy signifies our inner experience of God's presence in our lives.

This way of understanding about God's kingdom is involves in a holistic salvation—saving the whole person and the whole community in Myanmar. To do this in action, Christians in Myanmar should first and foremost claim Christ as a holistic Savior for the *Pyithu-Dukkha,* who need their wounded bodies to be healed, their empty stomachs fed, released from captivity and their souls saved from the bondage of sin.

What Jesus said to His disciples about how the Kingdom will look like in the future needs to be read as a present challenge in the life of the *Pyithu*, who cried the same: "I was hungry and you give me no food, I was thirsty and you gave me nothing to drink, I was a stranger and you did not welcome me, naked and you did

---

[36]Bruce Nicholls, "Theological Education and Evangelization," in *Let the Earth Hear His Voice*, ed. James D. Douglas (Minneapolis, MN: World Wide Publications, 1975), 634-635.

[37]Chris Sugden, "What is Good about Good News to the Poor? In *AD 2000 and Beyond—A Mission Agenda*, ed. Vinay Samuel and Chris Sudgen (Oxford: Regnum, 1990), 5.

[38]Moltmann, *The Trinity and the Kingdom*, 210.

[39]Moltmann, Experiences in Theology, 20-21.

[40]George Eldon Ladd, *The Gospel of the Kingdom* (Grand Rapids, MI: William B. Eerdmans Publishing Company, 1992), 114.

[41]Lesslie Newbigin, "The Gospel Among the Religions," in *Mission Trends No. 5*, ed. Gerald H. Anderson and Thomas F. Stransky (Grand Rapids, MI: William B. Eerdmans Publishing Company, 1981), 16.

not give me clothing, sick and in prison and you did not visit me" (Matt. 25:42-43). In the context of the *Pyithu*'s cry, "who is my neighbor?" (Lk.10:29), raised by a lawyer, who hesitated to cross the cultural boundary for the victim is not a relevant question. I must argue that the Christian question for the *Pyithu-Dukkha* is not to be associated with "who" but "whom."

We should ask a question in this way: how should we become neighbors to the *Pyithu-Dukkha*? Or to whom I could become a neighbor? This leads me to the second point.

The Kingdom Demands Border-Crossing Mission

In order to argue that God's kingdom demands border-crossing mission, I would like to read Luke 10:25-37 through the lens of Myanmar. As I read it through the lens of Myanmar, I would like to take both the Samaritan and the wounded victim as the paradigms of the *Pyithu-Dukkha*. First, both the oppressed Christians and Buddhists are the paradigms of the wounded victims in the parable. Both groups need liberation and healing. Second, the marginalized Christians represent the marginal Samaritan.

I consider the Samaritan's compassion to the wounded victim relevant for the Burmese Christians' practice of compassion to the *Pyithu-Dukkha* regardless of ethnicities and religiosities (Lk. 10:33-35). More interestingly, no one knows the accurate identity of the victim in this parable. This demands our compassionate act of solidarity with all victims, including strangers regardless of ethnicities and religions. First, what we see in this parable is the Samaritan's compassionate act of border-crossing. While the Levite and Priest hesitated to cross the border, the Samaritan dares to cross the cultural border and becomes neighbor to the victim. In light of this, it is imperative for the marginal Christians in Myanmar to cross the socio-cultural borders and to become the neighbors for the oppressed Buddhists and other victims. As Joel Green rightly notes, "the ultimate purpose of the parable of Samaritan is to show that "neighbor love knows no borders."[42]

The Levite and Priest know boundaries and decide not to cross and to become neighbors to the victims. But the Samaritan decides to cross the boundary and becomes a liberating and healing neighbor for the victim. Christians in Myanmar may not necessary be the liberators, but the visible witnesses of liberating Christ for their fellow oppressed Buddhists and others those who are beyond the borders. What is the interesting point of contrast between Christians in Myanmar and Samaritan is that Samaritan's border-crossing mission is the move from the margin to the margin; whereas the ethnic Christians' mission is the move from the margin to the majority Buddhists.

But if Christian mission is from everywhere to everywhere, it can be the move from the margin to the margin and the move from the margin to the center. Sometimes, it could even be the move from the center to the margin, depending on the context. Jesus' mission can be seen as the move from the center (heaven) to the margin (world). The common aim is to cross one's border. According to Peter

---

[42] Joel B. Green, *The Gospel of Luke* (Grand Rapids, MI: Eerdmans, 1997), 426.

Phan, Jesus was a border-crosser, and His incarnate life of trinitarian mission is border-crossing between heaven and earth by the power of the Spirit.[43] As Phan adds, border-crossing is a missiological imperative of imitating Christ. Without border-crossing, we cannot imitate and follow Christ.[44] Samaritan follows the footsteps of Jesus. Christians must embody both of them.

Most importantly, the act of border-crossing in a pluralistic world is witnessing to God's wider kingdom. There is no border in God's universal reign. But when God reconciles us to Him by destroying the dividing wall of hostility, He does not cancel our socio-political and religio-cultural and linguistic borders (Eph. 2:14-17). Our otherness, the simple fact of being different, such as Christian-ness and Buddhist-ness remains. In Myanmar's religiously and ethnically pluralistic societies, otherness poses a reality of challenge and opportunity for Christian theology. We should take otherness both as a challenge and as an opportunity for Christian theology in Myanmar. The challenge poses a prescriptive question of how we should witness to God's kingdom of freedom and shalom. On the other hand, but it is also a challenge for Christians on how to communicate faith to others those who are different from us in some way.

I would argue that socio-political and religio-cultural borders are to be understood not as the dividing walls of hostility between us and them in light of God's universal reign of cosmic reconciliation (Eph. 2:14-15; Col. 1:19-20), but as the identity markers of hospitality among human beings. If this is so, *Pyithu-Dukkha* theology must see the border-crossing as the privileged meeting where *Pyithu-Dukkha*—Christians and Buddhists and other faiths with different backgrounds—come and share a common vision of religious peace and social justice within God's kingdom of shalom in Myanmar.[45]

Defining Our *Oikos* in a Wider Horizon
Ecumenics, Ethics, Eschatology

Here our attention is drawn to three major themes: ecumenics, ethics and eschatology. First we will talk about God's *Oikos* from a wider perspective. The word *Oikos* in Greek was introduced into biology as a term in 1866 by Ernst Haeckel to describe the science of the relationships of the organism to the outward world surrounding it.[46] *Oikos* came to refer to the whole inhabited earth as God's realm. We confess that God created the world and sustains it—"God so loved the world that He sent Jesus to save it" (Jn.3:16). God created it and does not abandon it, but lives within it.

God intends to bring it into perfection and we, Christians, are called to be His partners in God's reconciling mission in the world. The concept of *Oikos* captures

---

[43] Peter C. Phan, "Crossing the Borders: A Spirituality for Mission in Our Times from an Asian Perspective," in *SEDOS Bulletin*, 35. (2003): 8-19.

[44] Ibid.

[45] Along these lines, see my article Moe, "The Word to the World," 68-85.

[46] Moltmann, *Ethics of Hope*, 131.

that Christ intends to bring all things and everyone under His rule, to reconcile all things to Himself, to restore that which is fallen and to overthrow all powers in opposition to His realm of justice and peace. God's *Oikos* is the whole world in which God rules.

> God's *Oikos* is not a religious institution, though it is manifested in the church; God's *Oikos* is not a nation, but is composed of people from different nations and ethnics (*embracing the 135 ethnic of Myanmar*); God's *Oikos* is not a moral code, though it calls all actions to submit to the justification of Christ; God's *Oikos* is not merely a political movement, though it confronts political power structures; God's *Oikos* is not an economic system, though it addresses the evils of poverty and exploitation; God's *Oikos* is not coercive, though it is persuasive in love."[47]

We now talk about God's *Oikos* from the ethical perspective. The Kingdom ethics comes from acknowledging Jesus as Lord of everything and everyone (Col. 1:16:20), speaking of vertical and horizontal relationships. This is evident in the Lord's Prayer in which Jesus taught His followers, saying "Father" (Matt. 6:9) and "Forgive us our debts as we also have forgiven our wrongdoers" (Matt. 6:12). As Luther stated well,

> As Heavenly Father has in Christ freely come to our aid in the midst of suffering and bondage of sin, we should also have freely to help our neighbors through our body and its works and each should become as it were a Christ to the other that we may be Christ to one another and Christ may be the same in all.[48]

Tom Wright said, the "Kingdom ethic work is rooted in worship."[49] According to Wright, Jesus exercises His rule through truly confessional worshippers. Wright went on to connect the Kingdom ethics with the Beatitudes or Sermon on the Mount. The Beatitudes are not simply about how to behave so that God will do something *nice* to you, but they are about the way in which Jesus rules the world. Jesus said "Blessings on the poor in spirit, the Kingdom is yours" (Matt.5:3). We should be one of those meek through whom the Kingdom of justice begins to appear on earth as it is heaven.[50]

When God wants to change the world, He does not send the tanks, but He sends in the meek and the mourners, those who are hungry and thirsty for justice, and the shalom-seekers. The Kingdom and the Cross work together in the ethical work. The Sermon on the Mount is the place where, the Kingdom-people are commanded to live our ethics, whereas the cross is the place where evil was overcome. Jesus rules the Kingdom in the world through the ethical church that "takes care for orphans and widows" (Jam.1:27).

---

[47]Snyder, *Models of the Kingdom*, 88.

[48]Timothy Lull, ed., *Martin Luther's Basic Theological Writings* (Minneapolis, MN: Fortress Press, 1989), 619.

[49]N. T. Wight, *Simply Jesus: A New Vision of Who He Was, What He Did and Why He Matters* (New York: Harper Collins, 2011), 217.

[50]Ibid., 218.

In light of this Kingdom ethics, churches in Myanmar have much to connect with Buddhists who are ethically-oriented people. At the heart of Buddhist teaching is moral life.[51] *Metta* (love) and *karuna* (compassion) sum up much of their moral teaching. *Metta* calls for our benevolence and *karuna* becomes a basis for an ethic of the other in *Dukkha*. Both *metta* and *karuna* are reciprocal in Kingdom work and in fulfilling Jesus' Golden Rule which says "Do to others as you would have them do to you" (Matt.7:12).

We will now turn to the third theme: eschatology. If *doxology* is the ultimate purpose of God's Kingdom, *eschatology* must be the hope of the Kingdom. Our Kingdom activity is not to convert this present society into the Kingdom of God—that will happen only when Jesus returns. We witness to the reality of God's Kingdom. The church will not realize the Kingdom in fullness, but will be a witness to the Kingdom as a light in the midst of despair until the great day of dawning occurs. As the foretaste of the Kingdom, the church must participate in Christ's *Dukkha* and anticipate His return.[52] Bosch said,

> As we pray your "Kingdom come; Your Will be done on earth as it is in Heaven;" we ourselves commit to initiate, here and now, approximates and anticipates of God's reign. Once again, God's reign *will* come since it has *already* come. It is both bestowal and challenge, gift and promise, present and future, celebration and anticipation. We have the firm assurance that its coming cannot be thwarted.[53]

Living in the time between the "already" and "not yet," Leslie Weatherhead's classification of God's *Oikos* into three types are helpful.[54] The first term is the one Weatherhead called "God's intentional will," second is "God's circumstantial will" and third is "God's ultimate will, future" (Eph.1:9-10). These three wills are closely related to each other. Strictly speaking, the first will traces back to the picture of the pre-distorted life in Eden while the middle one refers to the current church's life of solidarity amidst diversity and the third looks forward to the full realization of God's ultimate will.[55]

The God who creates this cosmos is the same God who uses the church as His image to bring the whole creation back to the restoration of harmonious Eden (Rev.21:1-5). Though chaotic and divisive forces seem strong in God's *Oikos*, God empowers churches to make great effort to be instrumental in bringing the whole creation to the integrity. The current situation in which we live calls for the churches in Myanmar to celebrate diversity as God's gift in a colorful *Oikos*, be united with one another in solidarity with victims and, combat the evils, which twist God's kingdom of justice.

---

[51]David Thang Moe, "Metta: Doing Pyithu-Thukha Theology of Reconciliation in Burma"(M.Div. Thesis, Sabbah Theological Seminary, Kota Kinabalu, 2009), 31.

[52]Oscar Cullmann, "Eschatology and Mission in New testament," in *The Theology of the Christian Mission,* ed. Gerald H. Anderson (Nashville, TN: Abingdon Press, 1961), 51.

[53]Bosch, *Transforming Mission*, 35.

[54]Leslie Weatherhead, *The Will of God* (Nashville, TN: Abingdon Press, 1944).

[55]Ibid., 9, 17.

Suffering unto Hope—*Dukkha* unto *Thukkha* Toward a New Messianic Kingdom

Suffering and hope are integrated in the crucified and risen Christ. While hope is essential to human life, suffering is an essential part of human existence and Messianic identity. Without the suffering of Christ, God's salvation would never get done as suffering belongs to the person and purpose of God. Two questions come in time of *Dukkha*—first why do we suffer? Second why is God in our suffering? My answer to the former is that God has a plan and purpose in all suffering. I am more interested in the second question as drawn from the crying Jesus on the cross (Mk.15:34; Ps.22).

What can one learn from the crying God-man Jesus? Two lessons should be learned: one is the very "visible crying Jesus," who is the paradigm of the crying *Pyithu* and the other is the "hidden God."[56] These two are quite real today! We claim that by faith we see God's hidden face in suffering as the Psalmist says: "God is a very present help in *Dukkha*" (Ps. 46:1b). But how do we understand suffering if Christ has overcome evil on the cross? This question will be answered by the "resurrection-hope."[57]

When Jesus rose from His death of suffering, He rose as the beginning of the new world. This is the most important thing to know about the power of hope. To Bultmann, Christ's resurrection is "the rise of faith in the disciples,"[58] calling forth their faith. Paul writes, "If Christ has not been raised, your faith is futile and you are still in your sins" (1Cor.15:17). As Christ's disciples today, we also have to experience the resurrection of faith and speak of the resurrected Christ, who comes and meets us in our *Dukkha*.

Crucifixion answers the meaning of suffering and resurrection promises the power of hope. Seeing hope as the link between life and death, the cross serves as a historical meaning of salvation and resurrection as the eschatological meaning of the cross—resurrection is the mark of Christ's victory over evil. Karl Barth was right when he nicely said, "Resurrection is God's yes against Satan's no and it is man's Amen to God's yes."[59] Resurrection fulfills the reality of history and establishes a world of hope.

The risen Christ, for Paul Tillich "was the bearer of New Being."[60] Having been raised bodily above transitoriness into the eternal presence of God as the Spirit, the risen Christ as the character of spiritual presence everywhere. The cross and the resurrection stand in the same relation to one another as death and new

---

[56]Martin E. Marty: "Looking Back, Summing Up," in *Echoes from Calvary: The Seven Last Words of Christ On the Cross,* ed. Richard Young (Oxford: Rowman & Littlefield Publishers, 2005), 203.

[57]George Hunsinger, "The Daybreak of the New Creation: Christ's Resurrection in Recent Theology," *Scottish Journal of Theology* 57, no. 2 (July 2004): 163.

[58]Rudolf Bultmann, "New Testament and Mythology," in *Kerygma and Myth: A Theological Debate*, ed. Hans Werner Bartsch (New York: Harper & Row, 1961), 1.

[59]Barth, *Church Dogmatics*, III/1:385.

[60]Paul Tillich, *Systematic Theology*, vol. 2 (Chicago, IL: University of Chicago, 1957), 156.

life. Whereas Christ's death was a historical event, His resurrection was an apocalyptic fact and this was the daybreak of new creation, holding out the promise that all things will be made new. As the whole Christ in person was raised from the death, body, soul, then the hope was all embracing in scope both physical and spiritual, both present and future.[61] As Moltmann stated,

> Resurrection hope is a hope for the transformation of this world, not a hope for escape from it. It is the hope that evil in all its forms will be utterly eradicated, the past will be redeemed and all the things that ever will be made new. It is the hope of new creation, a new heaven and a new world in which God is really honored as God, human beings are truly loving and peace and justice reign on earth.[62]

Life in this world means living with the open question of suffering, which springs from the open wound of life in this world, and seeking the future in which the desire for God will be restored.[63] The risen Christ is the Savior, who dies in our place to take away our sins and liberates our conscience and the fellow sufferer who holds our hands as we walk the valley of *Dukkha*. God's act of salvation in the risen Jesus is the point of departure for the *Pyithu's* hope for the liberation.[64] Liberation is not simply a human possession but a divine gift of freedom to those who struggle in faith against persecution in the world. Jesus said to His disciples, "in the world, you will face persecution but take courage, I have conquered the world" (Jn.16:33)—resurrection triumphs over death.

Christ's resurrection gives us the presence of peace and the promise of hope. The peace we have does not mean being in a place where there is no trouble but it means being in the midst of those things and still being calm in our heart and taking courage. Politically, peace is not an absence of tension but it is a presence of justice in combating evils. In the midst of *Dukkha*, the courage given by Christ is the dynamic that empowers us to bear our suffering. The courage to hope brings us to the presence of God, who holds future. It is possible that the promise of Christ's future coming and the vision of liberation is the key to why the *Pyithu* keep hoping even though their fight seems futile.

To hope in Jesus is to see the vision of His coming presence which is actualized on Easter. If Easter is about Jesus as the center of new creation, His *ascension* is about His *enthronement* as the one who is now "in charge" on earth as in heaven. According Tom Wright, "Easter tells us that Jesus is the first part of new creation, His ascension tells us that He is running it."[65] Below is Tom Wright's personal statement,

> Jesus is pictured as somebody who has two homes—heaven and earth. The homes are right next door to each other and there is a connecting door. They are meant to overlap and interlock and finally to be joined fully and forever. The partition wall

---

[61] Moltmann, *The Way of Jesus Christ*, 214.

[62] Jürgen Moltmann, "Response to the Opening Presentation," see in Ewert H. Cousins, *Hope and the Future of Theology* (Philadelphia, PA: Fortress Press, 1972), 59.

[63] Moltmann, *The Trinity and the Kingdom*, 49.

[64] Cone, *God of the Oppressed*, 127.

[65] Wright, *Simply Jesus*, 193-195.

will be knocked down and there will be one, glorious, heaven-and-earth mixture. This is a picture of new heaven and new earth (Rev.21:1-4)—death shall be no more, neither shall there be mourning nor crying nor pain anymore.[66]

To that goal, Christians should not be enticed to wait for the final realization of the Messianic Kingdom somewhere up in heaven, but they should transform this world of *Dukkha* into a Kingdom of *Thukkha*. Christians should be the "hosts" and share with their neighbors this vision. Sadly, a majority of Burmese Christians prefer to be "the guests rather than the hosts," as they piously long for a home in heaven dawn from what Jesus said to His disciples: "In my Father's house, there are many dwelling places" (Jn.14:2). To regard Christians as the "hosts," the Great Banquet (Lk.14:16-24) serves as the metaphor in which the host broke the barriers and embraced the poor into his home.

Many interpret this Banquet as "an eschatological story of the Messianic meal."[67] God's reign cannot be a classless society without the poor and the rich but crowded with different races and many nations (Lk.14:16-24). The Banquet reveals to us that God is the generous benefactor who provides for the needs of the people.[68] It is God Himself, who has broken down the barriers in Jesus' inclusion of the public sinners and restored them to the fellowship of the father's house (Lk.15:3-32). God's *Oikos* demands that sharing resources be extended to the outcast, the oppressed, and the crippled rather than confining these resources to our narrow milieu of friends, brothers and relatives.

The "Host" in the parable can be viewed as the Church in our context, which he redefined his *Oikos* by embracing the poor into his home. Such a Banquet can be interpreted as the Eucharist today, which bears witness to the reconciliation between God and humans and among creatures. The Eucharist is significant to both our participating in Christ's suffering ("do this in remembrance of me," Lk. 22:19) and our anticipating Christ's return. Joining the Eucharist, we are called to participate in Jesus' suffering for the sake of all those for whom He died (*Pyithu-Dukkha*). The reconciliation embedded in that Eucharist prompts the Church's responsibility to extend charity to all who suffer.[69]

The host in the parable challenges us to break the boundaries that prevent us from fellowship with God and His people and, more importantly, those whom we have long excluded as the outcast, and the poor. Sharing food around the Banquet table symbolizes the daily bread in our relationship with our neighbors.[70] In order for God's Kingdom to be full of many (as the host's house was full of guests, Lk. 14:23), our task is first and foremost to break these boundaries, to invite everyone to come in and to extend our helping hands to the *Pyithu-Dukkha*, who are outside

---

[66] Ibid.

[67] David B. Gowler, *Host, Guest, Enemy and Friend: Portraits of the Pharisees in Luke and Acts* (New York: Peter Lang, 1991), 246.

[68] Philip F. Esler, *Community and Gospel in Luke-Acts: The Social and Political Motivation in Lucan Theology* (Cambridge: Cambridge University, 1987), 179.

[69] Lee, *The Trinity in Asian Perspective*, 206-207.

[70] Ibid.

the church.⁷¹ If Jesus is Lord of all, all *Pyithu* deserve to be called brothers and sisters in God's *Oikos*. They remain non-Christians until they find salvation in Christ, but the Spirit is continually at work among them. The present Kingdom mirrors the Messianic Kingdom to come. As John said,

> The kingdom of the world will become the Messianic Kingdom and God will reign forever (Rev.11:15). Then I saw a new heaven and a new earth; for the first heaven and the first earth had passed away. And I heard a loud voice from the throne saying, "see the home of God is among mortals. God will dwell with them; they will be His peoples and God Himself will be with them; He will wipe every tear from their eyes. Death will be no more; mourning and crying and pain will be no more, for the first things have passed away" (Rev. 21:1-4).

John's Messianic Vision is associated with the same paradigm of the apocalyptic vision of hope among Israel enslaved by the Babylonian empire (Isa. 11; Ezek. 37). It is within the context of Jesus' past identity, present activity and His future coming that the *Pyithu-Dukkha*'s hope for the new Messianic Kingdom is grounded. Thus, we can speak of history Christologically, speak of hope eschatologically and speak of Christ soteriologically. These three aspects of dialectical theology formulate a complete "Christology from above" (Barth), "from below" (Pannenberg) and "from before, or yet to come" (Moltmann).⁷² Jesus, who entered in the history of humanity, is not a *docetic* Jesus or "banana-Jesus," but the "mango-Jesus"⁷³ who is in solidarity with the *Pyithu*.

The *Pyithu* come to combine the vision of the new messianic Kingdom with their struggle for freedom. They talk about Jesus not only as their Savior, who was born in Bethlehem, died on Calvary, but also as the One who would come again and take them home in glory—"suffering into glory" being a Messianic vision (Lk.24:26). This slight momentary *Dukkha* is preparing us for an eternal weight of glory beyond all measure, by faith we look not at what can be seen but at what cannot be seen (2Cor.4:17-18). As we are on the way, our divine brother-Christ is walking with us in the valley of *Dukkha*.

Paul writes, "Sufferings of this present time are not worth comparing with the *glory* about to be revealed" (Rom.8:18). Paul's eschatological vision of Jews and Gentiles shall one day praise God with One voice (Rom.15:9-12) is a powerful one. Yet do we, Christians in Myanmar, share such a vision with our neighbors who are in *Dukkha*?

---

⁷¹Willi Braun, *Feasting and Social Rhetoric in Luke 14* (Cambridge: Cambridge University Press, 1995), 18-19.

⁷²Cone, *God of the Oppressed*, 120.

⁷³Yung, *Mangoes or Bananas?* 240. The common fruits in tropical Asia are the mango and banana. Ripe banana is yellow outside but flesh-off-white inside (*Docetism*). Interestingly, ripe mango, an authentic Asian fruit, is golden yellow both *inside* and *outside* (*Homoousios*). The Mango symbolizes the Jesus who is truly divine and truly human, living in *both* heaven and on earth in the midst of the *Pyithu*.

Postscripts

Passion and Compassion: A Dialectical Theology of Divine Suffering and Human Suffering

This thesis is grounded in the threefold related theme —Christology, suffering and salvation. To put simply, it is about a theology of the cross. A theology of the cross is crucial for two main reasons today. First, it is a symbol of passion and compassion or love that opposes the impassibility of God. The patristic theology (with the exception of Origen) holds fast to the apathy axiom. According to patristic theology, God cannot suffer because passion stands against God's nature of omnipotence. However, we have noted earlier that the God of Israel is the God full of passion and compassion for the Israel and for justice.[74] The suffering of Christ echoes such passionate love of God. As Moltmann puts, "the suffering of Christ is the passion of the compassionate God."[75]

It is right to think that God suffers not because His power is limited, but because He chooses to show His sacrificial love. The weakness of divine impassibility is that God's essential impassibility distinguishes Deity from human beings who are subject to suffering. "If God were in every aspect of incapable of suffering, God would also be incapable of love,"[76] rightly said Moltmann. To quote Moltmann's convincing words;

> If God is love, God opens God's self for the suffering that love for others brings. God does not suffer, as we do, out of deficiency of being, but God suffers from love for creation, which is the overflowing superabundance of God's divine being. In this sense, God can suffer, will suffer, and is suffering in the world.[77]

Moltmann encourages us to hold the inseparable relationship between the suffering of Christ and the love of God. Compassion and passion coexists in the history of God's salvation. Love is the motivating power of Jesus' coming into the world (Jn. 3:16). As Daniel William righty puts it, "There can be no love without suffering. The active side of love requires our suffering for the sake of the other."[78] This is involved not only in the soteriological purpose, but also in the ethical participation. My point is that love is God's nature and suffering is His ethical act and salvation is His goal. Jesus' suffering is not in vain. It restores salvation. This leads me to my second point.

Second, a theology of the cross encourages Christians to look at the suffering of Christ through the lens of the suffering humans and to address the suffering

---

[74]Moltmann and Wendel, *Passion for God*, 74.
[75]Ibid.
[76]Ibid., 75.
[77]Ibid., 75.
[78]Daniel D. William, *The Spirit and the Forms of Love* (New York: Harper & Row Publishers, 1968), 117.

world's need in general and Myanmar's need in particular compassionately.[79] In looking at the suffering of Christ through the lens of the suffering humans, some liberal liberation theologians attempt to equate the suffering of Christ with the suffering of humans. The result is to criticize the suffering of Christ without appreciating its goal as salvation or redemption.[80] Paul indicates that God sent His son Jesus in order to redeem those under the law (Gal. 4:4-5). Likewise, it is stated in the Hebrews that there is no forgiveness without the shedding blood of Christ (Heb. 9:22). More importantly, Isaiah 53 predicts Jesus' sacrificial suffering (Is. 53:5). Of course, we must know that Jesus' suffering is also the result of His faithful commitment to the identification with the oppressed.[81]

In light of this, it is not wrong to criticize the sacrificial suffering of Christ only when the oppressors, for example, male Christians misuse the suffering of Christ as the ground for endorsing the sacrificial suffering of women.[82] However, it is not right to see the suffering of humans as equal to the suffering of Christ. Our suffering is not an offering to God nor is redemptive. Human suffering is not a quality of salvation or redemption. This is not to say that human suffering is not important to God. Rather the point of the crucified Christ is dialectically to present an alternative to human suffering.

Traditional theology teaches us that Christ suffers for sinful humans. As Jürgen Moltmann rightly asserts, Christ suffers for both God and humans. Two questions are important here. Why did God take the suffering of Christ onto God's self? Second, why did Jesus die for God and sinful humans? The first answer, according to Moltmann is *solidarity Christology*.[83] To say that God takes the suffering of Christ onto Himself means God is present in the suffering people regardless of religions and ethnicities. If God takes the road of crucifixion with Christ and God is where the humiliated Christ is (Phil. 2:7-8), then Christ brings Christ brings God's solidarity with the humiliated and oppressed people, such as *Pyithu-Dukkha* regardless of religions and ethnicities.[84]

The cross of Christ stands between our crosses as a sign of solidarity that God participates in our socio-political sufferings. The God who is mysteriously present in the crucified Christ does not merely understand the suffering of *Pyithu-Dukkha*, but He compassionately shares their sufferings. In other words, Christ does not merely suffer for us as a substitutionary savior, but He suffers with us as liberator and comforter. As I noted above, this was the insightful comfort of Bonhoeffer in

---

[79]Cited in Marit Trelstad, "The Cross in Context," in *Cross Examinations: Reading on the Meaning of the Cross Today*, edited by Marit Trelstad (Minneapolis, MN: Fortress, 2006), 1-18.

[80]For example, see Mary J. Streufert, "Maternal Sacrifice as a Hermeneutics of the Cross," in Marit Trelstad, "The Cross in Context," in *Cross Examinations: Reading on the Meaning of the Cross Today*, edited by Marit Trelstad (Minneapolis, MN: Fortress, 2006): 63-75.

[81]Ibid., 68.
[82]Ibid., 68-69.
[83]Moltmann and Wendel, *Passion for God*, 75.
[84]Ibid., 75.

the Gestapo Cell: "only the suffering God can help"[85] the suffering people. Matthew 8:17 makes it plain that "Christ helps us not by way of His omnipotence, but by way of His suffering."[86] Since Christ Himself experiences the human suffering, He is compassionately identified with those who pass through the valley of fear, rejection and socio-political suffering in Myanmar.

The second answer to the second question is *reconciliation Christology*.[87] To talk about the vicarious suffering of Christ as a mediation of reconciliation between God and sinful humans (1Tim. 2:5), we link Jn. 1:29 and 2Corin. 5:18 with Is. 53. The Suffering Servant of Isaiah takes away the sins of the people by carrying the people's sin. By carrying human sin (Jn. 1:29), God reconciles us to Himself through Christ and gives us a ministry of reconciliation (2Cor. 5:18).[88] This means that reconciliation is not an individualistic act between God and the self, but a communal act between God and the victims or *Pyithu-Dukkha* and the perpetrators.[89] As Jesus is the bridge of reconciliation God and us, so Christians are the bridge of reconciliation between the victims and the perpetrators. But how can we reconcile the oppressed with the oppressors in the face of social structural sin of the latter? This leads me to a holistic and inclusive liberation.

Sin and Suffering in the Context of *Pyithu-Dukkha Theology*: Toward a Holistic and an Inclusive Liberation

Sin and suffering are indivisible in their cause-effect relationship in Asia in general and Myanmar in particular.[90] Christ carries the suffering of the oppressed on the one hand, and resists the social structural sins of the perpetrators. Both sides of Christ belong together for the liberation of both the victims and the perpetrators.[91] To be sure, liberation is not explicitly a biblical term, but it is a biblical concept of God's salvation, redemption, justification/justice, reconciliation, healing, forgiveness, new creation and freedom from the power of sin and oppression.[92] The term "liberation" was first coined in 1971 by Gustavo Gutiérrez in his seminal book, *A Theology of Liberation*.[93] He introduced theology as a reflection on praxis against

---

[85]Bonhoeffer, *Letters and Papers from Prison*, 361.
[86]Ibid., 160-161.
[87]Moltmann and Wendel, *Passion for God*, 76.
[88]Ibid., 76.
[89]Ibid., 77.
[90]This section was first published in David Thang Moe, "Sin and Suffering: The Hermeneutics of Liberation Theology in Asia," in *Asia Journal of Theology*, vol. 30.2. (October 2016): 208-226.
[91]Moltmann and Wendel, *Passion for God*, 77.
[92]Elsa Tamez, *The Amnesty of Grace: Justification by Faith from a Latin American Perspective*, translated by Sharon H. Ringe (Nashville, TN: Abingdon, 1993), 19-36.
[93]Gustavo Gutiérrez, *A Theology of Liberation: History, Politics, and Salvation* (Maryknoll, NY: Orbis, 1973). Originally published in Spanish in 1971.

Marxism, born of the meeting of faith (orthodoxy) and work (orthopraxis).[94] He put orthopraxis alongside orthodoxy.

Gutiérrez's phrases, which became a kind of manifesto for liberation theology are: commitment to the poor as the first act, and theology as a critical reflection that follows the commitment for liberation as the second act.[95] Gutiérrez's liberation hermeneutics emerged as a critique of the traditional way of doing theology. In the classical form of doing theology, theologians think theologically, and then apply it. But quite differently, Gutiérrez stressed that the themes of doing theology must come from a Christian faith as commitment to the poor. By this way, he popularized the phrase "preferential option for the poor and the oppressed," which became a slogan for liberation theologies.

A New Testament scholar turned missiologist David Bosch also proposes "mission as liberation."[96] To make the liberation popular, the World Council of Churches held in Bangkok, Thailand in 1973 has replaced the terms "salvation with liberation and fellowship with solidarity."[97] The WCC, held in Melbourne, Australia in 1981, found the oppressed were put in the very center of missiological reflection.[98]

Some Asian and Burmese theologians adopted Latin American liberation theology without analyzing the contextual differences between two continents. Latin America is what Stephen Neill called "the only Christian continent in the Third World, and around 90 percent of its inhabitants are Christians."[99] By contrast, Asia is what Pieris asserted, "a continent of two realities: multireligiousity (in which Christianity is a minority)[100] and collective suffering (both Christians and non-Christians suffer together)."[101] In Asia in general and Myanmar in particular, most of the poor are non-Christians, while in Latin America, most of the poor are Christians. The Latin American way of struggling for physical liberating is crucial for the Asian way of struggling for liberation of oppressed, but God's salvation as holistic liberation, including saving lost souls has lost its meaning in Asia in general and Myanmar in particular. As a result, lay Asian Christians are not interested in liberation theology, but rather in saving lost souls.

In this context, Simon Chan in his book *Grassroots Asian Theology* rightly asserts that there is the contrast between the elite and the grassroots Christians in Asia.[102] For elite Asian and Burmese theologians, liberation is freedom from socio-political and economic oppression and poverty; for the grassroots liberation

---

[94]Ibid., 5, 15.
[95]Ibid., 6-15.
[96]Bosch, *Transforming Mission*, 442-457.
[97]Ibid., 445.,
[98]Ibid., 446.
[99]Neill, *A History of Christian Missions*, 462.
[100]Sunquist, *The Unexpected Christian Century*, xvii.
[101]Pieris, *An Asian Theology of Liberation*, 124.
[102]Simon Chan, *Grassroots Asian Theology: Thinking The Faith from the Ground Up* (Downers Grove, IL: IVP, 2014), 126.

is spiritual salvation.[103] I am convinced that Asian churches need to correct this imbalance if God's act of salvation is holistic. Another limitation of liberation theology is the struggle for liberation of the oppressed only, not for the oppressors as well. If God is God of all humans, His act of salvation must be "inclusive." The aim of this study is to appreciate the need of liberation theology and its hermeneutics as well as to criticize its limitations in the Asian context.

I speak of three types of liberation—holistic, exclusive and inclusive.[104] Yet, my aim is to note that holistic liberation is not just one type among the three, instead it is in a sense that provides the basis for an inclusive liberation. From this account, the first part will study God's holistic liberation in a broad sense, articulating the link between human sin and God's salvation. In the second part, I will discuss the link between sin and suffering by analyzing "God's preferential option for the oppressed," which often leads some Christians to believe that liberation is only for the oppressed. I call this an "exclusive liberation." I will highlight some important points of liberation hermeneutics and will also argue against its limitation. Finally, I will propose the need of an inclusive liberation theology in Myanmar. What I will argue in the final part is that God is the God of both the oppressed and oppressor, He loves both and thus, His liberation is inclusive.

Sin and Salvation: God's Holistic Liberation

As noted above, with their overemphasis on social justice, liberation theologians are interested more in physical liberation, whereas some grassroots Christians in Asia are interested in spiritual liberation. Liberation becomes a kind of "partial liberation"—grassroots Christians focus on spiritual liberation, whereas elite liberationists focus on physical liberation. Both groups need to reconsider a biblical concept of sin and salvation from a holistic perspective. I will address holistic liberation from the three perspectives.

First, consider the doctrine of the creation of humanity. God created humans to be holistic beings in terms of spiritual and physical compositions. Gerhard von Rad contends that "one should not split between body and soul because a holistic concept is grounded in a Hebrew worldview."[105] Let us now consider the doctrine of soteriology.

Second, consider the doctrine of soteriology, or new creation in the words of Paul (2Cor. 5:17). God's salvation is holistic, mainly because humankind is holistic creature, partly because sin and its effect are holistic in a sense that it distorts whole nature of humanity. Emphasizing sin as a cosmic disaster, Paul said, "just as one man's sin leads to condemnation for all humanity, so one man's act of righteousness leads to salvation for all" (Rom. 5:18). Holistic salvation has two meanings—spiritual and physical salvation, and personal and cosmic liberation. First, Paul uses the word "saved" as a term of holistic redemption of distorted

---

[103]Ibid., 126.
[104]Three types of liberation, Moe, "Sin and Suffering," 210.
[105]Gerald von. Rad, *Genesis*, trans. J.H. Marks (London: SCM, 1961), 56.

humanity. God sent his Son into the world to redeem us by restoring our distorted dignity and rights into a new communion with God (Gal. 4:4-5).[106]

Further, Paul's use of redemption is a synonym of cosmic restoration (Col. 1:19-20).[107] Two prominent New Testament scholars, Rudolf Bultmann and Ernst Käsemann are divided on the issue of interpreting Paul's doctrine of justification. For Bultmann, the justification of God (Rom. 1:17; 3:5, 21,22; 2Cor. 5:21) is a gift for the individual.[108] But for Käsemann, the righteousness or justification does not actually refer to the individual and is not to be understood exclusively as anthropology. Käsemann refers to Paul's use of righteousness as God's reestablishing His cosmic Lordship over the world.[109] Bultmann predicates his individualistic understanding of justification largely on Rom. 1-4, whereas Käsemann bases his cosmological-anthropological reading of Paul's justification on Rom. 6-8.[110] For the purpose of this paper, I will go along with Käsemann.

Salvation is holistic not only at the spiritual-physical level, but also the individual-cosmic level. The belief that human nature is not only a holistic dichotomy (body and soul) but also a holistic trichotomy (body, soul, and spirit) deserves to be studied.[111] But soul and spirit are synonymous. When Jesus said, "love your God with your heart, with all your soul, with all our mind, and with all your strength" (Mk. 12:3-31), he omitted "spirit." The holistic liberation is applied by Jesus saying, "I came that they may have life abundantly" (Jn. 10:10). Jesus' use of abundant life and salvation are held together for the present and future. Abundant life as holistic salvation continues beyond physical death through resurrection into life everlasting.[112]

Third, the concept of holistic salvation, as John Cooper argues, also serves as a pointer to the life after death. Just as holistic salvation keeps the unity of physical and spiritual healing, so it does not see death as a separation of the spirit from the body.[113] The belief in the continuing existence of life after death is acknowledged in Burmese ancestral veneration. A Burmese way of *Nat*-worship has no dichotomy between spirit and matter, sacred and secular, time and eternity. Everything

---

[106]Rudolf Bultmann, *Theology of the New Testament* (vol. 1; New York: Scriber, 1951), 192-195.

[107]Benjamin Myers, "A Tale of Two Gardens: Augustine's Narrative Interpretation of Romans 5," in *Apocalyptic Paul: Cosmos and Inthropos in Romans 5-8*, Beverly R. Gaventa, ed. (Waco, TX: Baylor University Press, 2013): 39-58.

[108]Bultmann, *Theology of the New Testament*, 273.

[109]Ernst Kasemann, "The Righteousness of God in Paul," in *New Testament Questions of Today* (Philadelphia, PA: Fortress, 1969), 180.

[110]Ernst Kasemann, *Commentary on Romans* (Grand Rapids, MI: Eerdmans, 1980), 163.

[111]Victor E. Frankl, *Man's Search for Meaning: An Introduction to Logotherapy* (Grand Rapids, MI: Eerdmans, 1968), 68.

[112]Koester, *Symbolism in the Fourth Gospel*, 111.

[113]John W. Cooper, *Body, Soul and Life Everlasting: Biblical Anthropology and Monism-Dualism Debate* (Grand Rapids, MI: Eerdmans, 1989), 73-80.

in the world is viewed as a unity.¹¹⁴ This holistic worldview enriches a Christian doctrine of holistic liberation of anthropos and cosmos (Col. 1:19). Sadly, Greco-Western Christianity and Buddhism distort the non-dichotomy implied in Burmese ancestral veneration. The former distorts it with its dualistic notion of here-and-now and hereafter, whereas the latter distorts it with its dualistic doctrine of this cosmic (*lokka*) and meta-cosmic (*lokkutra*) world.¹¹⁵

In its overzealousness to represent the oppressed, liberation hermeneutics has ends up as a "preferential option for the oppressed" for their political liberation, but some oppressed non-Christians have a "preferential option for becoming Christians"¹¹⁶ with the hope of securing a future for their souls. In order to overcome this imbalance, Burmese theologians should reconsider the need for a holistic hermeneutics. Holistic or both-and hermeneutics implies the idea that that physical and spiritual liberation depends on one another. Therefore, it is not right to divorce physical salvation from spiritual salvation, anthropological salvation from cosmological salvation, though anthropological liberation of *Pyithu-Dukkha* is the main focus of this study. Because God's first creation of humanity and the cosmos (creation out of nothing) is holistic in a comprehensive manner, so also is His new creation of restoration and redemption (new creation out of the old).

Sin and Suffering: The Oppressors and Oppressed

Liberation hermeneutics takes the interrelation of sin and suffering seriously. For example, a Mexican Pauline scholar Elsa Tamez detects correspondence between Paul's historical context and the Latin American contemporary context. Her claim is that sin and suffering are indivisible in their cause-effect relationship in Paul's imperial context (Rom. 8:18-23) as well as in the Latin American context.¹¹⁷ She goes on to redefine sin as being structural and as the cause of suffering in a Latin American context. Unlike traditional theologies, which see sin in private term, Tamez places it in a socio-political context. The sin of the oppressor is the cause of suffering of the oppressed.¹¹⁸

Similarly, a Korean theologian Andrew Sung Park states that "sin is of the oppressors and suffering is of the oppressed."¹¹⁹ Sin is redefined by the socio-politi-

---

¹¹⁴See my article David Thang Moe, "Nat-worship and Paul Tillich: Contextualizing a Correlational Theology of Religion and Culture in Myanmar," in *Toronto Journal of Theology*, Vol. 31, no. 1. (Spring 2015): 123-136. See also, Julia Ching, *Chinese Religions* (Maryknoll, NY: Orbis, 1993), 4-8.

¹¹⁵Ibid., 127. See also Julia Ching, *Chinese Religions* (Maryknoll, NY: Orbis, 1993), 35.

¹¹⁶I drew the ideas of discussion by a Pentecostal theologian Donald E. Miller, see Donald Miller and Tetsunao Yamamori, *Global Pentecostalism: The New Face of Christian Social Engagement* (Berkeley: University of California Press, 2007), 215. The statement goes like this: while liberation theology opts for the poor, the poor opts for Christianity.

¹¹⁷Tamez, *The Amnesty of Grace*, 13.

¹¹⁸Ibid., 14.

¹¹⁹Andrew Sung Park, *The Wounded Heart of God: The Asian Concept of Han and the Christian Doctrine of Sin* (Nashville, TN: Abingdon, 1993), 69

cal context of the unequal relation between the oppressors and the oppressed, and the former are the greater sinners. It is not because the oppressed are sinless; they are sinners too, if we see sin as a state, but they are *innocent* with respect to their being the victims of oppression, sin to speak.[120] Because domination of humans by humans stands against Christ's lordship, oppressors are the greater sinners. According to Raymond Fung, the oppressors are the greater sinners, whereas the oppressed are the "sinned against."[121]

Oppression stems from the sin of pride. In this connection, Reinhold Niebuhr is impressively right in defining "sin as pride."[122] In Asia, most of the political rulers commit the sin of pride by misusing their power. Their sins of omission have to do with the failures to uphold law and order for the welfare of people. The rulers' sin of pride and sins of omission are the root causes of the suffering of the ruled. For instance, the economic poverty of the people in Myanmar, a country blessed with rich natural resources, is not the result of their *karma*, but of the military rulers' behavioral *karma*.[123]

God's Solidarity with the Oppressed: An Exclusive Liberation?

In the context of the suffering of the innocent, how do we talk about God from the concrete situation of their suffering? With this question, Gutiérrez turns to the Book of Job, as the innocent suffering of Job helps us understand the love of God and the problem of evil in the world.[124] Gutiérrez refers to two ways of speaking God. One is a contemplative language and the other is a prophetic language. Both are interrelated. Contemplative language reveals God's preferential love for the innocent victim. In the early stages, Job was too concerned about his innocent suffering, but gradually he came to realize that he was not alone in his suffering. God was with him. Through contemplation, the sufferer knows God's solidarity with those who suffer.[125]

Prophetic language, on the other hand, attacks the structural causes of suffering. While Job knows God's solidarity with him, his suffering becomes the site of his protests in the name of other innocent victims. It is with this kind of language that we struggle for justice. In reading *On Job*, we see a methodological shift in Gutierrez's hermeneutics. As noted earlier, in his book *Liberation*, he proposes

---

[120]Tamez, *The Amnesty of Grace*, 21. Along these lines, see also David Thang Moe, "Postcolonial and Liberation Theologies as Partners in Praxis Against Sin and Suffering: A Hermeneutical Approach in Asian Perspective," in *EXCHANGE: Journal of Missiological and Ecumenical Research*, vol. 45.4. (2016): 321-343.

[121]Raymond Fung, "Compassion for the Sinned Against," in *Theology Today*, Vol. 37, no. 2. (July 1980): 162-169.

[122]Reinhold Niebuhr, *The Nature and Destiny of Man*, reprinted. (Louisville, KY: John Knox, 1996), 178.

[123]Aung San Suu Kyi, *Freedom From Fear* (New York, Penguin, 1991), 170.

[124]Gutiérrez, *On Job*, xviiii.

[125]Ibid.,

prophetic praxis as the first act and a theological reflection as the second act. But in his book *On Job,* he sees "meditation and practice as the first act, and theologizing as the second act.[126] Following Gutiérrez's twofold language, the major theme liberation theologians hold in common is God's solidarity with the oppressed and God's prophetic resistance to the oppressors.

Liberation theology is grounded in three historical and theological perspectives: (1) The Exodus as the model for God's liberation for the oppressed Israel (2) The prophetic writings as a critique of the structural evil which puts the oppressed and the margins in the unjust situation (3) Jesus' prophetic praxis against structural evil of injustice in the Galilean context and his resurrection as hope for the oppressed.[127]

From the Exodus story through the prophetic writings to the gospels, God is involved in history as the God who sides with the oppressed and fights against the oppressors. God's preferential option for the oppressed in the OT is summed up in Ps. 146:7-9, where God executes justice for the oppressed. The ethics of Jesus' preferential option for the margins in the NT are summed up in Lk. 4:18-19.[128] In the biblical traditions, God is never neutral, but always sides with the oppressed, the margins and the poor—all who are subject to prejudice.[129] Why is God so partial toward them?

First, because God is compassionate to them. The basis of God's preference for the oppressed is found in God's very essence of compassion. "The margins are privileged, not because they are morally superior, but because God is compassionate and prefers the least," rightly said Gutiérrez.[130] I would argue that Jesus prefers the least and identifies with them, partly because they are, as I have noted earlier, His humiliated images. Jesus comes not simply as humanity in general but comes as one margin from the center. As a noted Japanese theologian Koyama rightly said, "Christ the center-person comes to us in the true form of a periphery- person. For our sake, He was crucified at the periphery place outside Jerusalem" (Heb. 13:12).[131] Since Jesus was once a margin, He does not merely understand the suffering of the margins, but identifies with them.[132]

---

[126]Ibid.,

[127]R. S. Sugirtharajah, *Postcolonial Criticism and Biblical Interpretation*, reprinted. (Oxford: Oxford University Press, 2009), 66.

[128]Christopher J.H. Wright, *The Mission of God: Unlocking the Bible As A Grand Narrative* (Downers Grove, IL: InterVarsity Press, 2006), 48-70; 265-288.

[129]Walter Brueggemann, "Reading the Bible amid Israeli-Palestine Conflict," in *Theology Today,* Vol. 73. No. 1 (Princeton: SAGE, April 2016): 36-45.

[130]Gutiérrez, *On Job*, 94.

[131]Koyama, "Extend Hospitality to Strangers", 167.

[132]Moltmann, *The Crucified God*, 205.

God's Justice Toward the Oppressors: An Inclusive Liberation?

In the world of human injustice, Jesus shares His incarnational identification with the grassroots without ceasing to be divine. He sides with the oppressed and resists the oppressors. God is just because He restores the rights for those oppressed who have no rights. According to Moltmann, the highest form of divine justice is the "justice of compassion."[133] It is through God's justice of compassion that those without rights receive restorative justice. This is how God executes justice for the oppressed *Pyithu*.

Yet, liberation theologians never pause to think that God's justice is inclusive of the oppressors. As I will show later, God's justice must be inclusive. It must be inclusive because God's act of justice is not vindictive and reactive, but creative. God's justice is creative in a way that those deprived of their rights come to receive their rights and the unjust come to be converted to justice. This means God's resistance to the oppressors is not because He hates them, but partly because He wants them to be converted to justice, and partly because He is merciful to the oppressed. In short, God's solidarity with the oppressed and God's resistance to the oppressors brings mutual benefits of both groups.

As Jesus's disciples, Jesus commands us to be in solidarity with the oppressed. Matthew 25:35-45 provides a locus for what Jesus called "the least of these" (25:41a). Though Jesus does not make it plain who the "least of these" are, they are apparently not limited to those suffering from socio-political oppression. In Myanmar, it is not difficult to see who the least of these are. Since Christians represent 6.2% of the population,[134] they must first identify themselves with the least of marginalized community. As Jesus says, our relation to the least determines our relation to him (Matt. 25:41), so our solidarity with the least inside the church and outside the church is imperative. The margins are preferentially gifted by Jesus to represent justice on earth.

In his overzealousness for God's preferential option for the oppressed, Pieris proposes two ideas: "irrevocable covenant between Christ and the poor and the irreconcilable antagonism between God and mammon (exploiter)."[135] Put in this way, Asian liberation theology is applied exclusively to the oppressed. The same could be said of *Minjung* theology[136] and *Dalit* theology, Asian liberation theologies.[137] Much of what we know about *Minjung* and *Dalit* theologies have ended up

---

[133]Jürgen Moltmann, "Political Theology and the Ethics of Peace," in *Theology, Politics and Peace*, ed. Theodore Runyon (Maryknoll, NY: Orbis, 1989): 31-42, p. 38.

[134]See Myanmar's Christian population, https://www.worldwatchmonitor.org/2016/08/4576673/ (accessed on February 13, 2017).

[135]Pieris, *An Asian Theology of Liberation*, 75.

[136]Kim Young-Bock, ed, *Minjung Theology: People as the Subjects of History*, (Singapore: CCA, 1981).

[137]Arvind P. Nirmal, "Toward a Christian Dalit Theology," in *A Reader in Dalit Theology*, ed. Arvind P. Nirmal (Madras: Gurukual Theological College and Research Institute, 1990): 65-69.

as the struggle for an exclusive liberation of the oppressed. Divorcing Jesus' social ministry from his atonement is another weakness of liberation theology. Seeing the problem of human suffering, some liberationists criticize Jesus' death.[138] Since incarnation and atonement are one event of the person and work of Christ, we should not separate the two.

At the core of Christian faith lies the claim that Jesus died for our sins and he restored us to a communion with God (1Cor. 15:3; 2Cor. 5:18). Thus, the suffering of humans should not be seen as equal to or representative of the suffering of Jesus. While human suffering may appear aimless, the aim of Jesus' suffering is threefold: Jesus suffers *because* of our fall (1Cor. 15:3); Jesus suffers *for* the gift of reconciliation (2Cor. 5:18); the crucified Jesus suffers *with* those who suffer.[139] The cross is part of Jesus' struggle for reconciliation. This is what makes liberation holistic and inclusive.

In sum, while I appreciate liberation hermeneutics' privileging commitment to the oppressed, I am dissatisfied with its failures to integrate it with liberation of the oppressors. Because of its failure to integrate liberation of the oppressors and its choice of biblical themes, liberation theology is accused of a "pick and choose approach."[140] In its choice of biblical themes, liberation hermeneutics has its favored texts, such as Ex. 3:7-12; Lk. 4:18-19.[141] The problem is not liberation itself (God's act), but the way it has been applied (the theologizing of liberation). The question we must ask in Myanmar is not why God is partial to the margins, but how should we reconsider liberation theology in an inclusive sense. Does God's act of liberation exclude the oppressors?

An Inclusive Liberation: Liberation From and For

In order to establish an inclusive liberation theology in Myanmar, let us consider the following three claims together: "first, God is perfectly just; secondly, God is God of all peoples and the justice of God must be the justice for all peoples; thirdly, God's universal justice is the seed of universal peace."[142] Since the primary and ultimate goal of liberation theology is to achieve justice and peace, my argument will focus on justice and peace. In Psalms 85:10b, Psalmist says, "Justice and

---

[138]For a critique of Jesus' atonement, see Marit Trelstad, ed, *Cross Examinations: Readings on the Meaning of the Cross Today* (Minneapolis, MN: Augsburg, 2006). This book is not directly related to Asia, but some Asian liberationists do not take Jesus' atonement seriously by prioritizing over his social ministry.

[139]Fretheim, *The Suffering of God*, 107-148. Fretheim explores God's suffering in OT as a prototype of the suffering of Jesus in the NT.

[140]Eryl W. Davies, *The Immoral Bible: Approaches to Biblical Ethics* (London: T&T Clark, 2010), 64-76.

[141]C. Rowland, ed, *The Cambridge Companion to Liberation Theology* (Cambridge: Cambridge University Press, 1999).

[142]I draw the insights from Volf, *Exclusion and Embrace,* 197.

peace will kiss each other."¹⁴³ He stresses the integral relationship of justice and peace. The two are inseparable. But if one has to prioritize the two in the suffering context of socio-political oppression, I would argue that justice-doing has priority over peacemaking without excluding the latter.

My point is this: justice brings peace. Peace does not bring justice. There is no peace where injustice rules even when law and order are applied by force. In order to attain peace as an ultimate goal of liberation, we have first to seek and restore justice as the ultimate goal of liberation. What kind of justice? It has to be "restorative justice." Restorative justice is what John Rawls called the "justice of fairness."¹⁴⁴ The justice of fairness is based on Luke 1:52, which says, "God has brought down the oppressors from their thrones and lifted up the oppressed." In order to restore the justice of fairness, God uses the justice of compassion. It is through the justice of compassion that those deprived of their rights receive their rights, and the unjust are converted to justice.¹⁴⁵

God is just because He gives rights to those who have no rights and seeks to set right those who are unrighteous. God's restorative justice is not vindictive, but is creative, which leads to lasting peace.¹⁴⁶ God's act of restorative justice for lasting peace does not exclude the oppressors. Since God is the God of all peoples, the justice of God must be the justice for both the oppressed and oppressors. This means that justice is one and universal. There can be no two or more kinds of justices.¹⁴⁷ If there is more than one kind of justice, conflict of "justice*s*" is inevitable and no justice will ever be done. God's act of justice must be one and universal in a sense that when struggling for justice, one must be wrong and the other right. The oppressors are wrong and the oppressed are right.

Thus, in our struggle for justice and truth, our primary goal is to expose the injustice and deception of oppressors. Political and religious revolution should come hand in hand in the liberation movements. Theological reflection in such a socio-political context is known as "public theology." It would necessarily be dialogical and prophetic.¹⁴⁸ Christians must cooperate with other oppressed non-Christians or what I call *Pyithu-Dukkha* in their prophetic resistance to their common enemies of oppressors for a common goal of liberation. Our goal of prophetic struggle against injustice is not to hate oppressors but to let them know that we love them (persons) and hate their wrongs (deeds). Let us remember Jesus' command to love our enemies (Matt. 5:44). Jesus does not just command us to love our enemies, but He reveals the truth of how God loves both the righteous (op-

---

¹⁴³For an interpretation of Ps. 85:10b from a socio-political perspective, see my article https://pres-outlook.org/2016/08/justice-peace-will-kiss (accessed on February 13, 2017).

¹⁴⁴John Rawls, *A Theory of Justice* (Cambridge, MA: Harvard University Press, 1971). 251-257.

¹⁴⁵Moltmann, "Political Theology and the Ethnics of Peace," 38.

¹⁴⁶Ibid., 37.

¹⁴⁷Volf, *Exclusion and Embrace*, 197.

¹⁴⁸Noted in Felix Wilfred, "Asian Theological Trends," in *Oxford Handbook of Christianity in Asia*, ed. Felix Wilfred (Oxford: Oxford University Press, 2014): 31-50.

pressed) and the unrighteous (oppressors). Jesus said, "God causes His sun rise on the evil and on the good, and sends rain on the righteous and on the unrighteous" (Matt. 5:45). How should we practically apply this in Myanmar?

My proposal is that if "God causes His sun rise on the evil and on the good, and sends rain on the righteous and on the unrighteous," then his act of liberating justice must also be beneficial for both the oppressed and oppressors. Although God sides with the oppressed, God's resisting the oppressors does not mean that God hates them. The "God who causes His sun rise on the evil and on the good" loves both the oppressed and oppressors. But God does hate oppression, which causes the suffering of the oppressed.[149] The distinction between God's love of sinners and hatred of sins traces back to the history where Augustine "advised love for the persons and hatred for their vices."[150]

If God loves the sinners or enemies (Rom. 5:10), and hates their sins, we ought to love the oppressors and hate and resist their oppressive sin. The ultimate goal of loving oppressors without giving up the struggle against their oppressive sin is clear that they may be liberated from evildoing, and that justice and peace may triumph. It follows from this account that liberation needs to be done for both oppressed and oppressors. Liberation of the oppressors is a requirement for liberation of the oppressed. According to Moltmann, "liberation of the oppressors is psychological liberation and liberation of the oppressed is political liberation."[151] Moltmann's use of psychological liberation echoes Paulo Freire's notion of liberation of oppressors as "conscientization."[152]

Freire insists that the conscientization of the oppressors is gained only when the oppressed struggle against their oppression.[153] I will connect Freire's hermeneutics of conscientization to a Burmese Buddhist sense of *enlightenment*. Song calls the Buddhist sense of enlightenment "third eye."[154] The "third" eye is an inner eye that allows the oppressors to see the wrongs they commit toward their victims and to feel merciful toward them. But the oppressors will not be enlightened voluntarily. In order for them to be enlightened, we must keep resisting their oppressive sin. When the oppressors become conscious of their wrongs, they would feel guilty. But too often, they do not.

Thus, another way of enlightening the oppressors is to offer them forgiveness. In this regard, it is important to note that Paul's use of justification or righteousness (*dikaiosyne*), salvation, forgiveness and reconciliation has similarities with the concept of liberation, but I must argue that the processes are different. Loving

---

[149]For a full account, see Moe, "Sin and Suffering," 220

[150]*St. Augustine: Letters 211-270*, trans. Roland Teske [Hyde Park, NY: New York City, 2005], 211.11).

[151]Jürgen Moltmann, *The Crucified God*, 40th ann. (Minneapolis: MN: Fortress, 2015), 419-494.

[152]Paulo Freire, *Pedagogy of the Oppressed*, trans. Myra Bergman Ramos (New York: Herder and Herder, 1907).

[153]Ibid., 21-24.

[154]Song, *Third-Eye Theology*, 11. Song adopted "third eye" from a Japanese Zen master Daisetz Suzuki.

and forgiving oppressors should go hand in hand as the result of Jesus' command to love, forgive and pray for our enemies (Matt. 5:44). If the oppressors are repentant, forgiveness would come easier, but too often they are not. Thus, our task is not to wait for their repentance, but to offer them our forgiveness. I must acknowledge that to forgive someone in a religious context of Christian community is easier. But genuine forgiveness in a suffering context of socio-political injustice and oppression is a difficult act for a human victim. I imagine how difficult it must be for the most persecuted Kachin Christian brothers and sisters in Myanmar to offer their genuine forgiveness to the Burman perpetrators.

However, if the crucified Christ who said of the perpetrators on the cross, "Father forgive them for they do not know what they are doing" (Lk. 23:34) is the model for us, we ought to offer our forgiveness to the perpetrators without giving up the struggle against their injustice. In this respect, forgiving the oppressors is to let go of our hatred, not to forget their wrongs to us. To forgive the oppressors is to get them to feel guilty of their wrongs and to enlighten them of humanity, both their own and others. Becoming enlightened of their act of dehumanization and their common humanity begins the process of reconciliation. Reconciliation means new relationship with God and with one another. In other words, reconciliation (*katallasso* in Greek) means the exchange of hostility or enmity for hospitality.[155] Reconciling with the oppressors in the presence of social injustice, however, is cheap reconciliation. Cheap reconciliation perpetuates social injustice. Therefore, a certain degree of justice must first be restored before reconciliation can take place. In this sense, it is important to link reconciliation with social justice.

John de Gruchy notes the link between social justice and radical reconciliation:

> Reconciliation is properly understood as a process in which we become engaged at the heart of the struggle for justice and peace in the world.... to say that the God who reconciled the world to Himself in Jesus (2 Cor. 5:19-29) is another way of saying that God is busy restoring his universal reign of justice and peace.[156]

Universal peace rests upon universal divine justice (Mi. 4:2-4). God's "preferential option for the oppressed" should not be exclusive, rather includes the oppressors because God is interested in liberation of the whole human race. Thus, Myanmar Christians should defend not only individual human rights as in the West, but also socio-political rights of various groups with the hope of reconciling with oppressors. Paul reminds us to "live at peace with everyone" (Rom. 12:18). Living at peace with everyone means living in a new relationship with one another as a beloved community. A beloved community cannot be built by hatred but by love. When we seek peace with oppressors, we must avoid violence, but

---

[155] Stanley E. Porter, "Reconciliation as the Heart of Paul's Missionary Theology," in *Paul as Missionary: Identity, Activity, Theology and Practice*, eds. Trevor J. Burge and Brian S. Rosner (London: T&T Clark, 2011): 169-179 (here p. 173).

[156] John W. de Gruchy, *Reconciliation: Restoring Justice* (Minneapolis, MN: Fortress, 2002), 21.

resist them by peaceful means. As Paul said, we cannot overcome evil with evil, we can only overcome evil with good (Rom. 12:21).

Analogously, the Buddha declared, "Hatred is never appeased by hatred. Hatred is appeased by love."[157] Paul and the Buddha who lived in different parts of the world with the similar situations of imperialism had similar ethics of nonviolent revolt against violence. Both of them sought for peace by peaceful means. It is possible to overcome violence nonviolently. But it requires patience. Justice and peace will come in its time depending on how the oppressed put their hope into practice. As Buddhists believe in *kamma* (the link between act and consequence), so Christians believe in consistent *eschatos* of God's reign in which God fights with us for an inclusive liberation.[158]

An inclusive liberation demands that a tendency toward self-determination of seeking justice is an option for the oppressed or *Pyithu-Dukkha* and embracing the oppressors as their fellow citizens living in the same nation is an alternative for the mutual goal of a harmonious and peaceful communion between the conflictual groups.[159] This relates to the prophet Isaiah's apocalyptic vision: "the lamb and the lion shall lie down together" (Is. 11:6). I would like to take the lamb as the analogy of the oppressed or the vulnerable *Pyithu-Dukkha* and the lion as the analogy of the violent oppressors.

In order for the oppressed and oppressors to live together, liberation needs to take place on both sides. The oppressed need to be liberated *from* oppressors, and oppressors also need to be liberated *from* their sin of dehumanization. As original sin separates us from our ability to reconcile with God, so actual sin of oppression separate us from reconciling with oppressors. Liberation can only be achieved by the revolt of the victims against victimizers. The ultimate goal is *for* building a beloved community in which the victimizers will live side by side with their victims, rather than the exclusive visions of winners and losers that promote hatred. Love is the ground and goal of inclusive liberation in Myanmar.[160] Overcoming an exclusive view of liberation, we must insert liberation in a larger framework of what Volf calls "a theology of embrace."[161] Seeking justice against injustice and embracing perpetrator should coexist for inclusive liberation.

---

[157]Christopher S. Queen and Sallie B. King, *Engaged Buddhism: Buddhist Liberation Movements in Asia* (Albany, NY: State University of New York, 1996), v.
[158]Moe, "Sin and Suffering," 222-223.
[159]Noted in Volf, *Exclusion and Embrace*, 220-225
[160]Moe, "Sin and Suffering," 223.
[161]Volf, *Exclusion and Embrace*, 105.

Conclusion

Volf asked Moltmann, "who is God for you?" "Jesus Christ," Moltmann replied.[1] Echoing Colossians 1:15, "Jesus is the image of the invisible God," Moltmann convincingly argues that "the meaning of the crucified Christ is that this is God and God is like this."[2] Jesus defines who God is by His act of incarnation, death and resurrection. The incarnated and crucified Christ is the human face of God. Messianic story is not just an event that happened 2,000 years ago, but it is an ontological process. Jesus, the image of the invisible God, through whom the character of God's visibility serves as the reminder of divine transcendence and immanence in the midst of the *Pyithu-Dukkha*. The God in the crucified Christ by the power of the Spirit is present mysteriously among the suffering people. If Jesus defines who God is in terms of His divinity and humanity, the Holy Spirit defines where God is in terms of His presence both in the church among the suffering Christians and His cosmic presence among all those who suffer in Myanmar.

Adopting the *Pyithu-Dukkha* as a paradigm for a dialectical theology of divine and human *Dukkha*, I urge Christians in Myanmar to consider the components of Christ's suffering and solidarity with the sufferers in an interaction with the Buddhist view of *Dukkha* and *Karuna*. Compassion with all living creatures in *Dukkha* becomes a basis for ethic of the other. What we perceive a comparative approach to the Buddhist's notion of *Dukkha* and *Karuna* and the Christian's view of passion and compassion is the self-emptiness or *Anatta* by which God continually exists and is revealed to human struggle.

Therefore, Christians in Myanmar should not share an exclusive future with their neighbors, who share the same experience of *Dukkha*. If there is one theological vision for this study, it would be priestly *apostolic vocation* in reconciliation with one another and *prophetic vocation* in resistance to evil of *Dukkha*, by which the *broken* world and *wounded* people can be healed. An essential proposal is not the elimination of cosmic *Dukkha*, but overcoming and transforming suffering into divine *Dukkha* through the union of divine and human experience.

---

[1] https://www.youtube.com/watch?v=Z_XG7NywtjM (accessed on February 19, 2017).

[2] Moltmann, *The Crucified God*, 205.

Bibliography

Adams, Daniel J. *Cross-Cultural Theology: Western Reflections in Asia*. Atlanta, GA: John Knox Press, 1987.

Altmann, Walter. "*Interpreting the Doctrine of the Two Kingdoms: God's Kingship in the Church and in Politics.*" *Word and World* 7 (Winter 1987): 43-58.

Amaladoss, Michael. *Life in Freedom: Liberation Theologies from Asia*. Maryknoll, NY: Orbis Books, 1997.

Anderson, Bernhard W. *Understanding the Old Testament*. Englewood Cliffs, NJ: Princeton Hall, 1957.

Arbuckle, Gerald A. "*Inculturation and Evangelization: Realism or Romanticism?*" In *Missionaries, Anthropologists, and Cultural Change: Studies in Third World Societies*, edited by Vinson H. Sutlive, Nathan Altshuler, Mario D. Zamora, and Virginia Kerns, 171-214. Williamsburg, VA: College of William and Mary, 1983.

Aung, Maung Htin. *Folk Elements in Burmese Buddhism*. Oxford: Oxford University Press, 1962.

Balia, Daryl, and Kirsteen Kim, eds. *Edinburgh 2010 Witnessing to Christ Today*. Vol. 2. Eugene, OR: :LSI 6WRFN 2010.

Barth, Karl. *Against the Stream*. London: SCM Press, 1954.

———. *Church Dogmatics*. Edited by G.W. Bromiley and T.F. Torrance. 4 Vols. in 13. Edinburgh: T. & T. Clark, 1936-1969.

———. *Community, State and Church: Three Essays*. Garden City, NY: Anchor Books, 1960.

———. *Credo*. New York: Charles Scribner's Sons, 1962.

———. *Dogmatics Outline*. London: SCM Press, 1949.

———. *Fragments Grave and Gay*. London: Collins Fontana, 1971.

———. "*The Christian Community and Civil Community.*" In *Community, Church and State: Three Essays*. 149-189. Eugene, OR: Wipf & Stock, 2004.

———. *The Humanity of God*. Translated by J. Thomas and T. Wieser. London, UK: Collins, 1960.

Barton, John. *Understanding Old Testament Ethics: Approaches and Explorations.* Louisville, KY: John Knox Press, 2003.

Bethge, Eberhard. *Dietrich Bonhoeffer: A Biography.* Revised and edited by Victoria J. Barnett. Minneapolis, MN: Fortress Press, 2000.

Bock, Kim Young ed. *Minjung Theology: People as the Subjects of History*, Singapore: CCA, 1981.

Bodhi, Bhikku. *In The Buddha's Words: An Anthology of Discourses from the Pali Canon.* Boston, MA: Wisdom Publications, 2005.

Bonhoeffer, Dietrich. *The Cost of Discipleship.* Edited and translated by Reginald H. Fuller. New York: Macmillan Publishing Company, 1963.

———. *Discipleship.* Translated by Barbara Green and Reinhard Krauss. Minneapolis, MN: Fortress Press, 2003.

———. *Lettersand Papers from Prison.*Edited by Eberhard Bethge.Translated by Reginald H. Fuller. New York: Macmillan Publishing Company, 1953.

———. *Prisoner for God: Letters and Papers from Prison.* Translated by Reginald H. Fuller. New York: The Macmillan Company, 1954.

———. *A Testament to Freedom: The Essential Writings of Dietrich Bonhoeffer.* Edited by Geffrey B. Kelly & F. Burton Nelson. San Francisco, CA: A Division of Harper Collins Publishers, 1990.

Bornkamm, Gunther. *Jesus of Nazareth.*Translated by Fraser McLuskey and James M. Robinson. London: Hodder & Stoughton, 1960.

Bosch, David J. "God's Reign and the Rulers of this World: Missiological Reflections on Church-State Relationships." In *The Good News of the Kingdom*, edited by Charles Van Enen, Dean S. Gilliland and Paul Pierson, 89-95. Maryknoll, NY: Orbis Books, 1993.

———. *Transforming Mission: Paradigm Shifts in Theology of Mission.*20th anniversary edition. Maryknoll, NY: Orbis Books, 2011.

Braaten, Carl and Robert Jenson, eds. *Union with Christ: The New Finnish Interpretation of Luther.* Grand Rapids, MI: William B. Eerdmans Publishing Company, 1988.

Braun, Willi. *Feasting and Social Rhetoric in Luke 14.*Cambridge: Cambridge University Press, 1995.

Browning, Don S. *A Fundamental Practical Theology: Descriptive and Strategic Proposals.* Minneapolis, MN: Fortress, 1991.

Brueggemann, Walter. "Reading the Bible amid Israeli-Palestine Conflict." In *Theology Today,* Vol. 73. No. 1. (April 2016): 36-45.

Brunner, Emil. *The Christian Doctrine of Creation and Redemption: Dogmatics II.* Translated by Olive Wyon. Philadelphia, PA: The Westminster Press, 1952.

Bultmann, Rudolf. "New Testament and Mythology." In *Kerygma and Myth: A Theological Debate*, edited by Hans Werner Bartsch, 1-44. New York: Harper & Row, 1961.

———. *The Second Letter to the Corinthians.* Translated by Roy A. Harrisville. Minneapolis, MN: Augsburg Publishing House, 1985.

———. *Theology of the New Testament.* vol. 1; New York: Scriber, 1951.The Burma Socialist Program Party, Union of Burma. *The System of Correlation of Man And His Environment: The Philosophy of the Burma Socialist Party.* Rangoon: Sarpay Beikman Press, 1964.

Butler, Gerald A. "Karl Barth and Political Theology." In *Scottish Journal of Theology*, Vol. 27. Issue 4 (November 1974): 441-456.

Bwa, Saw Hlai. *Our Theological Journey in Honor of Professor Dr. Simon Pau Khan En.* Yangon: Myanmar Institute of Theology, 2012.

Chan, Simon. *Grassroots Asian Theology: Thinking the Faith from the Ground Up.* Downers Grove, IL: IVP, 2014.

———. *Liturgical Theology. The Church as Worshiping Community.* Downers, IL: IVP, 2006.

Ching, Julia. *Chinese Religions.* Maryknoll, NY: Orbis, 1993.

——— and Hans Küng. *Christianity and Chinese Religions.* London: SCM Press, 1989.

Chung, Paul S. *Christian Mission and A Diakonia of Reconciliation: Justification and Justice.* Minneapolis, MN: Lutheran University Press, 2008.

———. *Constructing Irregular Theology: Bamboo and Minjung in East Asia Perspective.* Leiden: Brill, 2009.

———. "Karl Barth and Religious Pluralism: A Conflict?" In *Theology Between East and West: Essays in Honor of Jan Milic Lochman*, edited by Frank D. Macchia and Paul S. Chung, 35-58. Eugene, OR: Cascade Books, 2002.

———. *Martin Luther and Buddhism: Aesthetics of Suffering.* 2nd edition. Eugene, OR: Pickwick Publications, 2008.

Clifford, Richard J. *Fair Spoken and Persuading: An Interpretation of Second Isaiah.* New York: Paulist, 1984.

The Commission on Theological Concerns of the Christian Conference of Asia (CTC-CCA). *Minjung Theology: People as the Subject of History.* Maryknoll, NY: Orbis Books, 1981.

Cone, James H. *God of the Oppressed.* New revised edition. Maryknoll, NY: Orbis Books, 1997.

Conze, Edward. *Buddhist Scriptures.* Baltimore, MD: Penguin Books, 1959.

Coogan, Michael D. *A Brief Introduction to the Old Testament.* New York: Oxford University Press, 2009.

Cooper, John W. *Body, Soul and Life Everlasting: Biblical Anthropology and Monism-Dualism Debate.* Grand Rapids, MI: Eerdmans, 1989.

Cousar, Charles B. *A Theology of the Cross: The Death of Jesus in the Pauline Letters.* Minneapolis, MN: Augsburg Publishing House, 1990.

Cousins, Ewert H. *Hope and the Future of Theology.* Philadelphia, PA: Fortress Press, 1972.

Cullmann, Oscar. "Eschatology and Missions in New Testament. "In *The Theology of the Christian Mission*, edited by Gerald H. Anderson, 42-54. Nashville, TN: Abingdon Press, 1961.

Cyris, Moon Hee-Suk. "An Old Testament Understanding of Minjung." In *Minjung Theology: Minjung as the Subjects of History*, edited by the Commission on Theological Concerns of the Christian Conference of Asia, 123-137. Maryknoll, NY: Orbis Books, 1983.

Davies, Alice. "And the Harvest Shall be Plentiful." *Economic: Voice of Burma* 6, no. 7 (1996): 7-20.
Davies, Eryl W. *The Immoral Bible: Approaches to Biblical Ethics*. London: T&T Clark, 2010.
D'Costa, Gavin. "Christ, The Trinity and Religious Plurality." In *Christian Uniqueness Reconsidered: The Myth of Pluralistic Theology of Religions*, ed. Gavin D' Costa. 16-29. Maryknoll, NY: Orbis, 1990.
──. *Christianity and World Religions: Disputed Questions in the Theology Of Religions*. Chichester: John Wiley & Sons, Ltd., 2009.
D'Souza, Joseph. *Dalit Freedom, Now and Forever: The Epic Struggle for Dalit Emancipation*. Greenwood Village, CO: Dalit Freedom Network, 2004
Deotis, Roberts J. *A Philosophical Introduction to Theology*. London: SCM Press, 1991.
Devasahayam, V. *Frontiers of Dalit Theology*. New Delhi: Indian Society for Promoting Christian Knowledge/ISPCK, 1997.
Dhammananda, K. Sri. *What Buddhist Believes*. Expended and revised edition. Kota Kinabalu, Malaysia: Laser Press Sdn. B.hd, 1999.
Diem, Hermann. "Karl Barth as Socialist: Controversy over a New Attempt to Understand Him." In *Karl Barth and Radical Politics*, edited and translated by George Hunsinger, 121-138. Philadelphia, PA: The Westminster Press, 1976.
Dong, Suh Nam.*Theology at Turning Point*. Seoul: Korean Theological Study, 1976.
Dumouln, Heinrich. *Understanding Buddhism Key Themes*. Translated by Joseph S. O'Leary. New York: Weatherhill, 1994.
Dunn, James D. G. *Romans 9-16*. WBC. Waco: Word, 1988.
Eliade, Mircea. *Images and Symbols: Studies in Religious Symbols*. Translated by Philip Mairet. New York: Sheed & Ward, 1952.
En, Simon Pau Khan. "Globalization and Inter-Religious Cooperation: A Myanmar Experience." *RAYS, MIT Journal of Theology* 7 (January 2006): 124-136.
──. "Gospel and Culture." *Engagement: Judson Research Center Bulletin* 7 (December 2006): 73-88.
──. "Nat-Worship: A Paradigm for Doing Ecumenical Theology in Myanmar." *Asia Journal of Theology* 8, no. 1 (April 1994): 42-53.
England, John C. "The Earliest Christian Communities in South East and North East Asia-An Outline of the Evidence Available in the Seven Centuries before A.D 1500." *Asia Journal of Theology* 4, no. 1 (April 1990): 174-185.
Esler, Philip F. *Community and Gospel in Luke-Acts: The Social and Political Motivation in Lucan Theology*. Cambridge: Cambridge University, 1987.
Forestell, Terence J. *The Word of the Cross: Salvation as Revelation in the Fourth Gospel*. Rome: Biblical Institute Press, 1974.
France, Richard T. *Divine Government: God's Kingship in the Gospel of Mark*. Grand Rapids, MI: William B. Eerdmans Publishing Company, 2003
Franfield, C. E. B. *The Gospel According to Saint Mark*. Cambridge: Cambridge University, 1959.

Frankl, Victor E. *Man's Search for Meaning: An Introduction to Logotherapy.* Grand Rapids, MI: Eerdmans, 1968.

Freire, Paulo. *Pedagogy of the Oppressed*, trans. Myra Bergman Ramos. New York: Herder and Herder, 1907.

Fretheim, Terence E. "Christology and the Old Testament." In *Who Do You Say That I Am? Essay on Christology in Honor of Jack Dean Kingsbury*, edited by Mark A. Powell and David R. Bauer, 201-215. Louisville, KY: John Knox Press, 1999.

———. "Divine Judgment and Warming of the World: An Old Testament Perspective." *Word & World* 4, Supplement Series (April 2000): 21-32.

———. *Exodus—Interpretation: A Bible Commentary for Teaching and Preaching.* Louisville, KY: John Knox Press, 1991.

———. *God and World in the Old Testament: A Relational Theology of Creation.* Nashville, TN: Abingdon Press, 2005.

———. *The Suffering of God: An Old Testament Perspective.* Philadelphia, PA: Fortress Press, 1984.

Fung, Raymond. "Compassion for the Sinned Against." In *Theology Today*, vol. 37, no. 2. (July 1980): 162-169.

Gaiser, Fredrick J. "I Will Carry and Will Save: The Carrying God of Isaiah 40:66." *Word and World* 5, Supplement Series (April 2006): 94-102. Gilhodes,

C. *The Kachins-Religions and Customs.* Calcutta: Catholic Orphan Press, 1922.

Gowler, David B. *Host, Guest, Enemy and Friend: Portraits of the Pharisees in Luke and Acts.* New York: Peter Lang, 1991.

Green, Clifford. ed, *Karl Barth: Theologian of Freedom.* Minneapolis, MN: Fortress, 1991.

Green, Joel B. *The Gospel of Luke.* Grand Rapids, MI: Eerdmans, 1997.

Greenwood, Nicholas, ed. *Burmese Then and Now*, 59-72. Bucks: Bradt, 1995

Grenz, Stanley J. *Theology for the Community of God.* Grand Rapids, MI: William B. Eerdmans Publishing Company, 1994.

Grieb, A. Katherine. *The Story of Romans: A Narrative Defense of God's Righteousness.* Louisville, KY: Westminster John Knox Press, 2002.

Gruchy, John W. de. *Bonheoffer and South Africa: Theology in Dialogue.* Grand Rapids, MI: Eerdmans, 1984.

———. *Reconciliation: Restoring Justice.* Minneapolis, MN: Fortress, 2002.

Gutiérrez, Gustavo. *On Job: God-Talk and the Suffering of the Innocent.* Translated by Matthew J. O'Connell. Maryknoll, NY: Orbis Books, 1997.

———. *A Theology of Liberation: History, Politics, and Salvation.* Maryknoll, NY: Orbis Books, 1973. Originally published in Spanish in 1971.

Haynes, Jeff. *Politics in the Developing World: A Concise Introduction.* Oxford: Blackwell Publishing, 2000.

Hennelly, Alfred T. *Liberation Theologies: The Global Pursuit of Justice.* Mystic, CT: Twenty-Third, 1995.

Hertz, Karl H., ed. *Two Kingdoms and One World: A Sourcebook in Christian Social Ethics.* Minneapolis, MN: Augsburg Publishing House, 1976.
Ho, Huang Po. *No Longer Stranger: Toward the Construction of Contextual Theologies.* Tiruvalla: Christava Sahitya Samithy, 2007.
Hollenweger, Walter J. "Ecumenical Significance of Oral Christianity." *Ecumenical Review* 41, no. 2 (1989): 259:265.
Hopkins, Martin K. *God's Kingdom in the New Testament.* Chicago, IL: Henry Regnery, 1964.
―――. *God's Kingdom in The Old Testament.* Chicago, IL: Henry Regnery, 1964.
Horsley, Richard A. "Jesus, Paul and the Arts of Resistance: Leaves from the Notebook Of James C. Scott." In *Hidden Transcripts And the Arts of Resistance, Applying the Work of James C. Scott to Jesus and Paul,* edited by Richard A. Horsley, 1-28. Leiden: Brill, 2004.
Huber, Wolfgang. "The Barmen Declaration and the *Kairos* Documents: On the Relationship between Confession and Politics." In *Journal of Theology for Southern Africa,* Vol. 27 (June 1991): 48-60.
Hultgren, Arland J. *Paul's Gospel and Mission: The Outlook from His Letter to the Romans.* Philadelphia, PA: Fortress Press, 1986.
Hunsinger, George. *Disruptive Grace: Studies in the Theology of Karl Barth.* Grand Rapids, MI: William B. Eerdmans Publishing Company, 2000.
―――. "The Daybreak of the New Creation: Christ's Resurrection in Recent Theology." *Scottish Journal of Theology* 57, no. 2 (July 2004): 163-181.
Hwa, Na Young. *A Critical Study of Korean Theology of Minjung in Comparison with Latin American Theology of Liberation.* St. Louis, MO: Covenant Theological Seminary, 1983.
Hyun, Young-Hak. "Minjung Theology and the Religion of Han." *East Asia Journal of Theology,* The Commission on Theological Concerns (1985): 354-375. Irvin, Dale T., and Akintunde E. Akinade, eds. *The Agitated Mind of God: The Theology of Kosuke Koyama.* Maryknoll, NY: Orbis Books, 1996.
Jeremias, Joachim. *New Testament Theology: The Proclamation of Jesus.* Translated by John Bowden. New York: Charles Scribner's Sons, 1971.
Kahler, Martin. *Schriften zur Christologie und Mission.* Munich: Verlag, 1971.
Kairos Theologians, Kairos Documents: Challenge to the Church, A Theological Comment on a Political Crisis in South Africa. Grand Rapids, MI: Eerdmans, 1986.
Kasemann, Ernst. *Commentary on Romans.* Grand Rapids, MI: Eerdmans, 1980.
―――. "The Righteousness of God in Paul." In *New Testament Questions of Today.* Philadelphia, PA: Fortress, 1969.
Kelly, Geffrey B., and F. Burton Nelson. *The Cost of Moral Leadership: The Scripture of Dietrich Bonhoeffer.* Grand Rapids, MI: William B. Eerdmans Publishing Company, 2003.
―――. *Reading Bonhoeffer: A Guide to Spiritual Classics and Selected Writing on Peace.* Eugene, OR: Cascade Books, 2008.

Khai, Sing Khaw. *The Theological Concept of the Zo in the Chin Tradition and Culture.* Yangon: Myanmar Institute of Theology, 1984.
Khawsiama, K. M. Y. "Toward A Theology of *Dukkha*: A Christian-Buddhist View on the Suffering of Ludu in Myanmar." *Asia Journal of Theology* 2, no. 26 (October 2012): 110-125.
Kitamori, Kazoh. *The Theology of the Pain of God.* Richmond, VA: John Knox Press, 1958.
Klein, Ralph W. *Israel in Exile, A Theological Interpretation.* Philadelphia, PA: Fortress Press, 1979.
Ko, Daw Sein. *Burmese Sketches.* Vol. 2. Rangoon: British Burma Press, 1920.
Koester, Craig R. *Symbolism in the Fourth Gospel: Meaning, Mystery, Community*, 2nd edition. Minneapolis, MN: Fortress Press, 2003.
Koyama, Kosuke. "The Crucified Christ Challenges Human Power." In *Asian Faces of Jesus*, edited by R. S. Sujirtharajah, 149-162. Maryknoll, NY: Orbis Books, 1993.
———. "Extend Hospitality to Strangers: A Missiology of Theologia Crucis." In *Currents In Theology and Mission*, Vol. 20, No. 30. (June 1993): 165-176.
———. *Mount Fuji and Mount Sinai.* London: SCM Press, 1984.
———. ed. *South East Asia Journal of Theology* 2 (Autumn 1969): 3-5.
———. *Three Mile an Hour God: Biblical Reflections.* Maryknoll, NY: Orbis, 1980.
———. *Water Buffalo Theology.* 25th anniversary edition, revised and expanded. Maryknoll, NY: Orbis Books, 1999.
Kraus, Hans-Joachim. *Psalms 1-59: A Continental Commentary.* Minneapolis: Augsburg Publishing House, 1989.
Küng, Hans. *Global Responsibility: In Search of A New World Ethic.* Eugene, OR: Wipf & Stock, 1991.
Kung, Lap Yan. "Love Your Enemies: A Theology for Aliens in Their Native Land: The Chin in Myanmar." *Studies in World Christianity* 15, no. 1(April 2009): 81-99.
Kuo-Wei, Peng. *Hate the Evil, Hold Fast to the Good: Structuring Romans 12:1-15:13.* Bloomsbury: T&T Clark, 2006.
Kushner, Harold S. *When Bad Things Happen to Good People.* New York: Anchor Books, 2004.
Ladd, George Eldon. *The Gospel of the Kingdom.* Grand Rapids, MI: William B. Eerdmans Publishing Company, 1992.
Larbeer, P. Mohan. "Mission: Ambedkar's Perspective." In *Dalit-Minjung Theological Dialogue: On Being A New Community and Ecclesia of Justice and Peace*, edited by James Massey and Noh Jong Sun, 159-174. Bangalore: BTESSC, 2010.
Latourette, Kenneth Scott. *Introducing Buddhism.* New York: Friendship Press, 1999.
Lee, Jea Hoon. *The Exploration of the Inner Wounds-Han.* Atlanta, GA: Scholar Press, 1994.

Lee, Jung Young. *God Suffers For Us: A Systematic Inquiry into a Concept of Divine Passibility.* The Hague: Martinus Nijhoff, 1974.

———. "Minjung Theology: A Critical Introduction." In An *Emerging Theology in World Perspective: Commentary on Korean Minjung Theology,* edited by Jung Young Lee, 3-29. Mystic, CT: Twenty-Third Publications, 1988.

———. *The Theology of Change: A Christian Concept of God in an Eastern Perspective.* Maryknoll, NY: Orbis Books, 1979.

———. *The Trinity in Asian Perspective.* Nashville, TN: Abingdon Press, 1996.

Lienhard, Marc. *Luther: Witness to Jesus Christ.* Translated by J. A. Bouman. Minneapolis, MN: Augsburg Publishing House, 1982.

Ling, Samuel Ngun. "In the Midst of the Stupas: Revitalization the Christian Presence in Myanmar." *RAYS, MIT Journal of Theology* 3 (January 2003): 113-125.

———. *Theological Themes for Our Times, Reflections on Selected Themes of The Myanmar Institute of Theology.* Yangon: Judson Research Center, 2007.

Loewenich, Walther V. *Luther's Theology of the Cross.* Translated by Herbert J. A. Bouman. Minneapolis, MN: Augsburg Housing Publishing, 1976.

Lull, Timothy, ed. *Martin Luther's Basic Theological Writings.* Minneapolis, MN: Fortress Press, 1989.

Lundbom, Jack J. *Jeremiah Among The Prophets.* Eugene, OR: Cascade Books, 2012.

———. *Jeremiah 21-36.* Anchor Bible 21B. New York: Doubleday, 2004.

Magnus, Richard. "The Christian Role in a Pluralistic Society, with Specific Reference to Singapore." In *Pilgrims and Citizens: Christian Social Engagement in East Asia,* edited by Michael Nai-Chiu Poon. 169-178. Singapore: ATF Press, 2006.

Mang, Pum Za. "Separation of Church and State: A Case Study of Myanmar (Burma)." *Asia Journal of Theology* 25, no. 1 (April 2011): 42-58.

Marsh, Charles. *Reclaiming Dietrich Bonhoeffer: The Promise of His Theology.* New York: Oxford University Press, 1994.

Marty, Martin E. "Looking Back, Summing Up." In *Echoes from Calvary: The Seven Last Words of Christ on the Cross,* edited by Richard Young, 199-208. Oxford Rowman & Littlefield Publishers, 2005.

Massey, James. *Another World is Possible: Dalit Perspective on Human, Globalization and Just Society.* CDS Pamphlet 6. New Delhi: ISPCK, 2004.

———. *Indigenous People: Dalits, Dalit Issues in Today's Debates.* Bangalore: ISPCK, 1994.

Maung, Maung, *Aung San of Burma.* The Hague: Martinus Nijhoff, 1962.

McLeish, Alexander. *Christian Progress in Burma.* London: World Dominion Press, 1929.

McMahon, A. R. *The Karens of the Golden Chersonese.* London: Paall Mall, 1876.

McWilliams, Warren. *The Passion of God: Divine Suffering in Contemporary Protestant Theology.* Macon, GA: Mercer University Press, 1985.

Mendenhall, George E. *Ancient Israel's Faith and History: An Introduction to the Bible in Context.* Louisville, KY: John Knox Press, 2001.

Miller, Donald E and Tetsunao Yamamori, *Global Pentecostalism: The New Face of Christian Social Engagement.* Berkeley, Calif: University of California Press, 2007.

Moe, David Thang. "Being Church in the Midst of Pagodas: A Theology of 'Embrace' in Myanmar." In *Mission Studies: Journal of the International Association for Mission Studies*, vol. 31.1. (2014): 22-43.

———. "The Crucified Mind: Kosuke Koyama's Missiology of Theology of the Cross." In *Exchange: Journal of Contemporary Christianities in Context*, 46/1. (2017): 5-28.

———. "The Significance of Karl Barth's Political Theology for the Politics of Myanmar." In *International Journal of Public Theology* (forthcoming 2017).

———. "Metta: Doing *Pyithu-Dukkha* Theology of Reconciliation in Burma." M.Div. Thesis, Sabah Theological Seminary, Kota Kinabalu, 2009.

———. "Nat-worship and Paul Tillich: Contextualizing a Correlational Theology of Religion and Culture in Myanmar." In *Toronto Journal of Theology*, Vol. 31, no. 1. (Spring 2015): 123-136.

———. "Postcolonial and Liberation Theologies as Partners in Praxis Against Sin and Suffering: A Hermeneutical Approach in Asian Perspective." In *EXCHANGE: Journal of Missiological and Ecumenical Research*, vol. 45.4. (2016): 321-343.

———. "Reading Romans 13:1-7 as a Hidden Transcript of Postcolonial Theology in Myanmar." In *Journal of Theology for Southern Africa*, 157. (March 2017): 71-98.

———. "Sin and Evil in Christian and Buddhist Perspectives: A Quest for Theodicy." In *Asia Journal of Theology*, vol. 29.1. (April 2015): 22-46.

———. "Sin and Suffering: The Hermeneutics of Liberation Theology in Asia." In *Asia Journal of Theology*, vol. 30.2. (October 2016): 208-226.

———. "A Trinitarian Theology of Religions: Themes and Issues in Evangelical Approaches." In *Evangelical Review of Theology*, vol. 40.2. (July 2017).

———. 'The Word to the World: Johannine Trinitarian Missiology (John 20: 21-22)." In *Journal of Pentecostal Theology*, 26. (2017): 68-85.

Moe, Joel Tin. "Korean Theology of Han and Its relevance to *Pyithu-Dukkha* Theology Of Myanmar." M.Th. Thesis, Hanil University & Presbyterian Theological Seminary, Jeonbuk, 2000.

Moltmann, Jürgen. *The Church in the Power of the Spirit: A Contribution to Messianic Eschatology.* Translated by Margaret Kohl. New York: Harper & Row, 1977.

———. *The Crucified God: The Cross of Christ as the Foundation and Criticism of Christian Theology.* Minneapolis, MN: Fortress Press, 1993.

———. *The Crucified God*, 40th ann. Minneapolis: MN: Fortress, 2015.

———. "Political Theology and the Ethics of Peace." In *Theology, Politics and Peace*, ed. Theodore Runyon. 31-42. Maryknoll, NY: Orbis, 1989.

———. "A Definitive Study Paper: A Christian Declaration of Human Rights." In *A Christian Declaration on Human Rights: Theological Studied of the World Alliance of Reformed Churches*, edited by Allen O. Miller, 129-143. Grand Rapids, MI: William B. Eerdmans Publishing Company, 1977.

———. *Ethics of Hope*. Translated by Margaret Kohl. Minneapolis, MN: Fortress Press, 2012.

———. *Experiences in Theology: Ways and Forms of Christian Theology*. Translated by Margaret Kohl. Minneapolis, MN: Fortress Press, 2000.

———. "Minjung Theology for the Ruling Classes." In *Asian Contextual Theology for the Third Millennium: Theology of Minjung in Fourth-Eye Formation*, edited by Paul S. Chung, Veli-Matti Karkkainen, and Kim Kyoung Jae. Eugene, OR: Pickwick Publications, 2007.

———. *Passion for God: Theology in Two Voices*. Louisville, KY: Westminster John Knox Press, 2003.

———. *The Source of Life: The Holy Spirit and the Theology of Life*. Translated by Margaret Kohl. Minneapolis, MN: Fortress Press, 1997.

———. *The Spirit of Life: A Universal Affirmation*. Minneapolis, MN: Fortress Press, 2001.

———. *The Trinity and the Kingdom*. Minneapolis, MN: Fortress Press, 1993.

———. *The Trinity and the Kingdom of God: The Doctrine of God*. Translated by Margaret Kohl. San Francisco, CA: Harper & Row, 1981.

———. *The Way of Jesus Christ: Christology in Messianic Dimensions*. Translated by Margaret Kohl. San Francisco, CA: Harper & Row, 1990.

Montague, George T. *The Holy Spirit: Growth of a Biblical Tradition-A Commentary on The Principal Texts of the Old and New Testaments*. New York: Paulist Press, 1970.

Moon, Chris H. "An Old Testament Understanding of Minjung." In *Minjung Theology*, edited by Kim Yong-Bock, 27-40. Singapore: The Christian Conference of Asia, 1981.

Moon, Joshua N. *Jeremiah's New Covenant*. Winona Lake, IN: Eisenbruans, 2011.

Moreau, A. Scott, Gary R. Corwin, and Gary B. McGee, *Introducing World Missions: A Biblical, Historical and Practical Survey*. Grand Rapids, MI: Baker Academic, 2004.

Mu, Ahn Byung."Jesus and the Minjung in the Gospel of Mark." In *Minjung Theology: People as the Subjects of History*, edited by the Commission on Theological Concerns of the Christian Conference of Asia/CCA, 138-152. Maryknoll, NY: Orbis Books, 1981.

Muck, Terry C, and Frances S. Adeney. *Christianity Encountering World Religions*. Grand Rapids, MI: Baker Academic, 2009.

———. "Instrumentality, Complexity and Reason: A Christian Approach to Reli- gious Diversity." In *Christian-Buddhist Studies*, 22 (2002): 115-121.

———. *Why Study Religion? Understanding Humanity's Pursuit of the Divine*. Grand Rapids, MI: Baker Academic, 2016.

Muilenburg, James. "The Office of the Prophet in Ancient Israel." In *The Bible in Modern Scholarship*, edited by J. Philip Hyatt, 74-100. Nashville, TN: Abingdon Press, 1965.

Myers, Benjamin. "A Tale of Two Gardens: Augustine's Narrative Interpretation of Romans 5." In *Apocalyptic Paul: Cosmos and Inthropos in Romans 5-8*, edited by Beverly R. Gaventa, 39-58. Waco, TX: Baylor University Press, 2013.

Miyahira, Nozamu. *Towards a Theology of the Concord of God: A Japanese Perspective On the Trinity*. Carlisle: Paternoster, 2000.

Nagel, Norman E. "Martinus: Heresy, Doctor Luther, Heresy! The Person and Work of Christ."In *Seven-Headed Luther, Essays in Commemoration of a Quincentenary 1483-1983*, edited by Peter Newman Books, 25-49. Oxford: Clarendon Press, 1983.

Neill, Stephen. *A History of Christian Missions*. 2nd edition. Owen Chadwick: Penguin Books, 1986.

Netland, Harold A. *Dissonant Voices: Religious Pluralism and the Question of Truth*. Grand Rapids, MI: William B. Eerdmans Publishing Company, 1991.

Newbigin, Lesslie. "The Gospel Among the Religions." In *Mission Trends No. 5*, edited by Gerald A. Anderson and Thomas F. Stransky, 16-38. Grand Rapids, MI: William B. Eerdmans Publishing Company, 1981.

———. *The Gospel in A Pluralistic Society*. Grand Rapids, MI: William B. Eerdmans Publishing Company, 1989.

———. *The Household of God: Lectures on the Natures of the Church*. London: SCM Press, 1953.

———. *The Open Secret: An Introduction to the Theology of Mission*. Revised edition. Grand Rapids, MI: William B. Eerdmans Publishing Company, 1995.

Ngien, Dennis. *The Suffering of God: According to Martin Luther's Theologia Crucis*. Eugene, OR: Wipf and Stock Publishers, 2001.

Nicholls, Bruce. "Theological Education and Evangelization. "In *Let the Earth Hear His Voice*, edited by James D. Douglas, 634-648. Minneapolis, MN: World Wide Publications, 1975.

Niebuhr, Reinhold. *The Nature and Destiny of Man*, reprinted. Louisville, KY: John Knox, 1996.

Niebuhr, Richard H. *Christ and Culture*. New York: Happer Torch Book, 1951.

Nirmal, Arvind P., and V. Devasahayam. *A Reader in Dalit Theology*. New Delhi: Indian Society for Promoting Christian Knowledge/ISPCK, 1990.

———. "Toward a Christian Dalit Theology." In *A Reader in Dalit Theology*, ed- ited by Arvind P. Nirmal. 65-69. Madras: Gurukual Theological College and Research Institute, 1990.

Ott, Craig, Stephen J. Strauss, and Timothy C. Tennent. *Encountering Theology of Mission: Biblical Foundations, Historical Developments, Contemporary Issues*. Grand Rapids, MI: Baker Academic, 2010.

Pannenberg, Wolfhart. *Jesus: God and Man*. Translated by L. L. Wilkins and D. A. Priebe. Philadelphia, PA: The Westminster Press, 1968.

Park, Andrew Sung. *The Wounded Heart of God: The Asian Concept of Han and the Christian Doctrine of Sin*. Nashville, TN: Abingdon, 1993.

Perrin, Norman. *Rediscovering the Teaching of Jesus.* New York: Harper & Row Publishers, 1967.

Phan, Peter C. "Crossing the Borders: A Spirituality for Mission in Our Times from an Asian Perspective." In *SEDOS Bulletin,* 35. (2003): 8-19.

Pieris, Aloysius. *An Asian Theology of Liberation.* Maryknoll, NY: Orbis Books, 1988.

———. "The Buddha and the Christ: Mediators of Liberation." In *The Myth of Christian Uniqueness: Toward a Pluralistic Theology of Religions,* edited by John Hick and Paul F. Knitter, 162-177. Maryknoll, NY: Orbis Books, 1987.

———. "Buddhism as a Challenge for Christians." In *Christianity Among World Religions,* edited by Jürgen Moltmann and Hans Küng, 60-66. Edinburgh: T&T Clark, 1986.

Pirriere, Benedicte brac de la. "The Taungbyon Festival." In *Burma at the Turn of the 21st Century,* edited by Monique Skidmore, 65-89. Honolulu, HI: University of Hawaii Press, 2005.

Porter, Stanley E. "Reconciliation as the Heart of Paul's Missionary Theology." In *Paul as Missionary: Identity, Activity, Theology and Practice,* eds. Trevor J. Burge and Brian S. Rosner. 169-179. London: T&T Clark, 2011.

Prenter, Regin. *Luther's Theology of the Cross.* Philadelphia, PA: Fortress Press, 1971.

Queen, Christopher S. and Sallie B. King, *Engaged Buddhism: Buddhist Liberation Movements in Asia.* Albany, NY: State University of New York, 1996.

Rad, Gerald von. *Genesis,* translated by J.H. Marks. London: SCM, 1961.

Rahula, Walpola Sri. *What the Buddha Taught.* Revised and expanded edition. New York: Grove Press, 1979.

Ratnam, M. V. Ram Kumar. *Dukkha: Suffering in Early Buddhism.* New Delhi: Discovery Publishing House, 2003.

Rawls, John. *A Theory of Justice.* Cambridge, MA: Harvard University Press, 1971

Rowland, C. Rowland, ed. *The Cambridge Companion to Liberation Theology.* Cambridge: Cambridge University Press, 1999.

Razu, I. John Mohan. "Being Dalits and Becoming A New Community in A Globalizing Context." In *Dalit-Minjung Theology: On Being A New Community and Ecclesia of Justice and Peace,* edited by James Massey and Noh Jong Sun, 116-143. Bangalore: BTESSC, 2010.

Richards, Lawrence O. *Expository Dictionary of Bible Words.* Grand Rapids, MI: Zondervan, 1985.

Robinson, H. Wheeler. *The Cross in the Old Testament.* London: SCM Press, 1955.

Sanneh, Lamin. *Whose Religion is Christianity? The Gospel Beyond the West.* Grand Rapids, MI: William B. Eerdmans Publishing Company, 2003.

Say, Saw Doh. "A Brief History and Development Factors of the Karen Baptist Church of Myanmar." M.Th. Thesis, Fuller Theological Seminary, Pasadena, 1990.

Schattauer, Thomas A., *Inside Out: Worship in an Age of Mission*. Minneapolis, MN: Fortress, 1999.
Scott, James C. *Domination and the Arts of Resistance: Hidden Transcripts*. New Haven, CT: Yale University Press, 1990.
Shik, Oh Jae. "The People: Come of Age." In *Toward A Theology of People*, 51-68. Tokyo: Christian Conference of Asia & Urban -Rural Mission, 1977.
Simundson, Daniel J. *Where is God in My Suffering? Biblical Responses to Seven Searching Questions*. Minneapolis, MN: Augsburg Publication House, 1983.
Smeaton, Donald Mackenzie. *The Loyal Karens of Burma*. London: Kegan Paul Trech & Co., 1887.
Smith, Wilfred Cantwell. *The Faith of Other Men*. New York: New American Library, 1963.
Snyder, Howard A. *Models of the Kingdom*. Nashville, TN: Abingdon Press, 1991.
Sobrino, Jon S.J. *Christology at the Crossroads: A Latin American Approach*. Translated by John Drury. Maryknoll, NY: Orbis Books, 1978.
Song, C. S. *The Compassionate God*. Maryknoll, NY: Orbis Books, 1982.
———. *Jesus, The Crucified People*. Minneapolis, MN: Fortress Press, 1996.
———. *Jesus and The Reign of God*. Minneapolis, MN: Fortress Press, 1993.
———. *Theology From The Womb of Asia*. Maryknoll, NY: Orbis Books, 1986.
———. *Third-Eye Theology: Theology in Formation in Asian Settings*. Maryknoll, NY: Orbis Books, 1979.
Spiro, Melford E. *Buddhism and Society: A Great Tradition and Its Burmese Vicissitudes*. Berkeley: CA: University of California Press, 1982.
St. Augustine: Letters 211-270, trans. Roland Teske [Hyde Park, NY: New York City, 2005], 211.11).
Stackhouse, Max L. *Public Theology and Political Economy: Christian Stewardship in Modern Society*. Lanham, MD: University Press of America, 1991. Stanley, Brian. *The History of Baptist Missionary Society (1792-1992)*. Edinburgh: T&T Clark, 1992.
———. *The World Missionary Conference, Edinburgh 1910*. Grand Rapids, MI: Eerdmans, 2009.
Stott, John R.W. *The Contemporary Christian*. Downers Grove, IL: Inter Varsity, 1992.
Study Catechism. Edited by the Presbyterian Church (USA). Louisville, KY: Weatherspoon Press, 1998.
Streufert, Mary J. "Maternal Sacrifice as a Hermeneutics of the Cross." In *Cross Examinations: Reading on the Meaning of the Cross Today*, edited by Marit Trelstad. 63-75. Minneapolis, MN: Fortress, 2006.
Sugden, Chris. "What is Good about Good News to the Poor? In *AD 2000 and Beyond—A Mission Agenda*, edited by Vinay Samuel and Chris Sudgen, 5-23. Oxford: Regnum, 1990.
Sugirtharajah, R.S. *Postcolonial Criticism and Biblical Interpretation*, reprinted. Oxford: Oxford University Press, 2009.

Suh, David Kwan-sun "A Biographical Sketch of an Asian Theological Consultation." In *Minjung Theology*, edited by Kim Yong-Bock, 15-37. Singapore: The Christian Conference of Asia/CCA, 1981.

Suh, Nam-dong."Toward a Theology of *Han*."In *Minjung Theology*, edited by Kim Young-Bock, 55-69. Singapore: The Christian Conference of Asia/CCA, 1981.

Sunquist, Scott W. *The Unexpected Christian Century: Reversal and Transformation of Global Christianity 1900-2010*. Grand Rapids, MI: Baker Academic, 2015.

Suu Kyi, Aung San. *Freedom From Fear*. New York, Penguin, 1991.

Tambiah, Stanley J. *The Buddhist Saints of the Forest, the Cult of Amulets*. New York: Cambridge University Press, 1984.

Tamez, Elsa. *The Amnesty of Grace: Justification by Faith from a Latin American Perspective*, translated by Sharon H. Ringe. Nashville, TN: Abingdon, 1993.

Tanner, Kathryn. *Christ the Key*. New York: Cambridge University Press, 2010.

The Significance of Barth's Political Theology for the Context of *Pyithu-Dukkha*, Carmen Krieg, and Thomas Kucharz, eds. *The Future of Theology: Essays in Honor of Jürgen Moltmann's 70th Birthday*. Grand Rapids, MI: William B. Eerdmans Publishing Company, 1996.

Thomas, M. M. "Christ-Centered Syncretism." *Religion and Society* 26, no. 1 (March 1979): 24-61.

Tillich, Paul. *Theology of Culture*. New York: Oxford University Press, 1959.

———. *Systematic Theology*.Vol. 2. Chicago, IL: University of Chicago, 1957.

Todt, Heinz Eduard. *Authentic Faith: Bonhoeffer's Theological Ethics in Context*, edited by Ernst-Albert Scharffenorth. Translated by David Stassen and Ilse Todt. Grand Rapids, MI: William B. Eerdmans Publishing Company, 2007. Tracy, David. *The Analogical Imagination: Christian Theology and Culture of Pluralism*. New York: Crossroad, 1981.

Trelstad, Marit ed. *Cross Examinations: Readings on the Meaning of the Cross Today* Minneapolis, MN: Augsburg, 2006.

———. "The Cross in Context," in *Cross Examinations: Reading on the Meaning of the Cross Today*, edited by Marit Trelstad. 1-18. Minneapolis, MN: Fortress, 2006.

Vanhoozer, Kevin J., N. T. Wright, Daniel J. Treier, and Craig Bartholomew, eds. *Dictionary for Theological Interpretation of the Bible*. Grand Rapids, MI: Baker Academic, 2005.

Vicedom, George F. *The Mission of God: An Introduction to a Theology of Mission*. Translated by Gilbert A. Thiele and Dennis Hilgendorf. St. Louis, MO: Concordia, 1965.

Volf, Miroslav. *After Our Likeness: The Church as the Image of the Trinity*. Grand Rapids, MI: William B. Eerdmans Publishing Company, 1998.

———. *Exclusion and Embrace: A Theological Exploration of Identity, Otherness and Reconciliation*. Nashville, TN: Abingdon Press, 1996.

———. "Forgiveness, Reconciliation and Justice: A Christian Contribution to a More Peaceful Social Environment." In *Theology Between East and West: Es-*

Von Rad, Gerhard. *Old Testament Theology*, translated by D. M. G. Stalker. Vol. 1. New York: Harper & Row, 1962.
Warren, Rick. *The Purpose Driven Life: What On Earth Am I Here For?* Grand Rapids, MI: Zondervan, 2002.
Weatherhead, Leslie. *The Will of God*. Nashville, TN: Abingdon Press, 1944.
Webster, Douglas. *Unchanging Mission*. Britain: Hodder Stroughton, 1965.
Weinanday, Thomas G. *Does God Suffer?* Edinburgh: T&T Clark, 2000.
Wilfred, Felix. "Asian Theological Trends." In *Oxford Handbook of Christianity in Asia*, ed. Felix Wilfred. 31-30. Oxford: Oxford University Press, 2014.
William, Daniel D. *The Spirit and the Forms of Love* (New York: Harper & Row Publishers, 1968.
Williams, James G. *The Bible, Violence, and the Sacred: Liberation from the Myth of Sanctioned Violence*. Valley Forge, PA: Trinity Press International, 1991.
Woolnough, Brian and Wonsuk Ma, ed. *Holistic Mission: God's Plan for God's People*. Eugene, OR: Wipf & Stocks, 2010.
Wright, Christopher J. H. *Knowing the Holy Spirit through the Old Testament*. Downers Grove, IL: InterVarsity Press, 2006.
———. *The Mission of God: Unlocking the Bible As A Grand Narrative*. Downers Grove, IL: InterVarsity, 2006.
Wright, N. T. "The Letter to the Romans: Introduction, Commentary and Reflection." In *New Interpreter's Bible*, edited by Leander E. Keck, 712-740. Vol. 10. Nashville, TN: Abingdon Press, 2002.
———. *Simply Jesus: A New Vision of Who He Was, What He Did and Why He Matters*. New York: Harper Collins, 2011.
Wright, William J. *Martin Luther's Understanding of God's Two Kingdoms*. Grand Rapids, MI: Baker Academic, 2010.
Yong-Bock, Kim. "Korean Christianity as a Messianic Movement of the People." In *Minjung Theology*, edited by Kim Yong-Bock, 80-119. Singapore: The Christian Conference of Asia/CCA, 1981.
———. *Messiah and Minjung: Christ's Solidarity with the People for New Life*. Hong Kong: The Christian Conference of Asia/CCA, 1992.
———. "Reading the Bible from Below." In *World Christianity in the 20th Century*, edited by Noel Davies and Martin Conway, 40-41. London: SCM Press, 2008.
Young, Edward. *The Book of Isaiah*. Vol. 2. Grand Rapids, MI: William B. Eerdmans Publishing Company, 1972.
Yung, Hwa. *Mangoes or Bananas? The Quest for an Authentic Asian Christian Theology*. Oxford: Regnum, 1997.
Zachariah, Aleyamma. *Modern Religious and Secular Movement in India*. Bangalore: Sevasadan Training Institute, 1994.
https://pres-outlook.org/2016/08/justice-peace-will-kiss (accessed on February 13, 2017).
https://www.worldwatchmonitor.org/2016/08/4576673/ (accessed on February 13, 2017).
https://www.youtube.com/watch?v ∴ z XG7Nyw jlv.f (accessed on February 19, 2017)

www.ingramcontent.com/pod-product-compliance
Lightning Source LLC
Chambersburg PA
CBHW051102230426
43667CB00013B/2412